IMPRESSIONS OF NEWFOUNDLAND

THE ART OF Tingting Chen

BREAKWATER

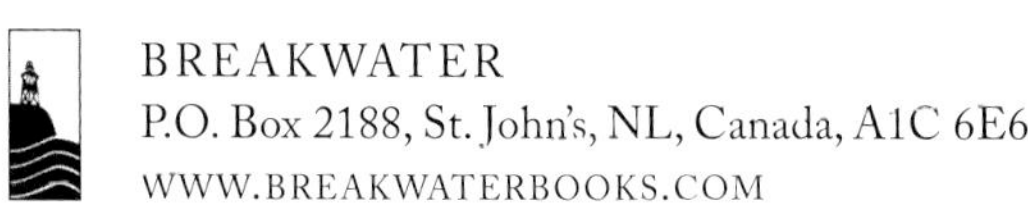
BREAKWATER
P.O. Box 2188, St. John's, NL, Canada, A1C 6E6
WWW.BREAKWATERBOOKS.COM

Library and Archives Canada Cataloguing in Publication
Title: Impressions of Newfoundland : the art of Ting Ting Chen.
Other titles: Art of Ting Ting Chen
Names: Chen, Ting Ting, photographer, author.
Identifiers: Canadiana 2023018376X | ISBN 9781550819830 (softcover)
Subjects: LCSH: Chen, Ting Ting. | LCSH: Photography, Artistic. | LCSH: Photography—Newfoundland and Labrador. | LCSH: Landscape photography—Newfoundland and Labrador. | LCSH: Portrait photography—Newfoundland and Labrador. | LCSH: Newfoundland and Labrador—Pictorial works.
Classification: LCC TR647 .C46 2023 | DDC 779.092—dc23

We acknowledge the support of the Canada Council for the Arts. We acknowledge the financial support of the Government of Canada through the Department of Heritage and the Government of Newfoundland and Labrador through the Department of Tourism, Culture, Arts and Recreation for our publishing activities.

PRINTED AND BOUND IN CANADA.

Breakwater Books is committed to choosing papers and materials for our books that help to protect our environment. This book is printed on paper that is certified by the Forest Stewardship Council®.

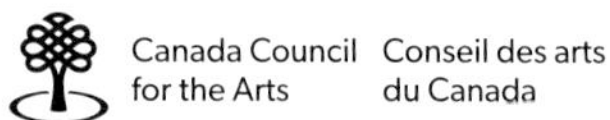

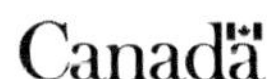

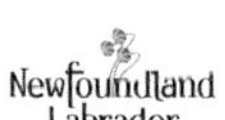

To Robert Tilley:

loyal friend, dear companion, and eternal muse

INTRODUCTION

The name "Impressions of Newfoundland" came to mind initially when I visited Newfoundland for the first time in the fall of 2017 as a tourist. I was a beginner in photography then. After staying in St. John's for a month, I made some friends—Robert Tilley was one of them—and created a simple photo album under the name "Impressions of Newfoundland," featuring the photos I took during my short trip. At that time, I could never have imagined that "Impressions of Newfoundland" would develop into a beautiful photography book six years later. Nor did I realize a precious friendship would unfold in the following years between Robert and me.

I returned to Newfoundland in 2018 to pursue my second PhD in folklore, settled in St. John's, and haven't left. Robert has become my best buddy, and we've travelled across most parts of Newfoundland taking photos. This experience changed my life. It enabled me to discover the artist's spirit inside me and gave me the passion to evolve from a beginner in photography to an award-winning visual artist. If I hadn't come to Newfoundland and met Robert, perhaps I wouldn't have found my enthusiasm for art. I found here not only my new home but also my muse. And my trips around Newfoundland with Robert are my trips of self-discovery.

This book, which includes landscape photos and fine art portraits, briefly summarizes my artwork in the past few years. Every photo in this book is about Newfoundland—these are Newfoundland landscapes and portraits of Newfoundlanders. My landscape photos reveal the rhythms and moods hidden in the natural scenery, which are personified through my eyes. My fine art portraits explore people's personalities, life experiences, and identities. My best friend, Robert Tilley, is the model in most of the portraits, which are a unique demonstration of our beautiful friendship.

My journey as an artist is still going on. I hope my impressions of Newfoundland will continue to impress you.

My sincere gratitude goes to all the friends who have helped me since I came alone to Newfoundland. Your encouragement and support give me the strength to grow as an artist. My special thanks go to Rebecca Rose and Marnie Parsons, whose kindness and efforts made the publication of this book possible.

LANDSCAPE

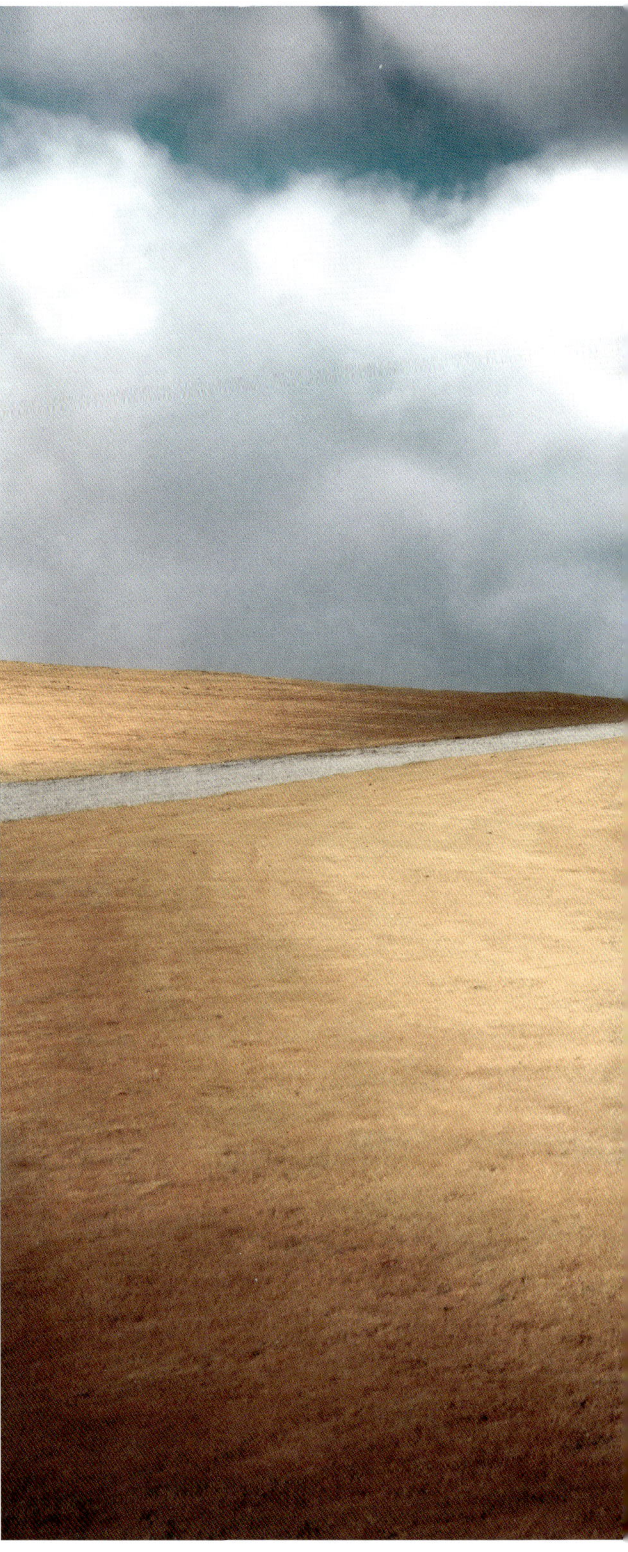

SURREALNESS IN BOWRING PARK My friend Robert Tilley and I both like to visit the century-old Bowring Park, in St. John's. I took this photo when Robert was standing beside the trees in autumn colours. Time seems to freeze in this photo, and the picture is shrouded in a surreal aura.

YEAR: 2020

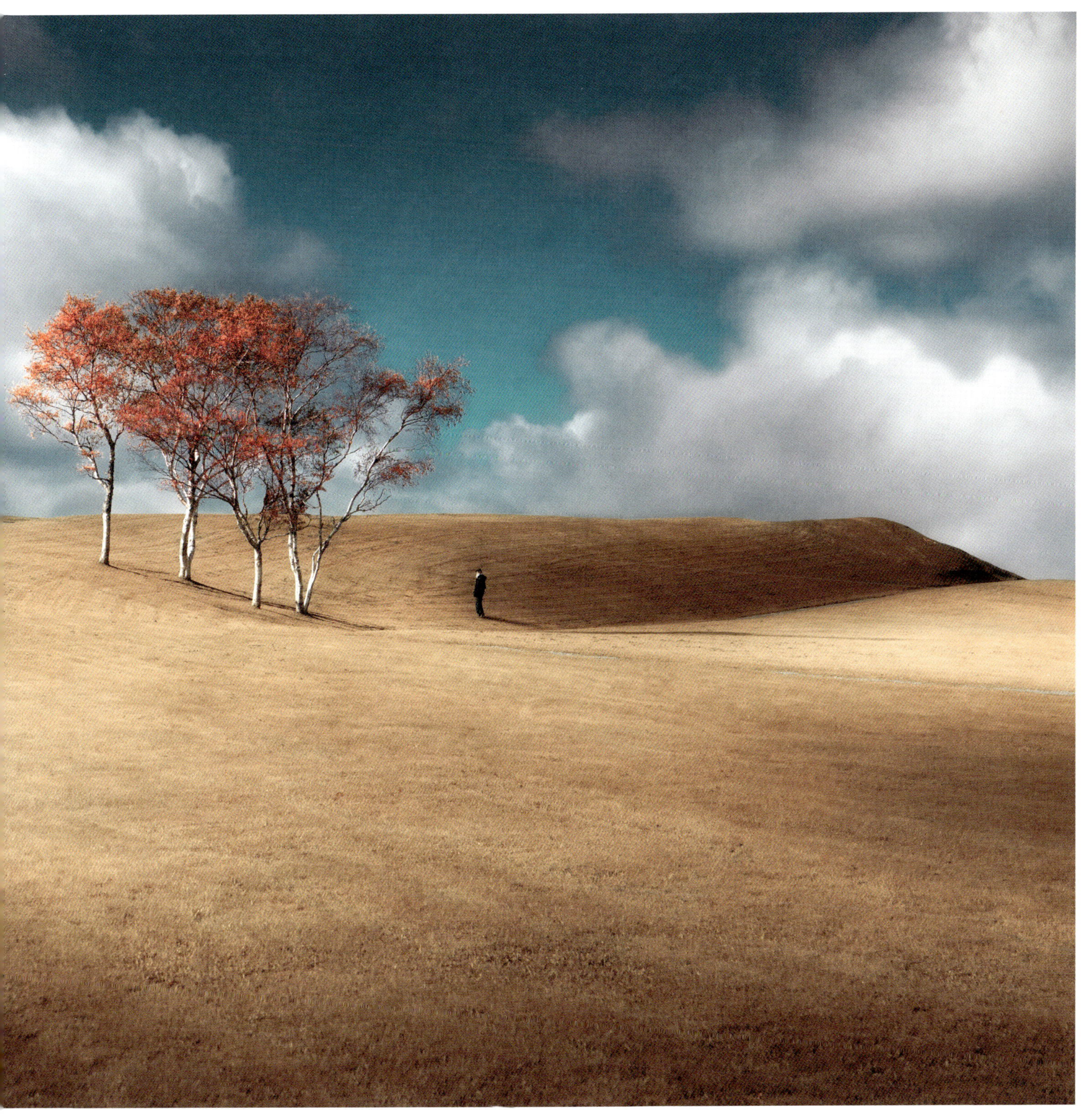

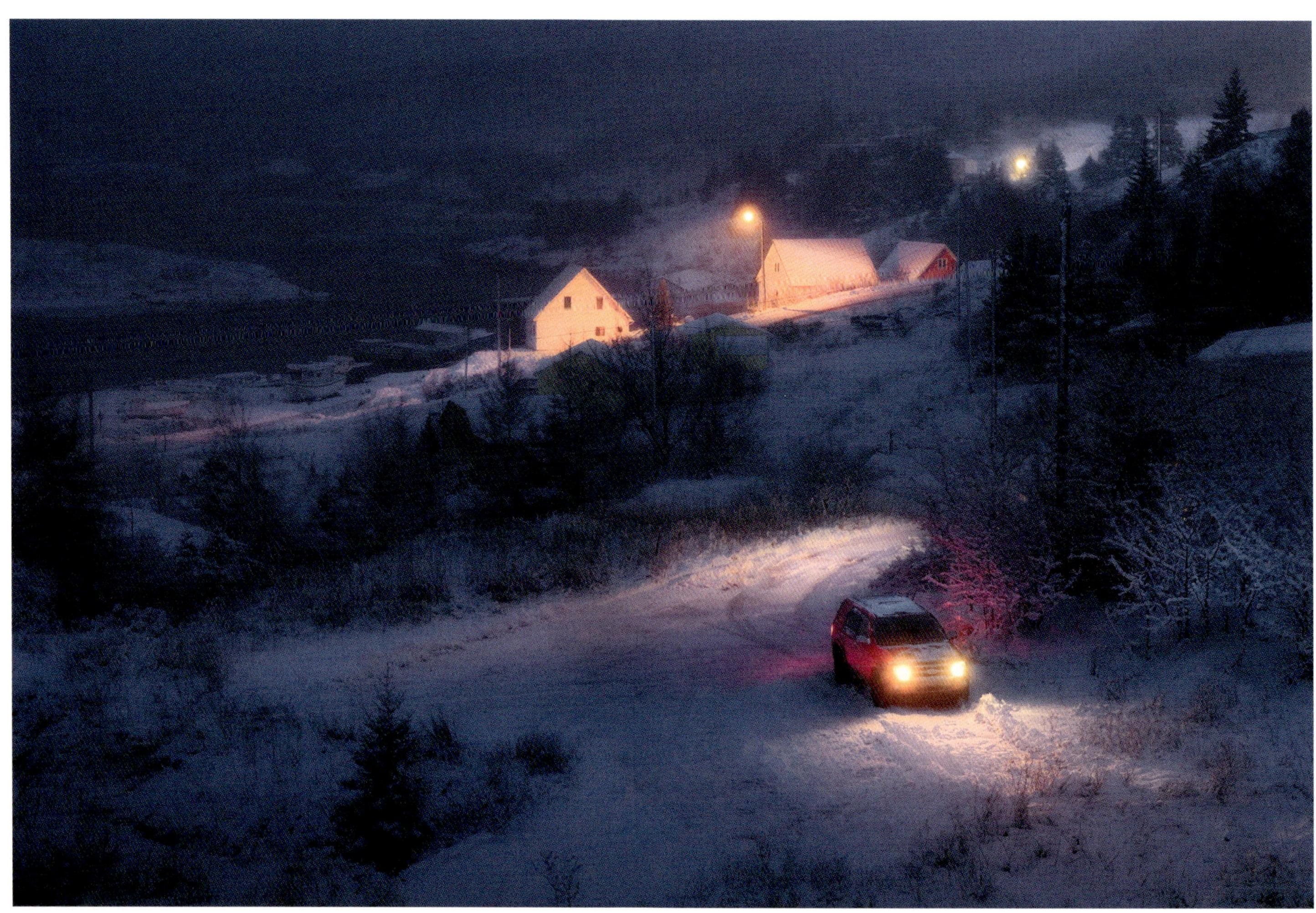

ABOVE

HEADING HOME A snowy night in Brigus South. Robert was heading home in his red vehicle.

YEAR: 2021

OPPOSITE

QUIDI VIDI ARTIST STUDIOS The Quidi Vidi Artist Studios were created in St. John's for artisans and craftspeople. I took this photo at night, when a leather craft artist, Stephen, was still working in his studio.

YEAR: 2021

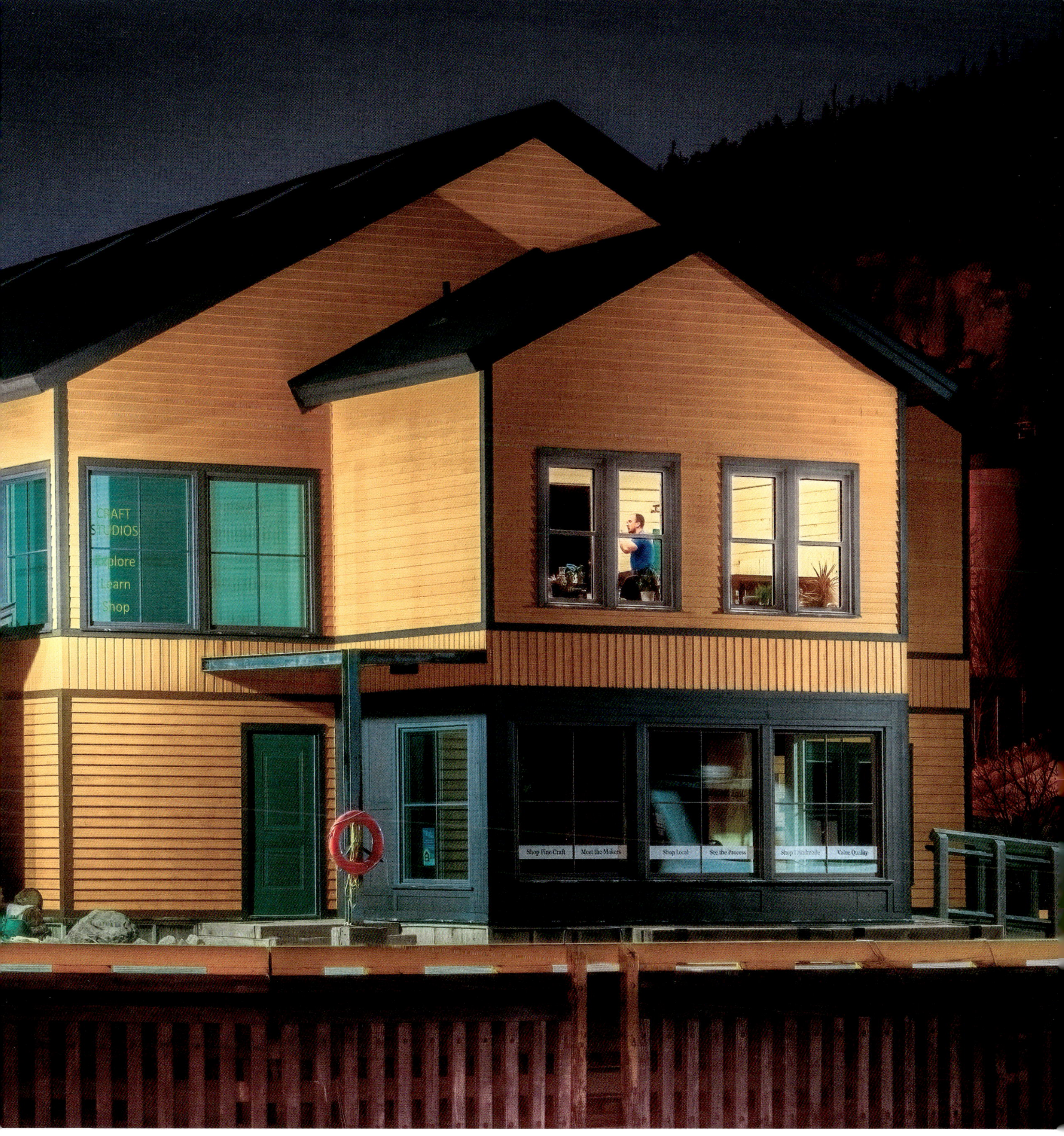
CRAFT
STUDIOS
Explore
Learn
Shop
Shop Fine Craft
Meet the Makers
Shop Local
See the Process
Value Quality

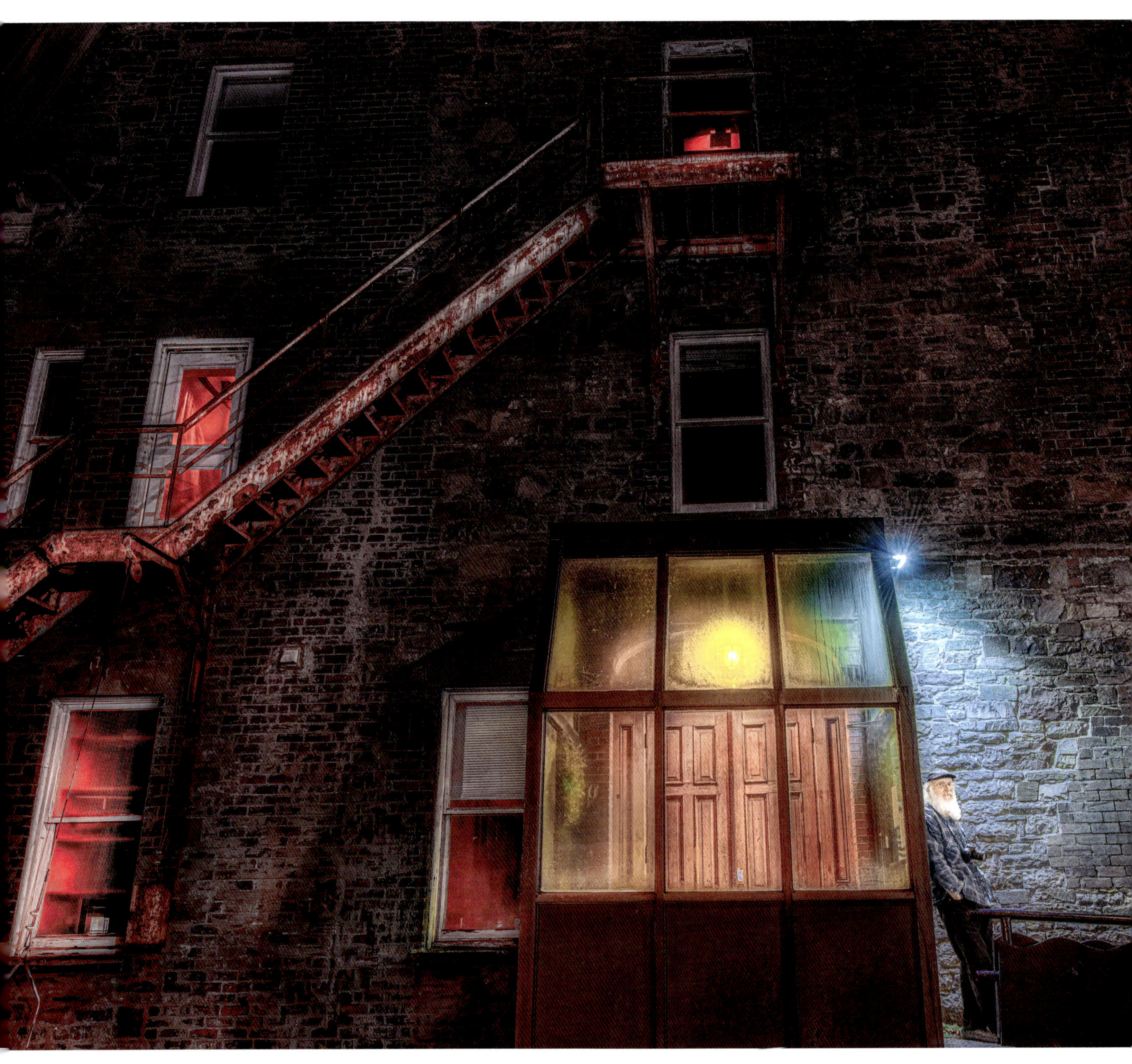

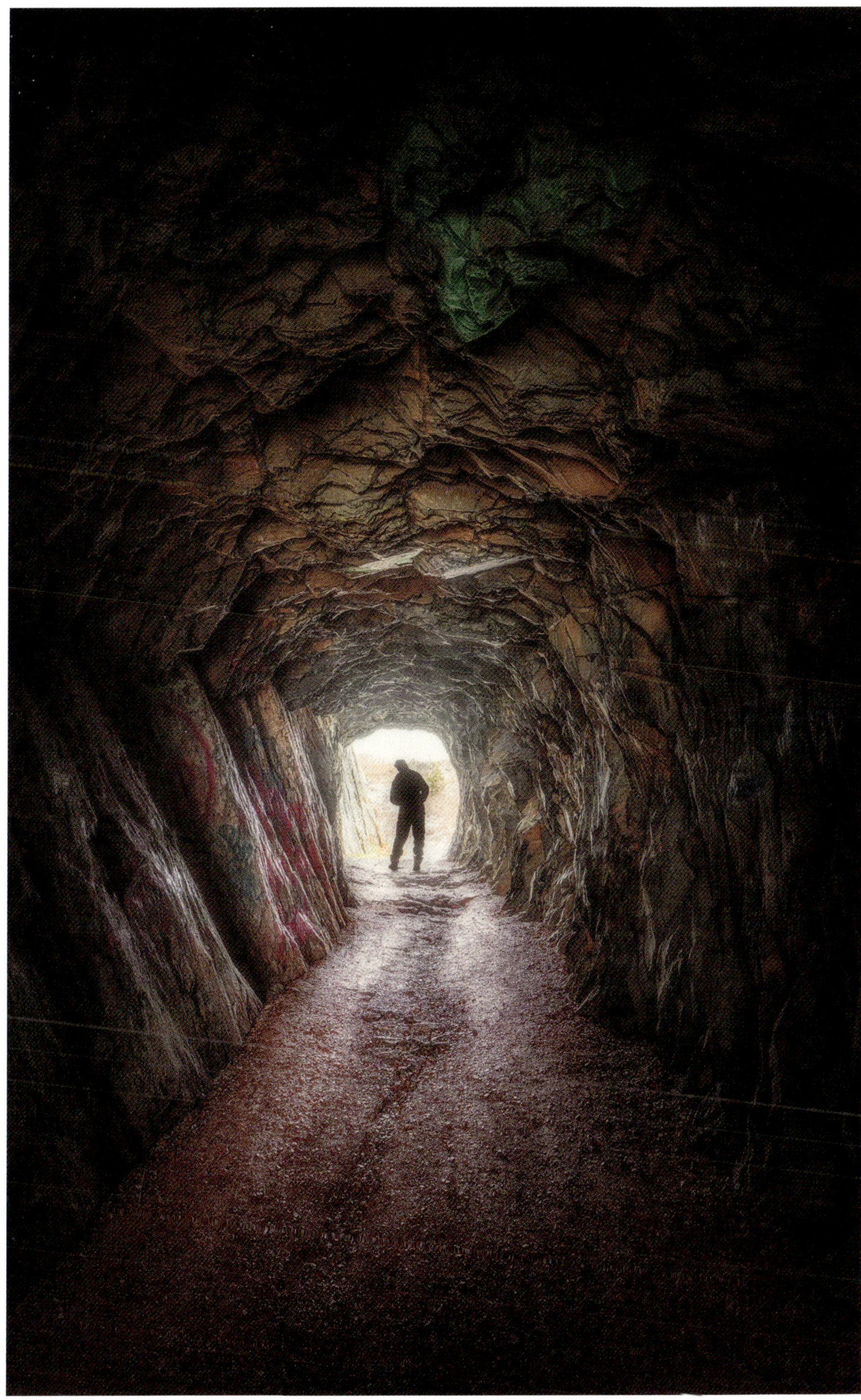

OPPOSITE

DEVON HOUSE The Craft Council of Newfoundland and Labrador used to operate in Devon House, a heritage structure located at 59 Duckworth Street, St. John's. Robert, who is leaning on the door of this closed building, took a class on clay-making here in the early 1990s.

YEAR: 2021

LEFT

AT THE END OF DARKNESS THERE IS LIGHT Cornish miner John Hoskins created the Brigus Tunnel around 1860 for the famous Captain Abram Bartlett, to allow easy access to his ship and make offloading of his catch more convenient. This tunnel was used until about 1910 and has become a place of interest in Brigus. In this photo, Robert is standing at the end of the tunnel, looking up.

YEAR: 2021

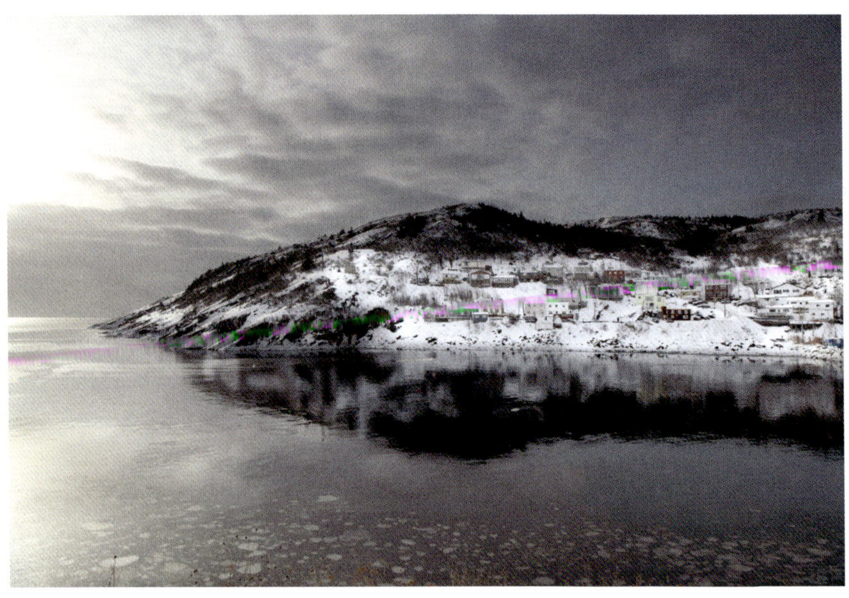

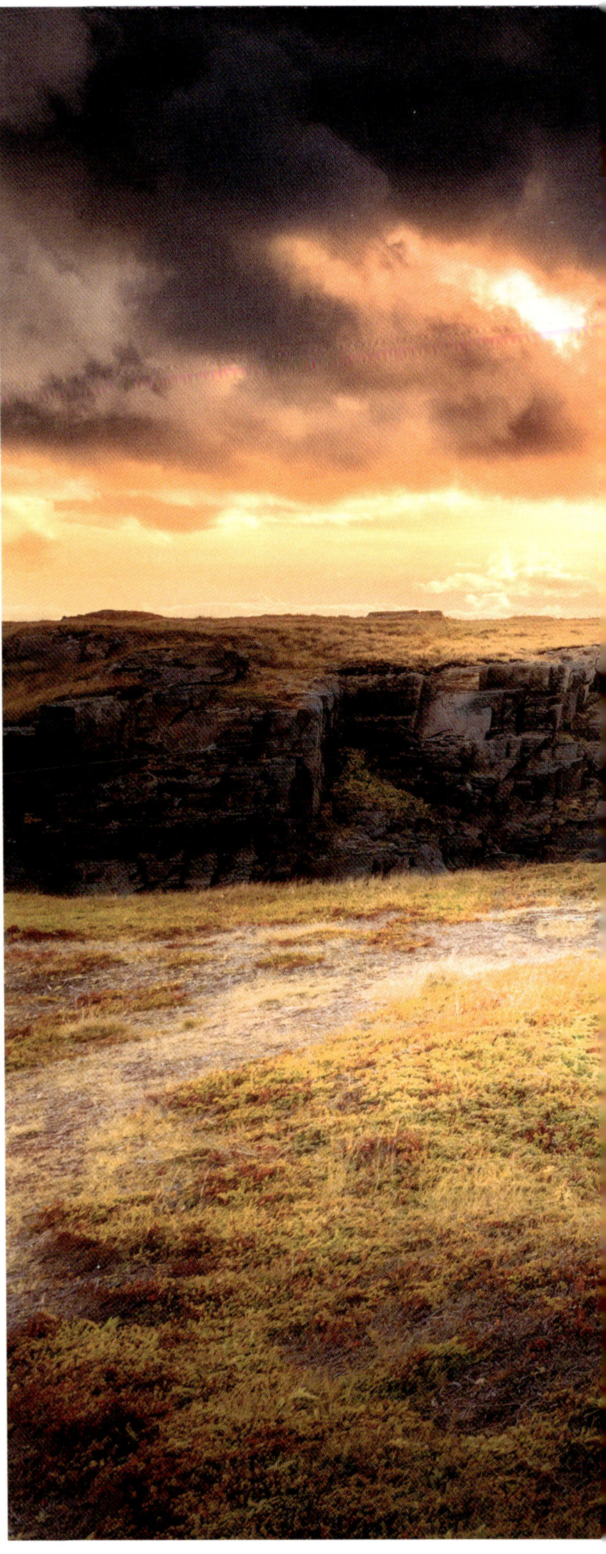

ABOVE

PETTY HARBOUR MORNING Early morning in Petty Harbour. The reflections of the hill swing gently in the Atlantic Ocean.

YEAR: 2019

RIGHT

A NEW DAY In 2019, Robert and I visited his hometown, Elliston. In this photo, Robert was watching the glorious sunrise. His ancestors must have seen the same vista. Robert now lives elsewhere, but he still feels connected to this place where his home used to be. Bathed in the golden sunshine, we knew a new day had come.

YEAR: 2019

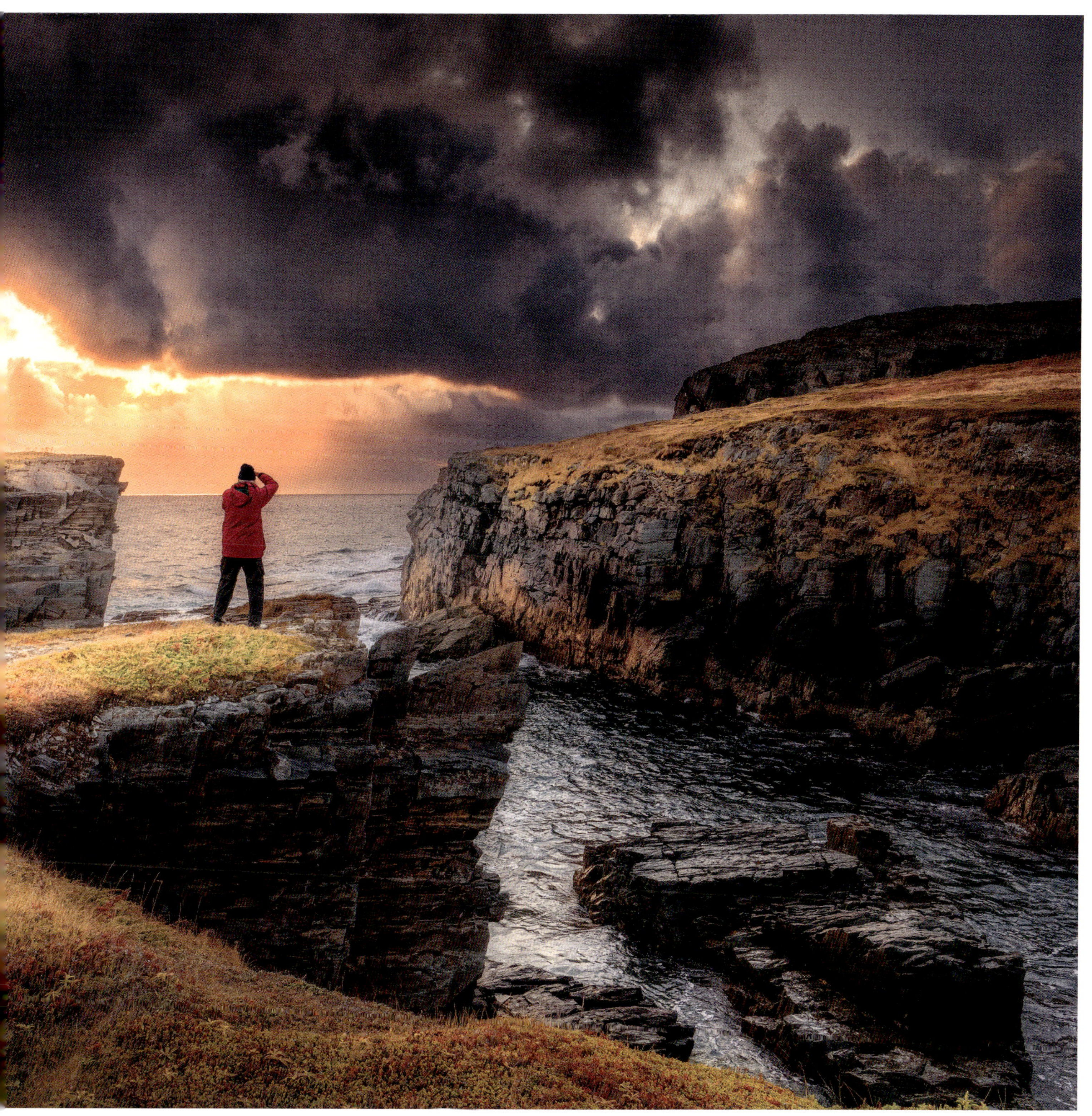

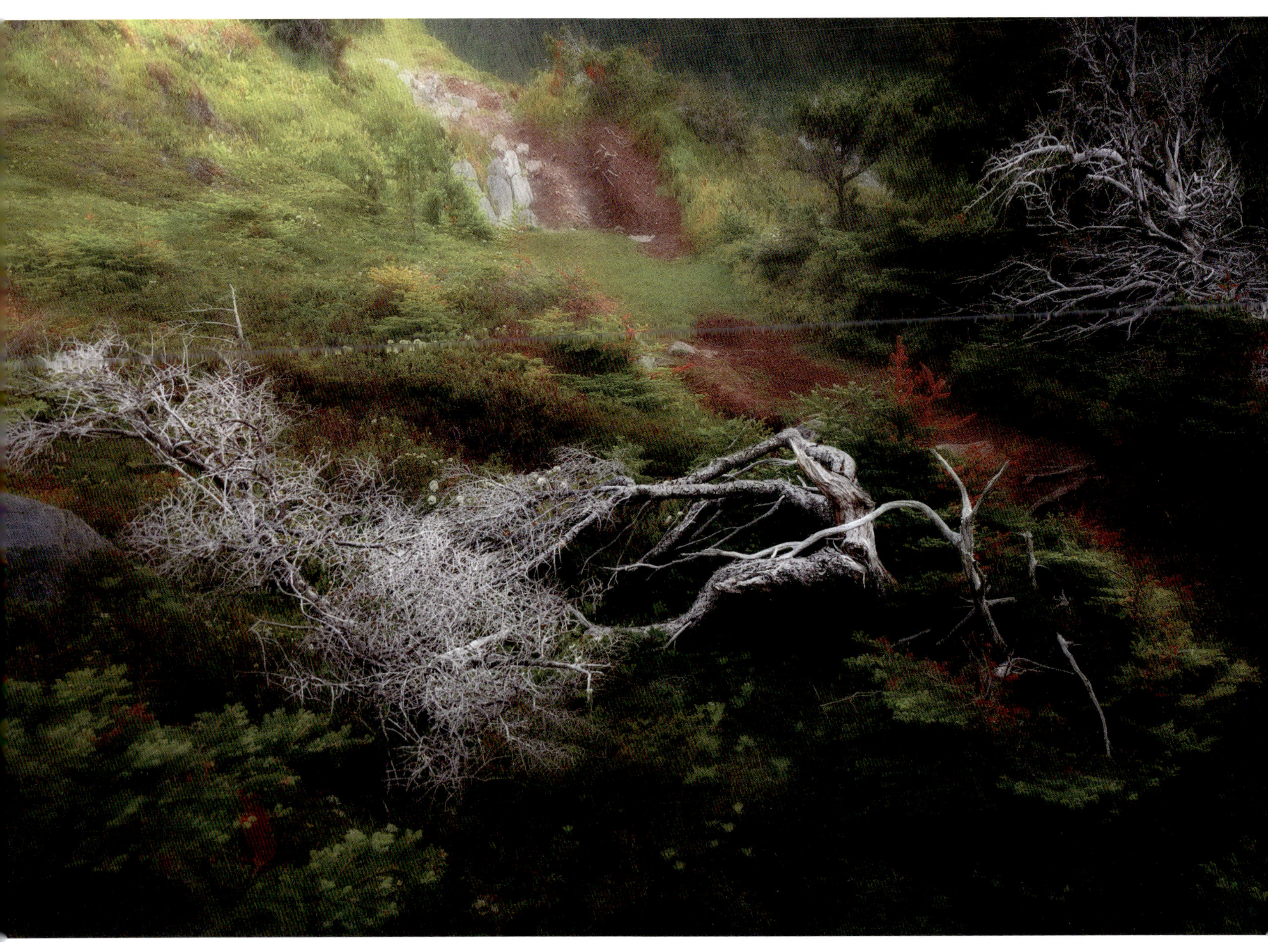

LEANING TREES AT FLATROCK Like many other parts of Newfoundland, Flatrock is close to the sea, and the trees lean away from the wind.

YEAR: 2020

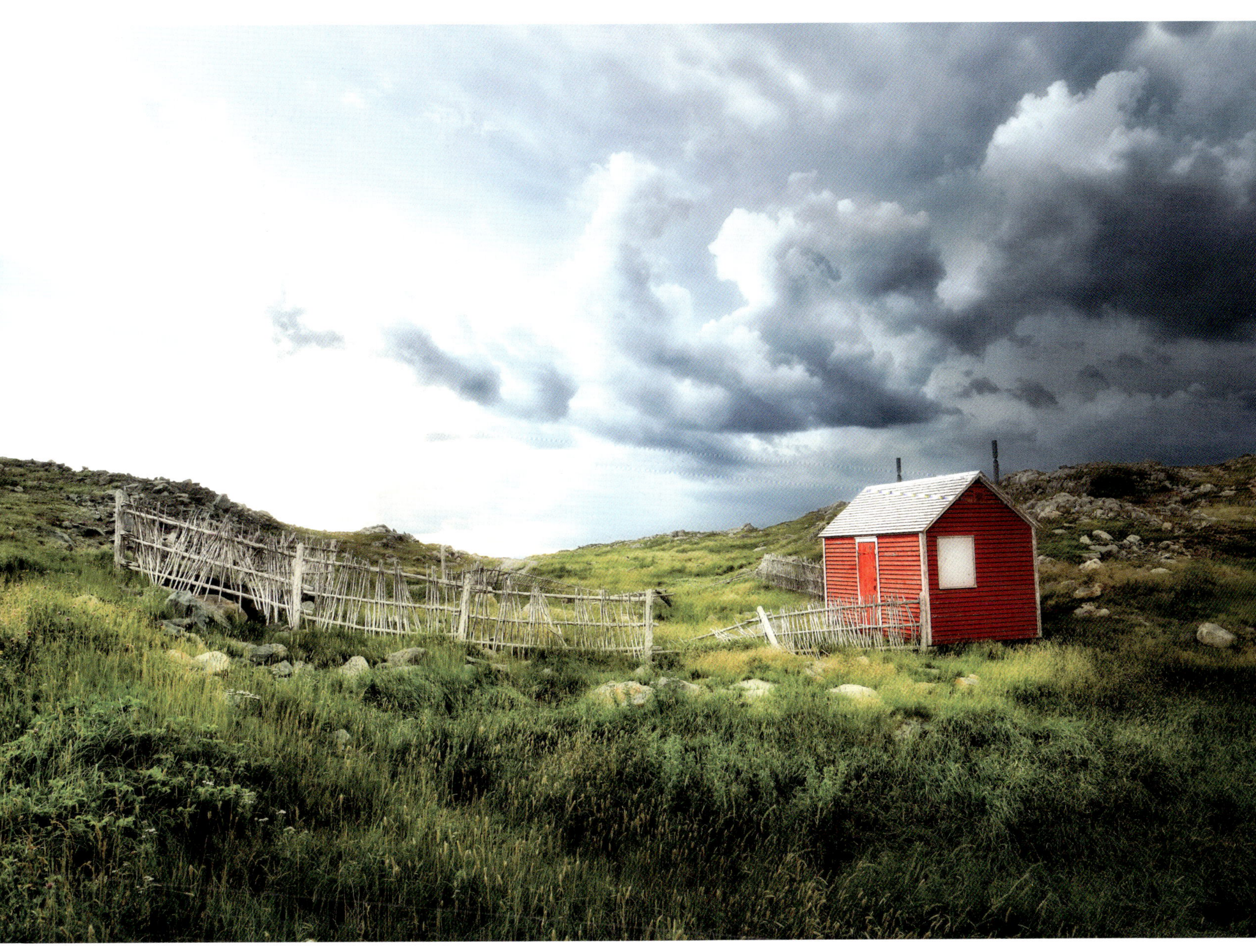

THE RED SHED This red shed just below the lighthouse is one of my favourite scenic spots in Bonavista.

YEAR: 2021

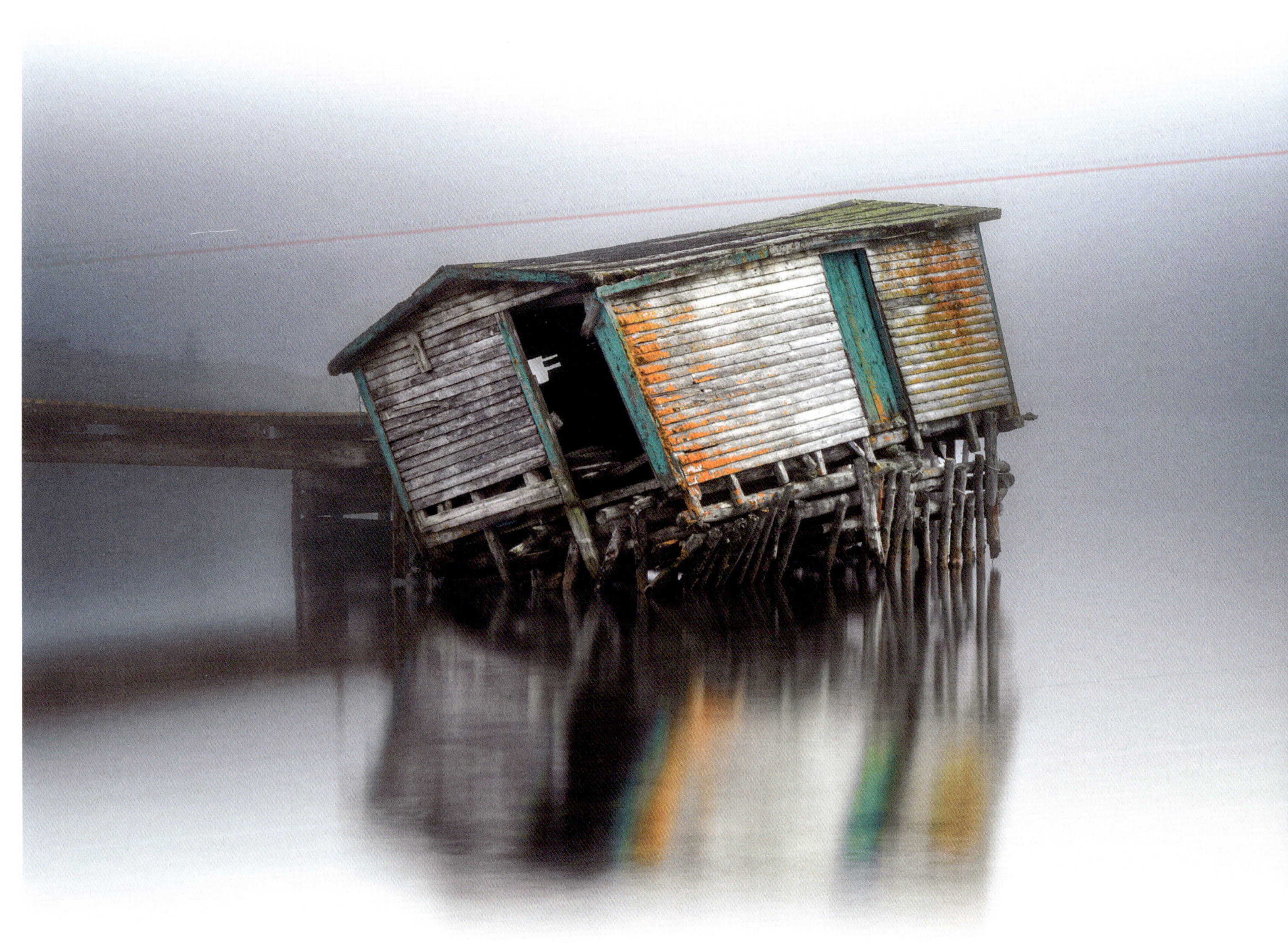

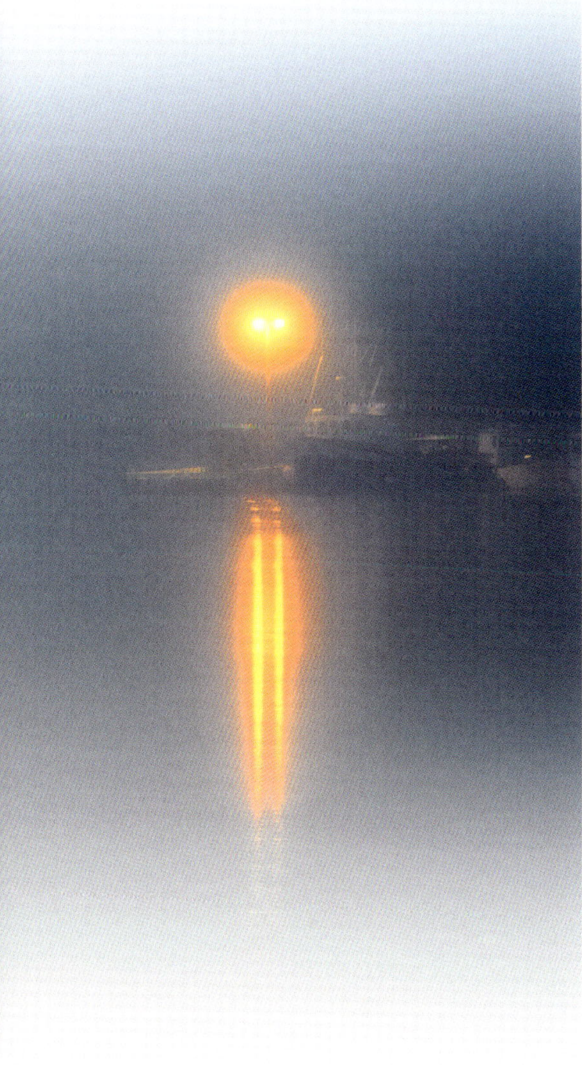

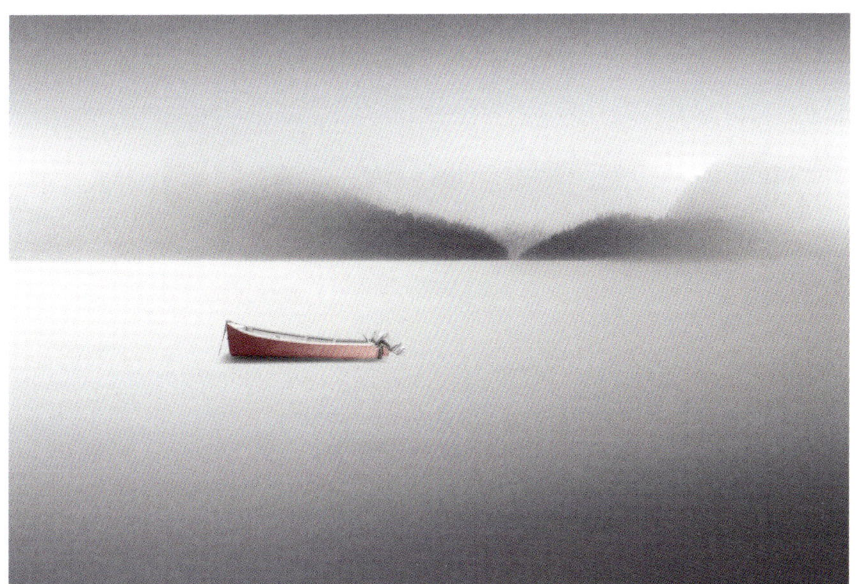

LEFT

GONE WITH THE TIDES A fishing stage is a wooden vernacular structure associated with the cod fishery in Newfoundland. To many Newfoundlanders, especially the older generation, fishing stages were reminiscent of home. Francis Power Stage, the fishing stage in this photo, was located in Brigus South, a small fishing community I visit occasionally. Before this stage was taken away by the tides on March 8, 2021, it had stood for around seventy years. Some community members came to the harbour to see it off that day, as if they were saying goodbye to an old friend, to part of their memories of home.

YEAR: 2020

ABOVE

SERENITY IN MONKSTOWN Monkstown is a fishing village located in the northern part of the Burin Peninsula, at the end of a thirty-minute drive on a dirt road. Robert and I went there in the summer of 2021. When we arrived, the fog began to rise and gave the hills different shades of grey.

YEAR: 2021

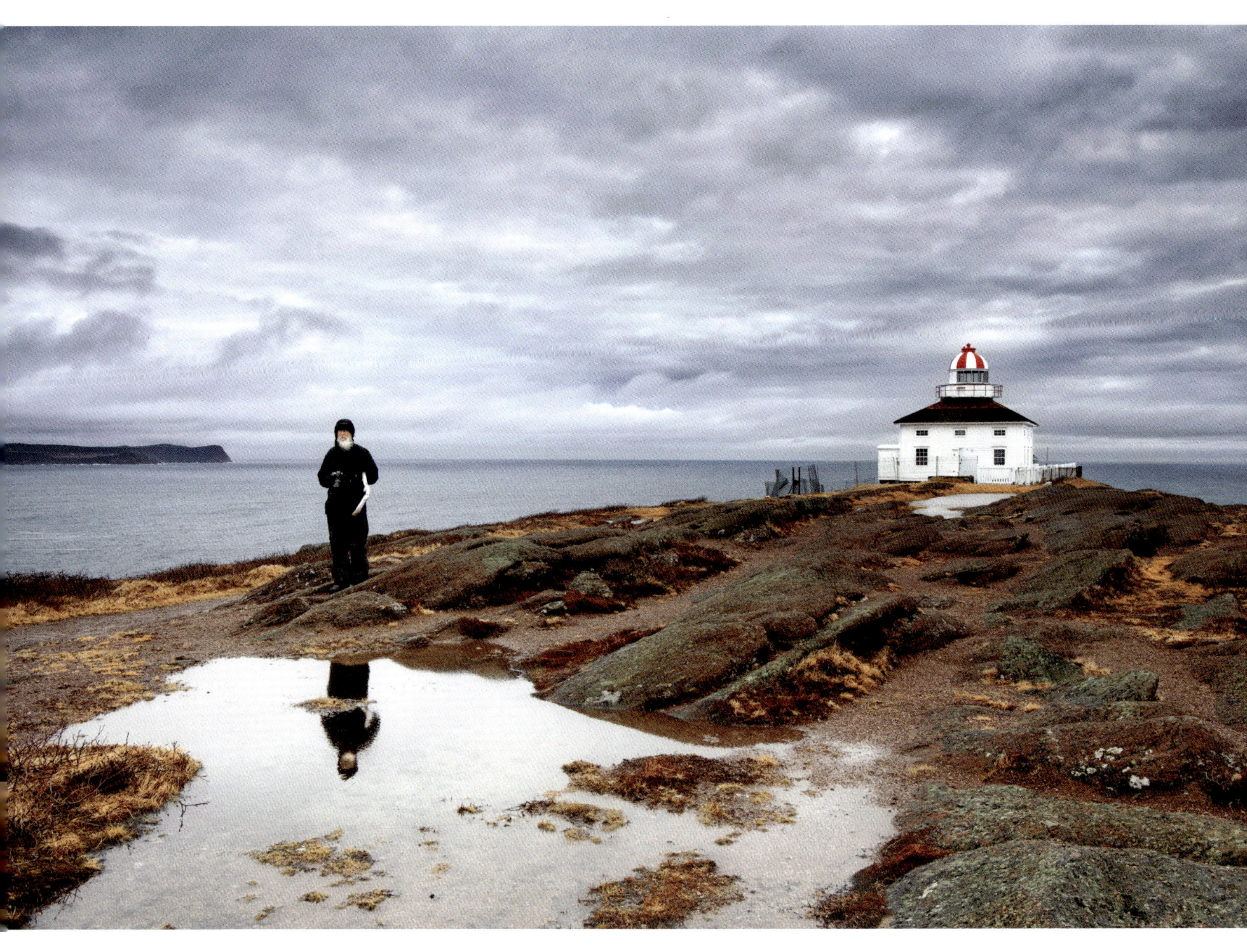

ROBERT AT CAPE SPEAR Robert and I visited the Cape Spear lighthouse after a rain shower. Robert's reflection was in the puddle, with the lighthouse behind him.

YEAR: 2019

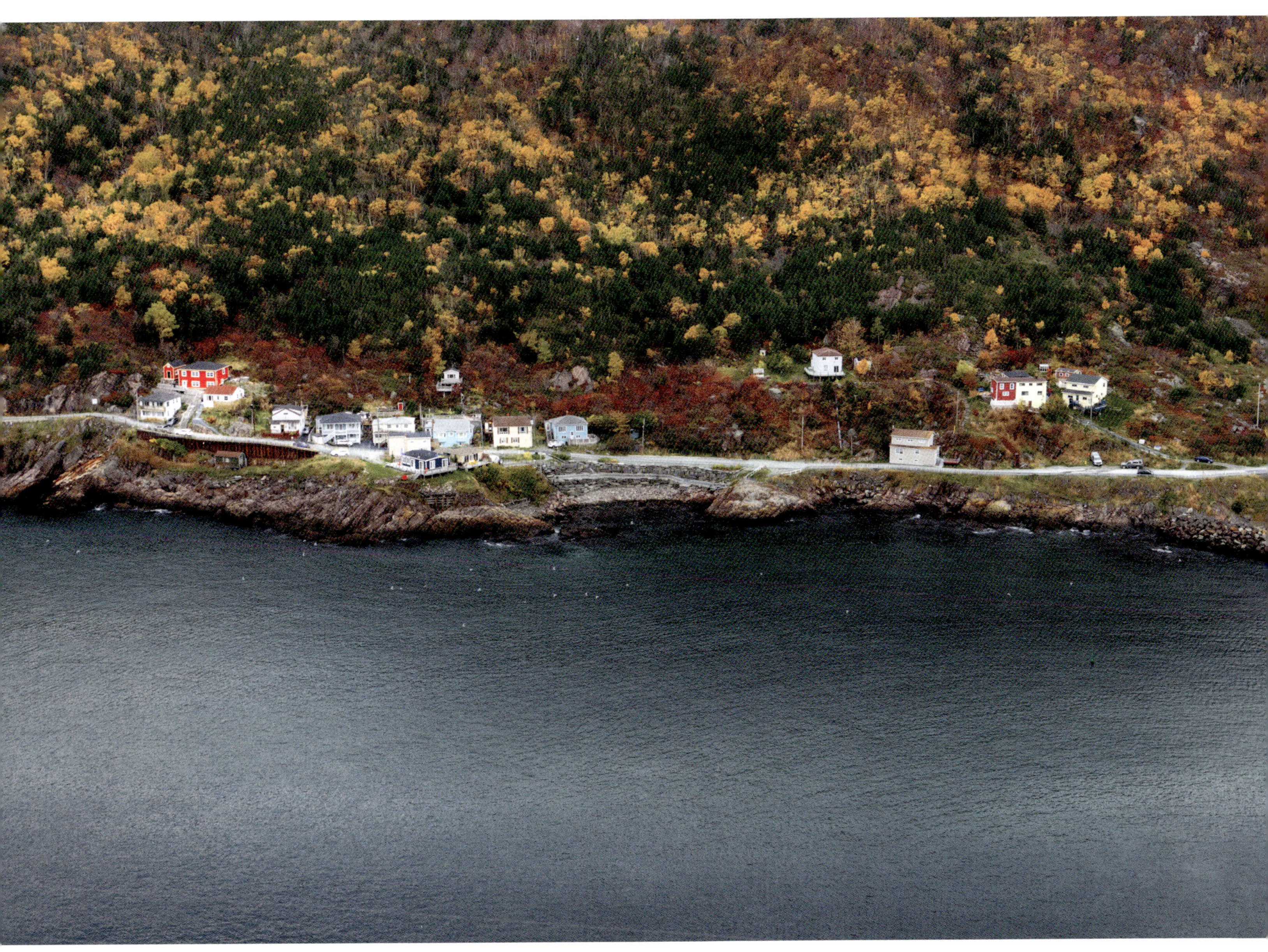

ATLANTIC BLUE When Canadian autumn colours meet the Atlantic blue: the sea gently shines and looks like a silky ribbon. The little white dots on the sea are seagulls flying by. I do like this small community of Fort Amherst.

YEAR: 2019

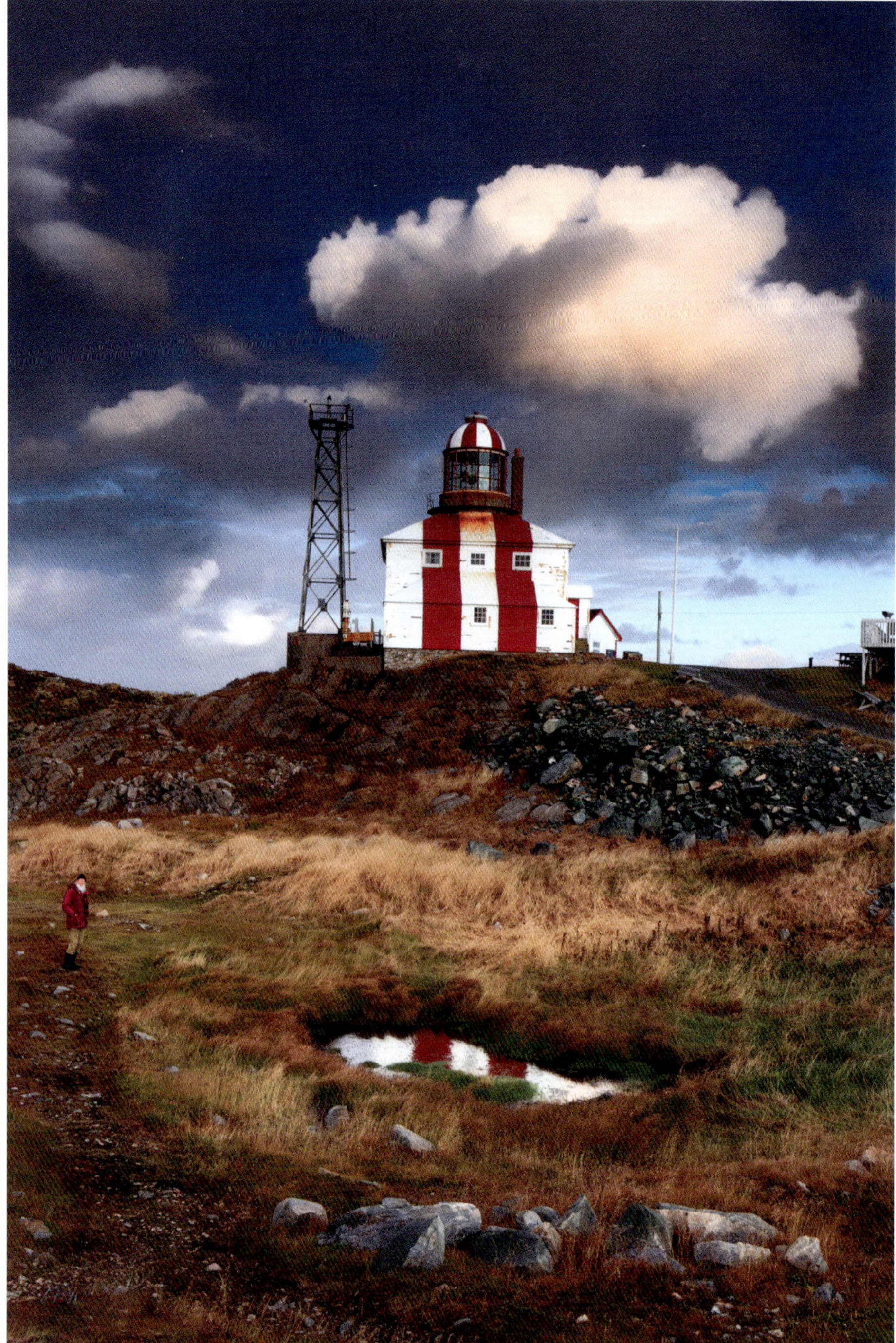

BONAVISTA LIGHTHOUSE

A very windy day at Cape Bonavista, but I was lucky to find a puddle with a reflection in it.

YEAR: 2019

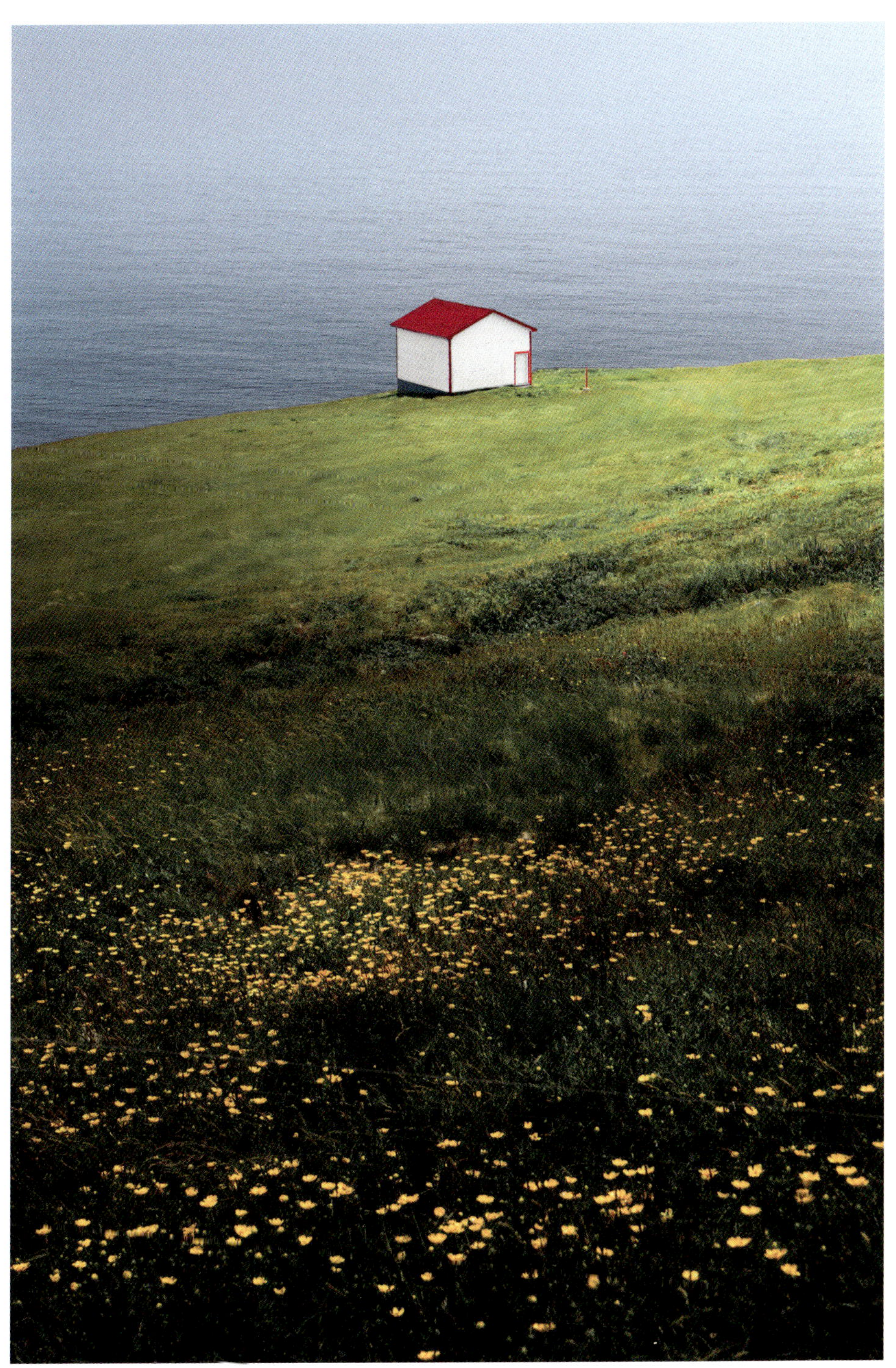

CAPE PINE A small shed, some lovely wildflowers, and the Atlantic blue. This is a painterly view around Cape Pine lighthouse.

YEAR: 2022

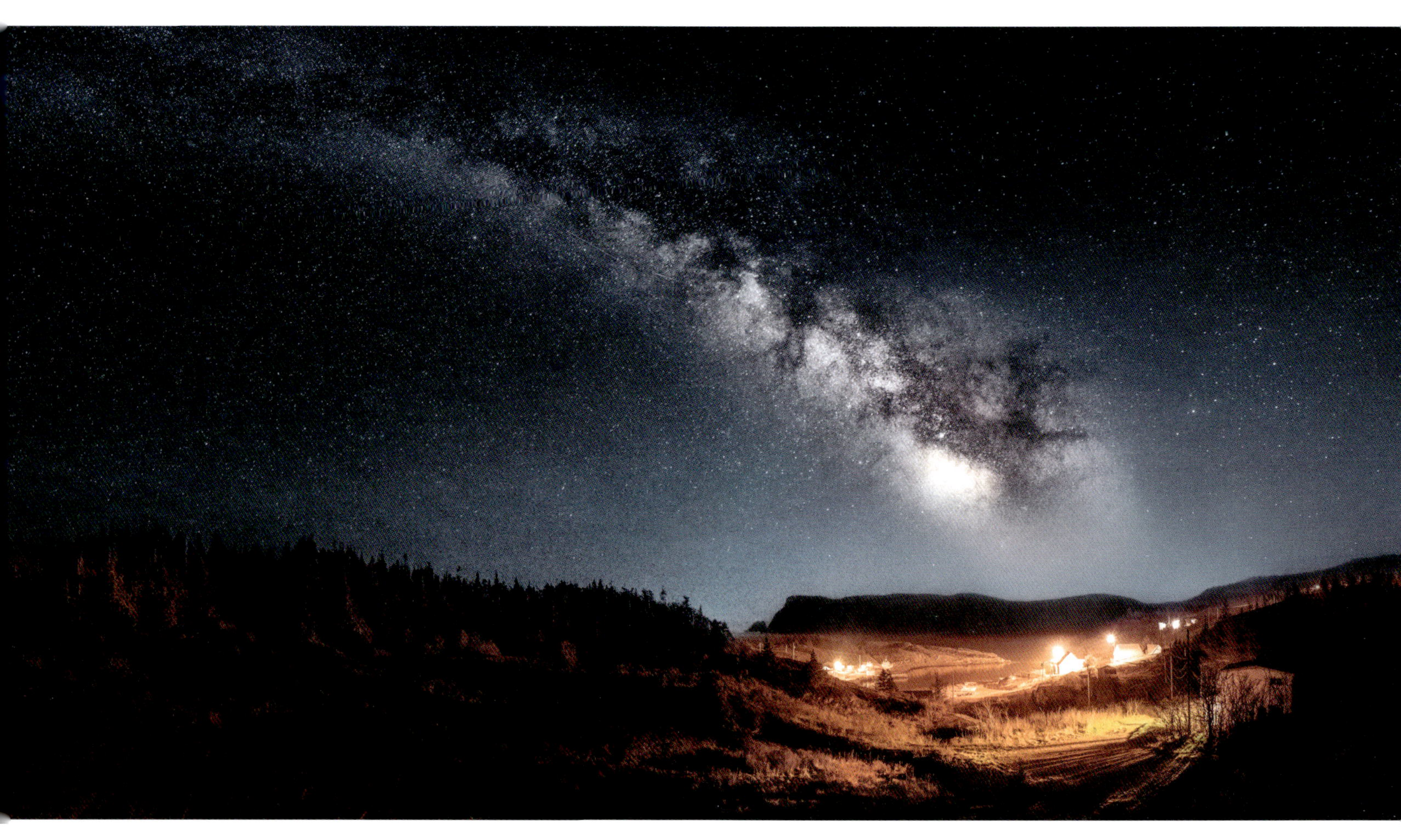

A NIGHT AT BRIGUS SOUTH The Milky Way shines above the quiet community of Brigus South.

YEAR: 2021

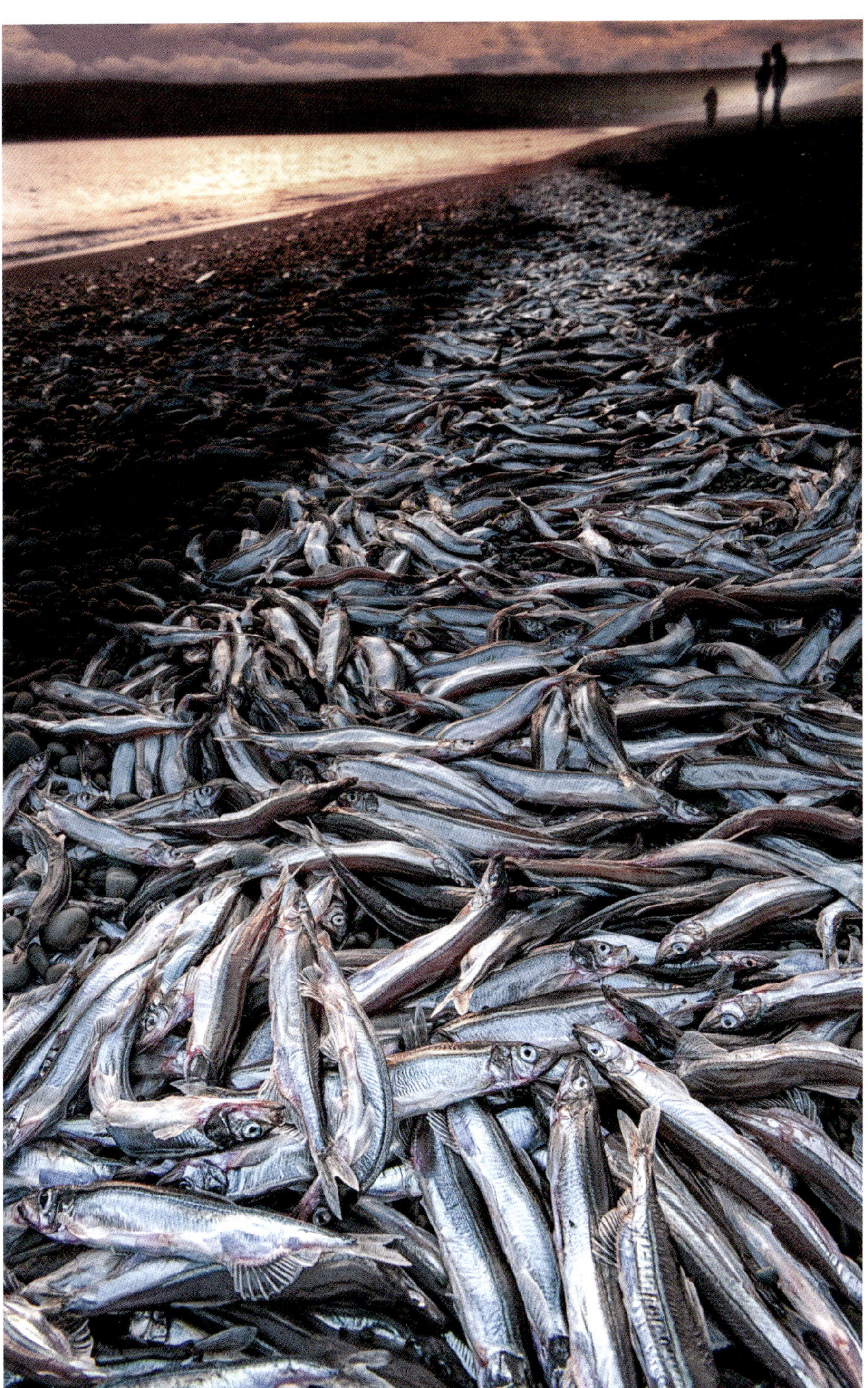

CAPELIN ROLLING IN THE DUSK Capelin rolling has been a big event in Newfoundland for decades. This is not fish mass suicide. This is capelin's natural life circle—they come near the shore to spawn every summer and are washed up on the beach. Thousands of capelin roll on Newfoundland's beaches every year, and people go there with nets to catch them. Capelin are multi-purpose fish: they can be bait, food, and great fertilizer in your garden. I took this photo at St. Vincent's beach.

YEAR: 2020

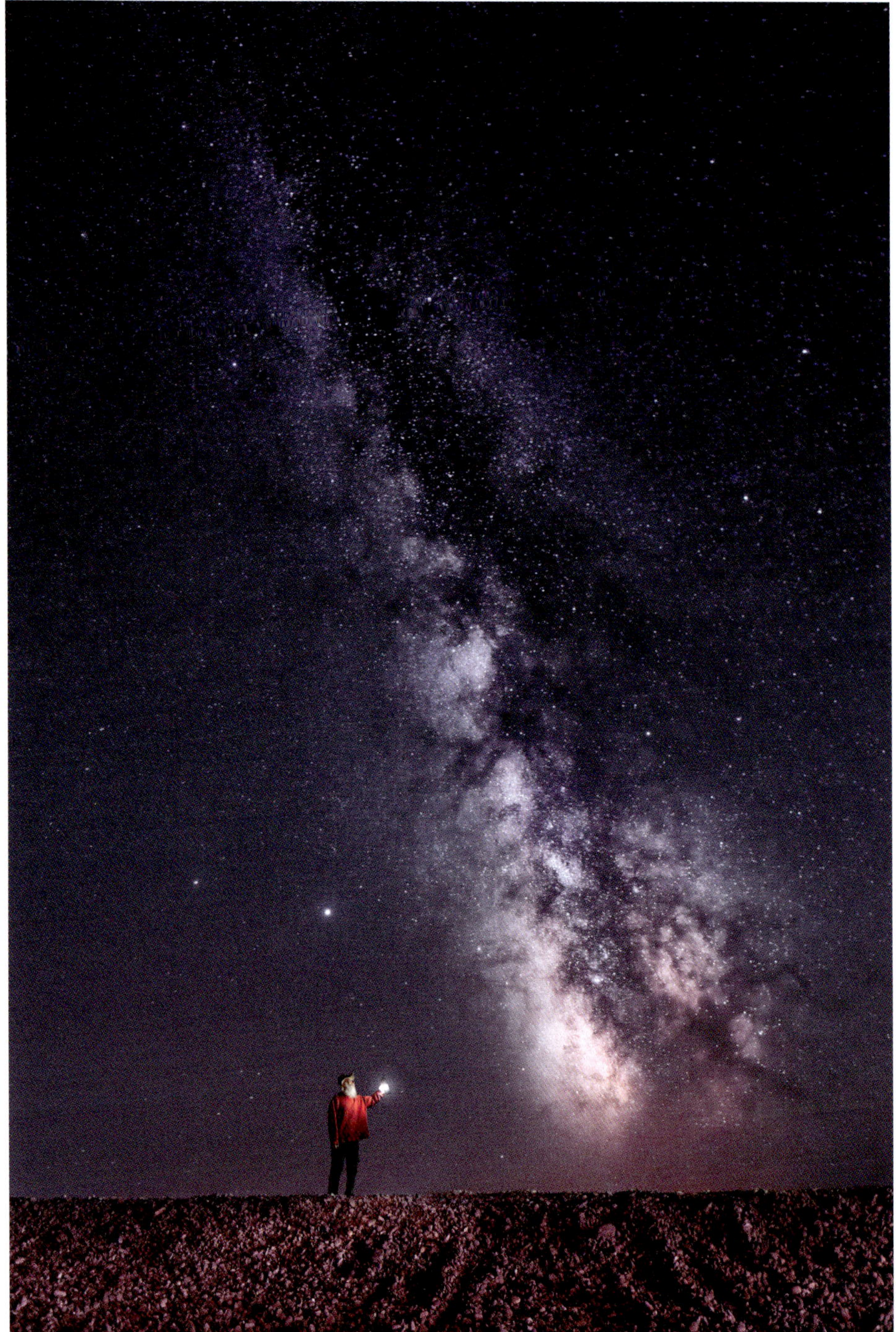

LADDER TO THE SKY

When Robert and I visited the Chance Cove beach, I saw the clearest night sky that I have ever encountered. The Milky Way is like a ladder leading to the heavens. Robert is in red, holding a lamp. He looks like a Santa Claus who climbs down the ladder from the sky and wanders around the world before Christmas.

YEAR: 2020

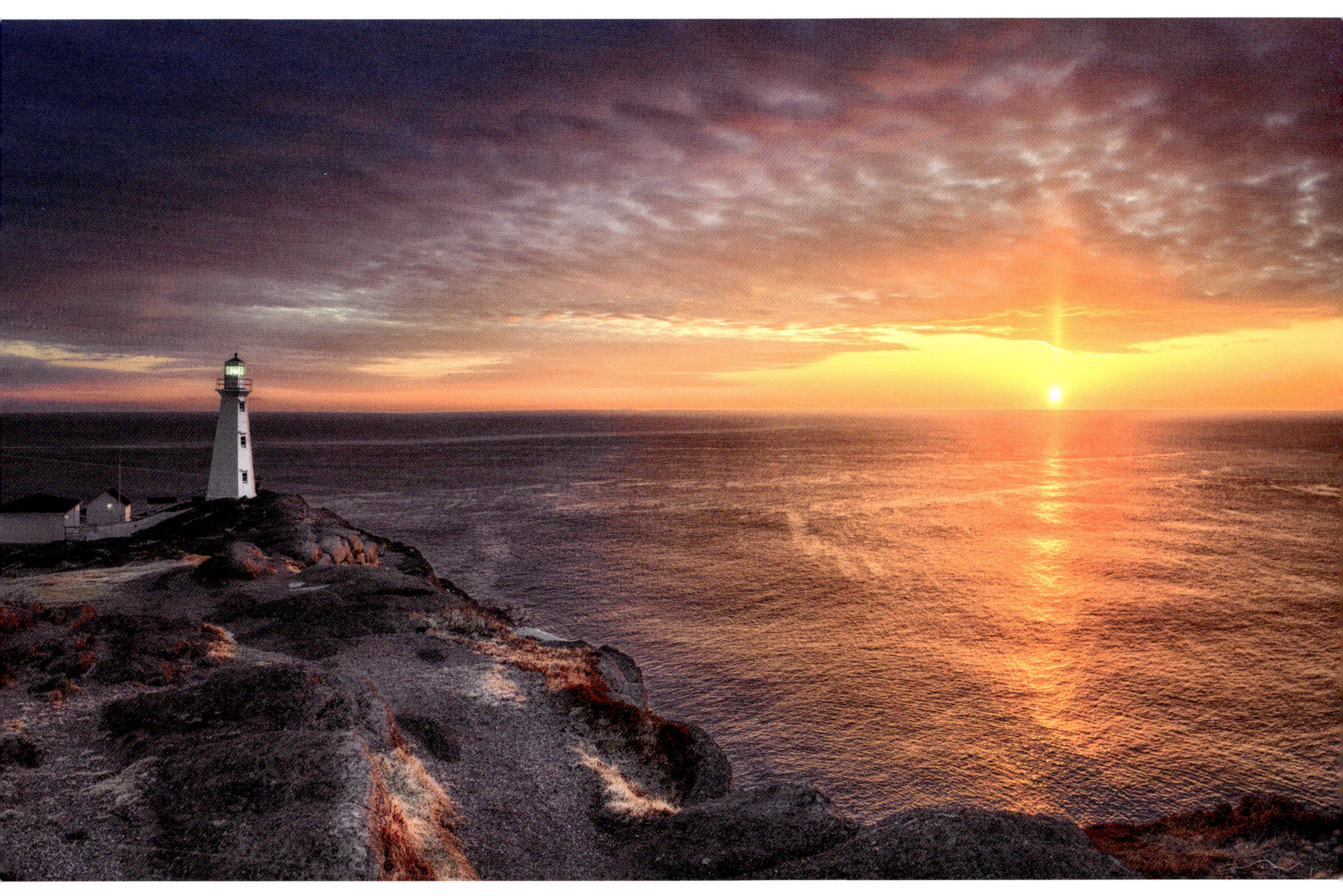

SUNRISE AT CAPE SPEAR An early morning in the spring: it's still cold in Newfoundland. Robert and I climbed up to the Cape Spear lighthouse and saw this gorgeous sunrise above the Atlantic Ocean.

YEAR: 2020

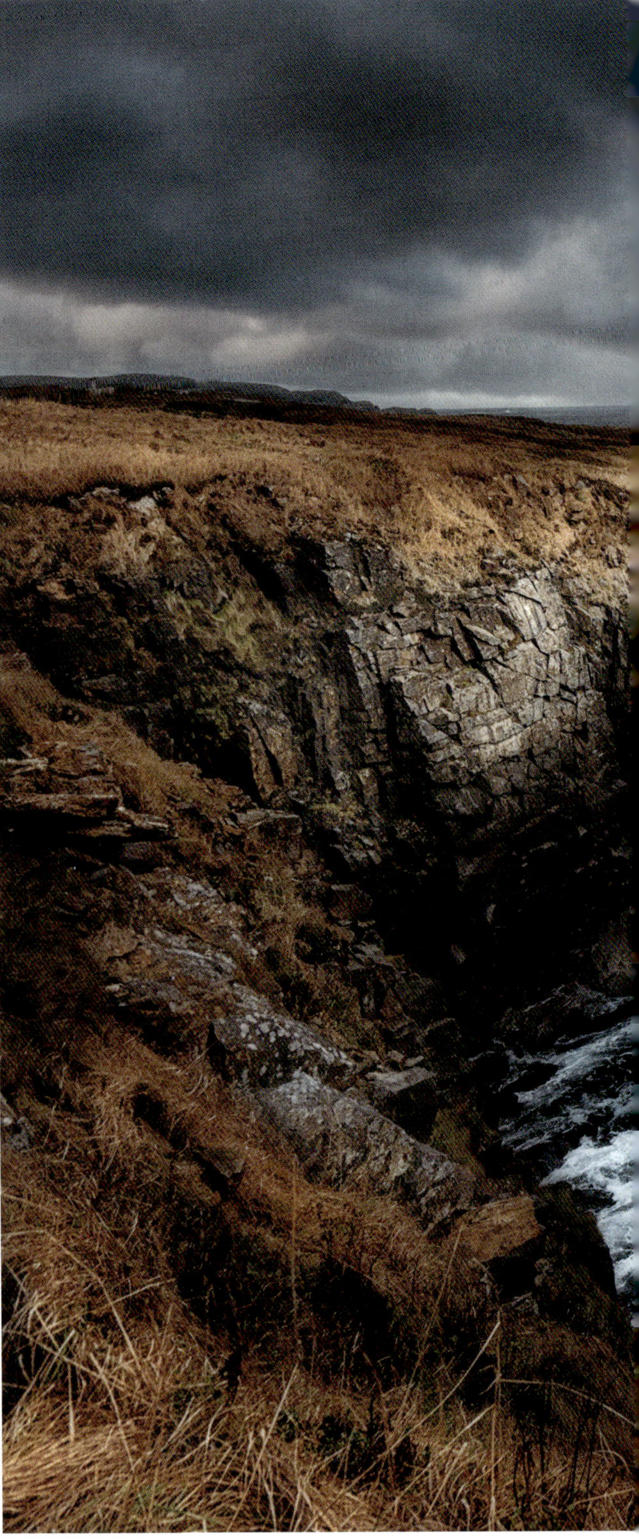

RIGHT

THE ROCKS AT ELLISTON Robert is walking on the rocks at Elliston. Robert's family settled in this fishing village on the Bonavista Peninsula in the mid-nineteenth century. These rocks have known his great-great-grandfather, his great-grandfather, his grandfather, and his father, and he used to play on them when he was a young boy. It was early morning in October 2019 when Robert and I went out to catch the sunrise and the morning light. The colours of his coat, the rocks, and the grass made a beautiful contrast.

YEAR: 2019

FOLLOWING

A MAGICAL NIGHT AT BRIGUS SOUTH This photo could be in a children's storybook: the Milky Way is shining bright; Uncle Robert hops in his flying truck and can't wait to drive to the sky. This is not a composite photo, but a real panorama picture taken at Brigus South, in front of Robert's house. Brigus Head, the landmark of Brigus South, is on the right.

YEAR: 2021

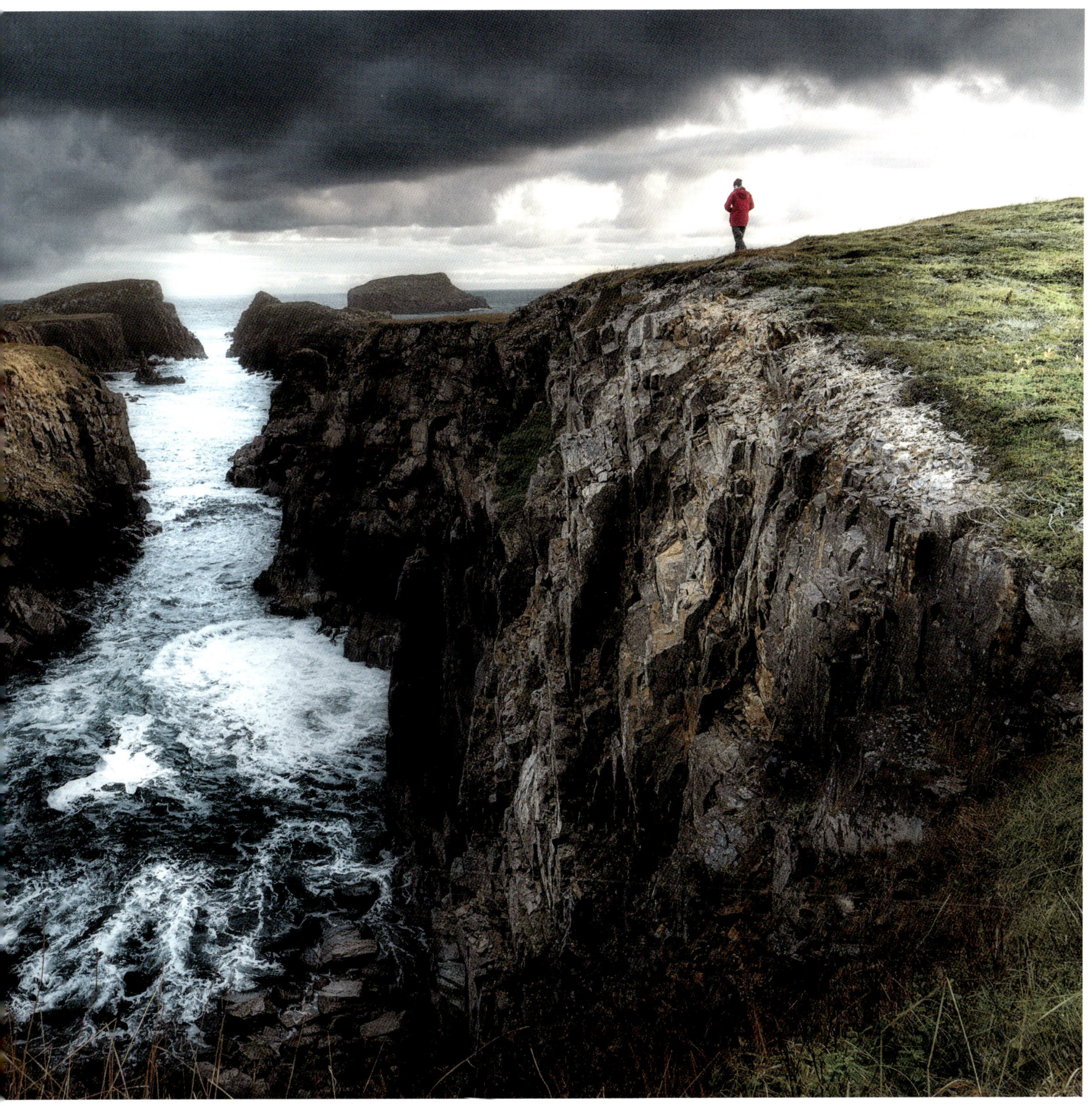

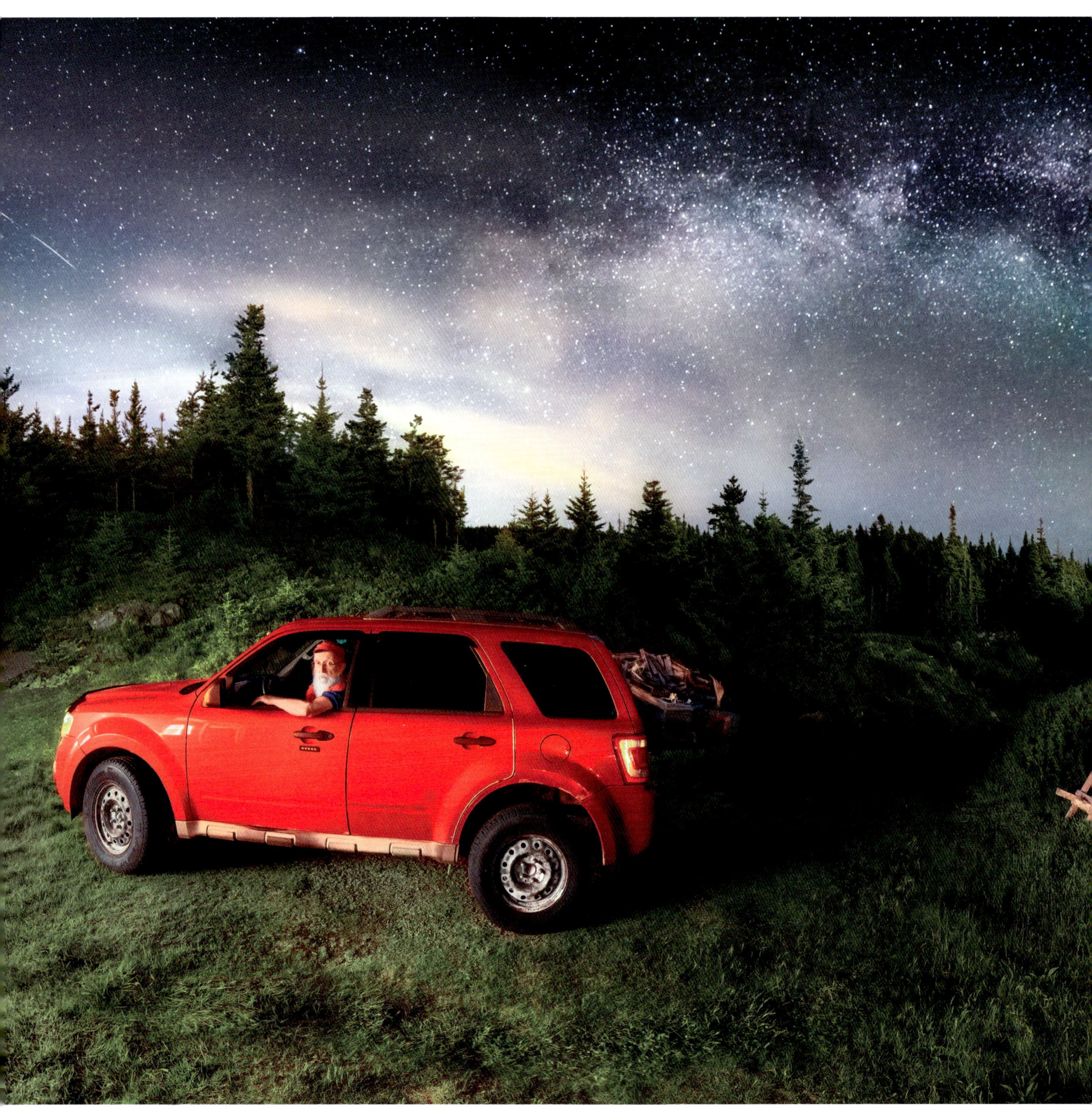

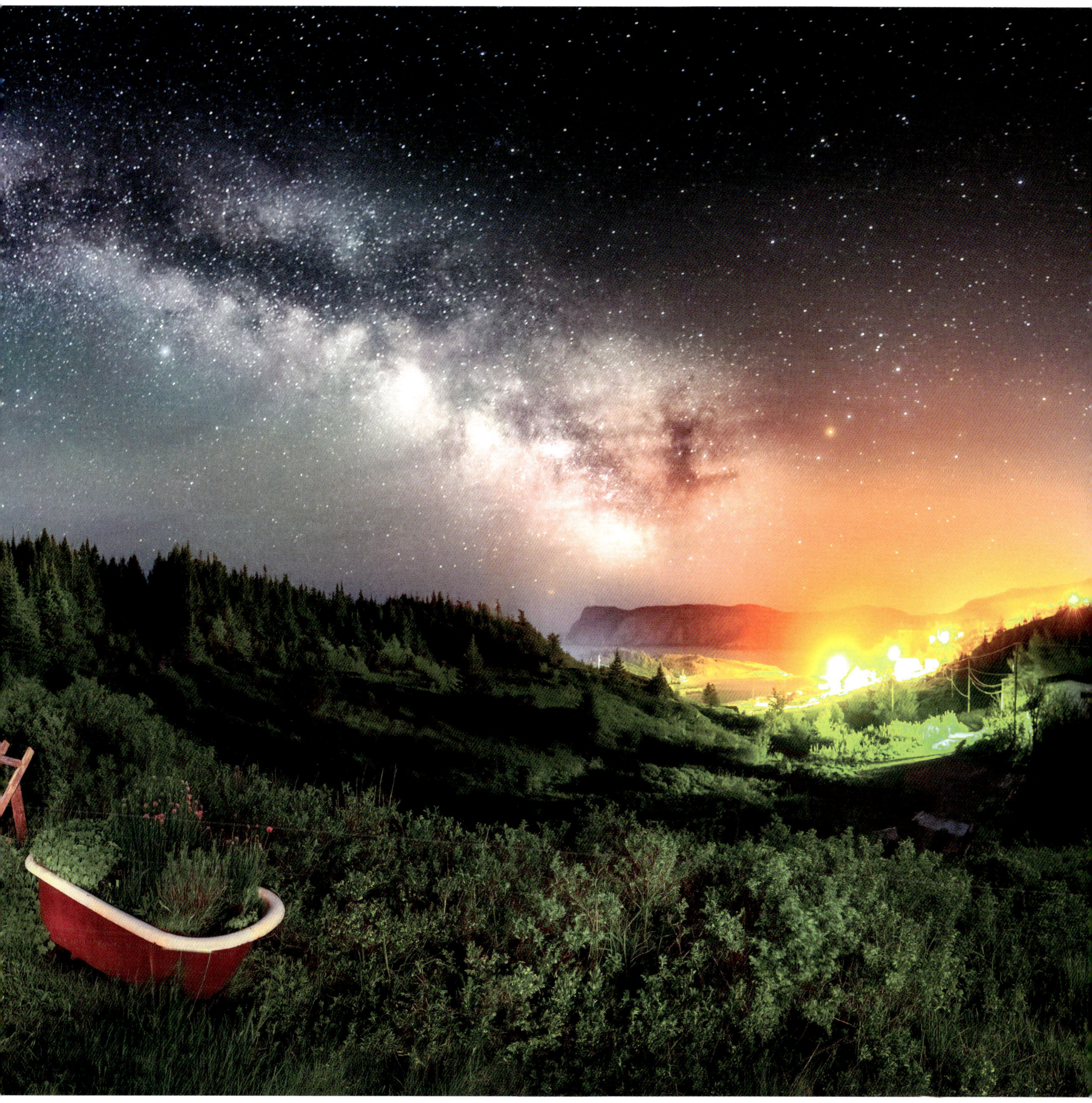

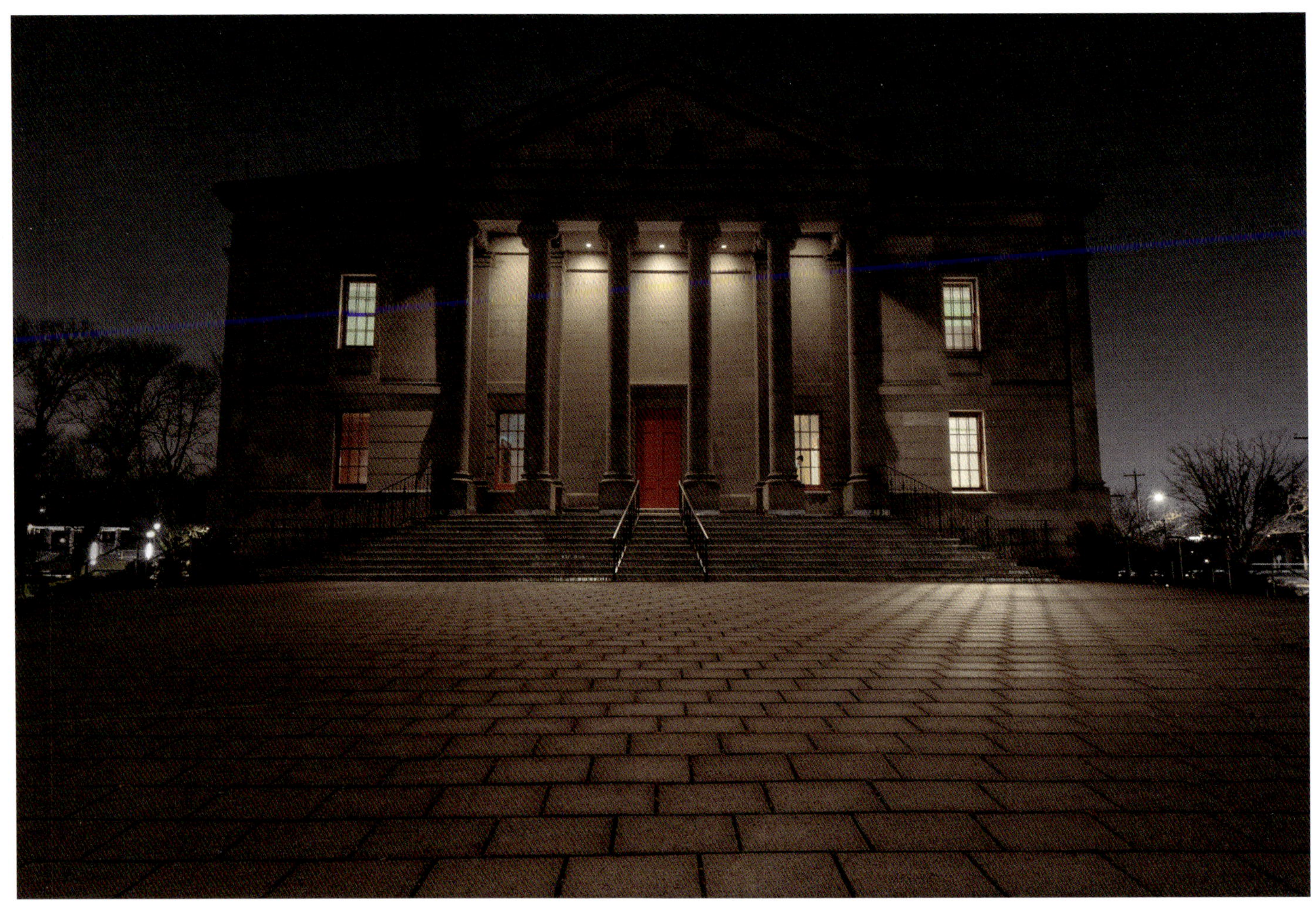

NOBLE SIMPLICITY AND QUIET GRANDEUR The Colonial Building is one of the most important historic sites in Newfoundland. It witnessed the historic moment when Newfoundland joined Canada in 1949. Robert, who was born one year before Newfoundland became part of Canada, is peeking behind one column in this photo. This great building with its soft light at night always reminds me of what Johann Joachim Winckelmann, a German art historian and archaeologist said—"edle Einfalt, stille Größe": "noble simplicity and quiet grandeur."

YEAR: 2020

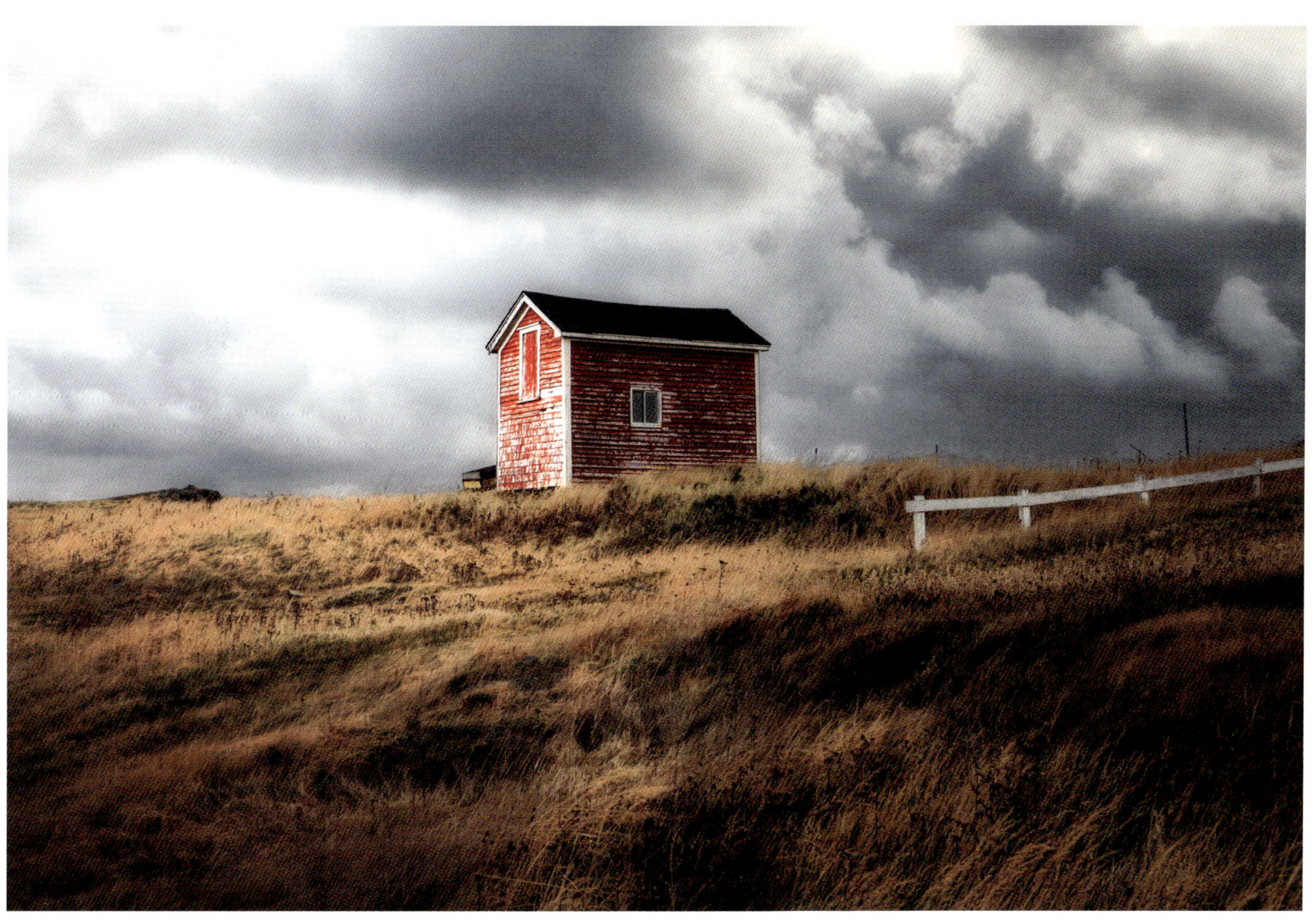

CHANGING CLOUDS IN ELLISTON I took this photo in Elliston when the clouds were constantly changing and forming dramatic layers.

YEAR: 2021

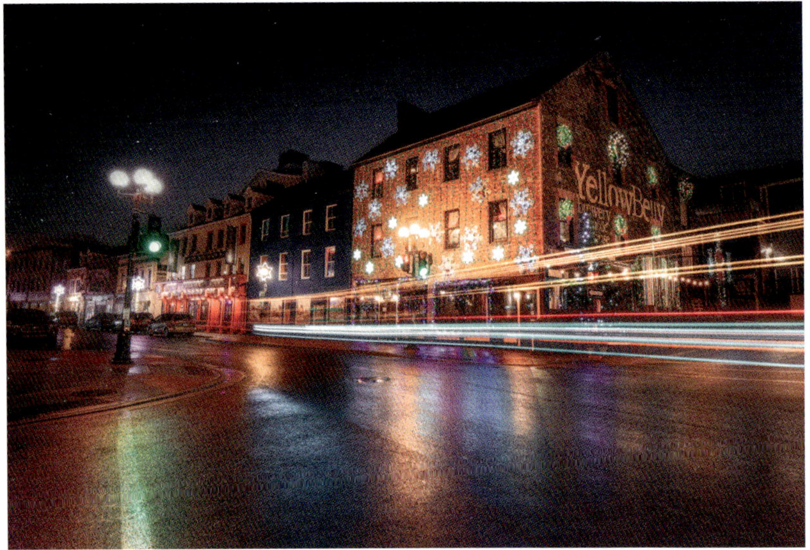

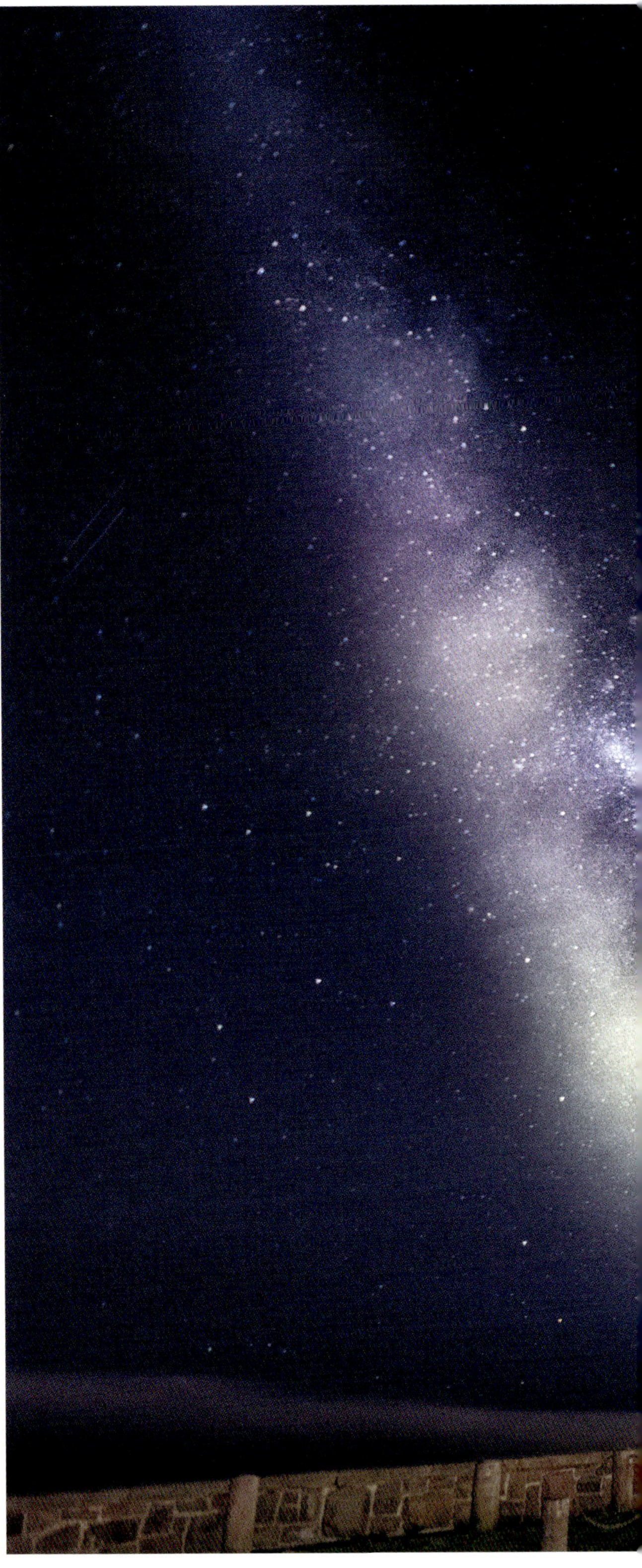

ABOVE

DELIGHTFUL LIGHTS The delightful lights in downtown St. John's around Christmastime.

YEAR: 2020

RIGHT

THE MILKY WAY ABOVE CABOT TOWER When I came to Newfoundland as an international student, Cabot Tower was the first historic site I visited. Robert, my first friend in Newfoundland, showed me around. I took this photo in the summer of 2020. Robert posed in this photo with a headlamp, and the Milky Way rises behind him. Cabot Tower is also a symbol of our friendship.

YEAR: 2020

FOLLOWING

BOAT LIGHTING IN PORT DE GRAVE Every year, fifty to sixty boats are lit with thousands of lights in Port de Grave from early December to early January, to celebrate Christmas and New Year. The boat lighting in Port de Grave has become a must-see in Newfoundland. Robert and I visited Port de Grave in 2019, before Christmas.

YEAR: 2019

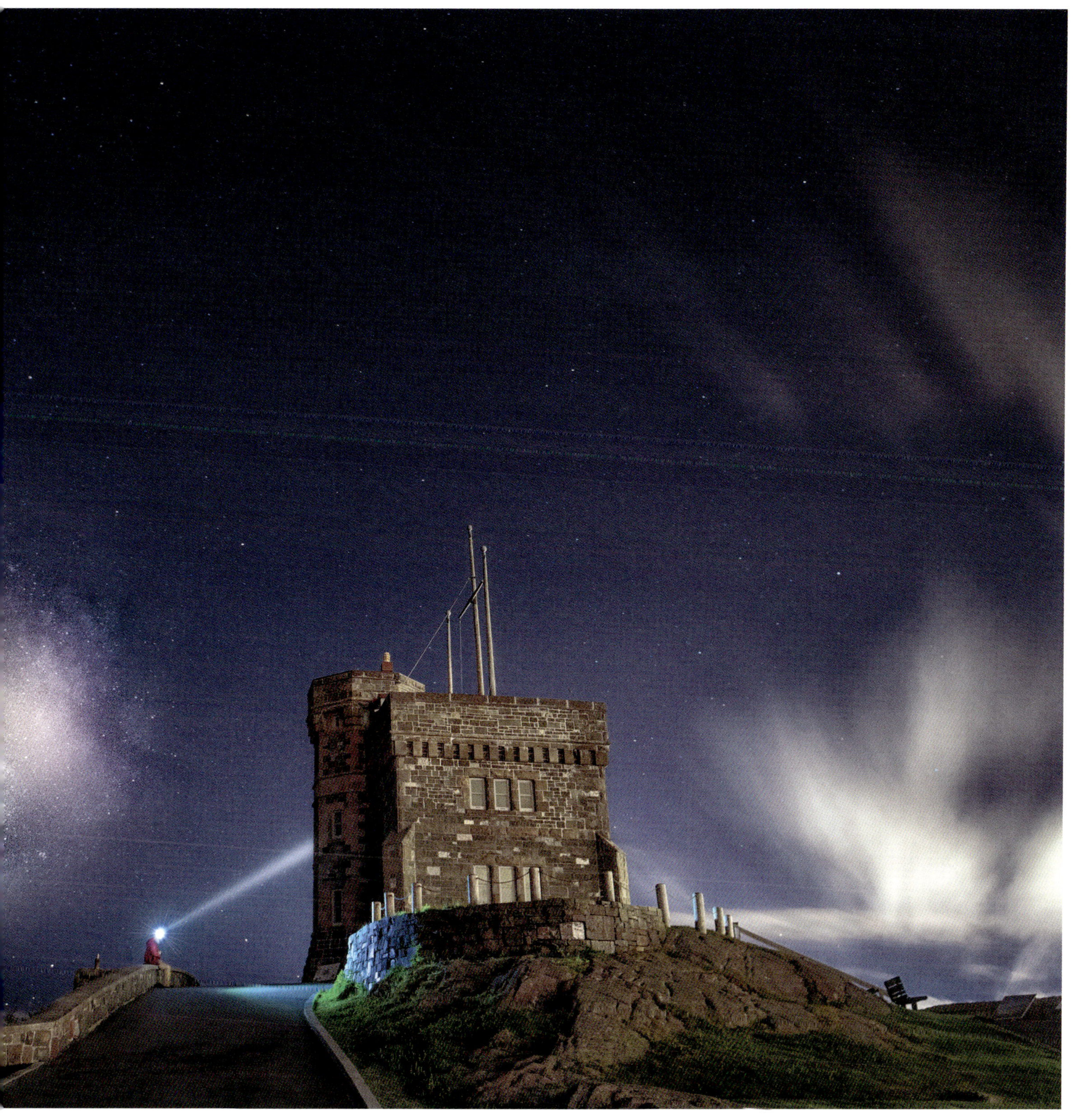

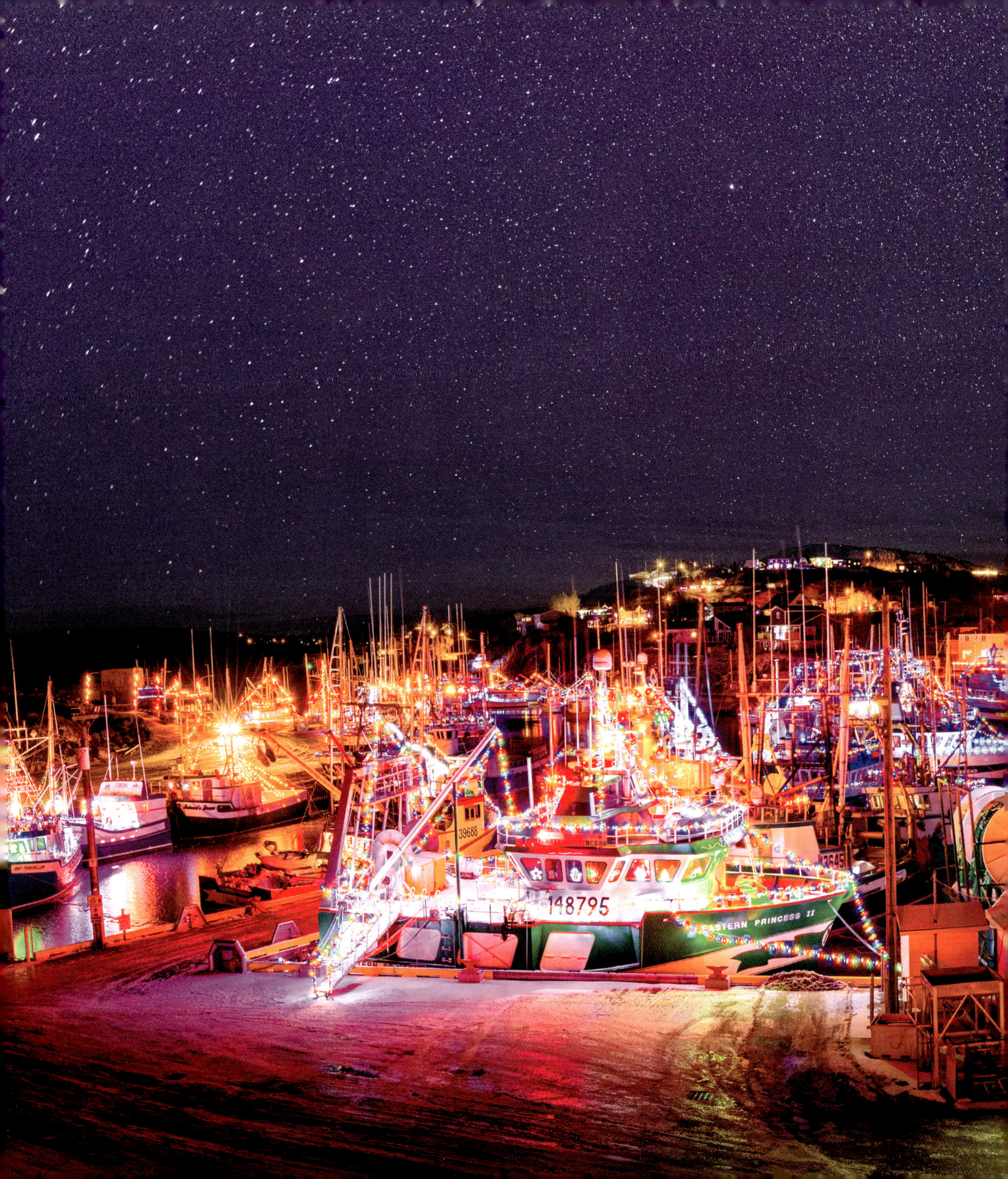
39688
148795
EASTERN PRINCESS II

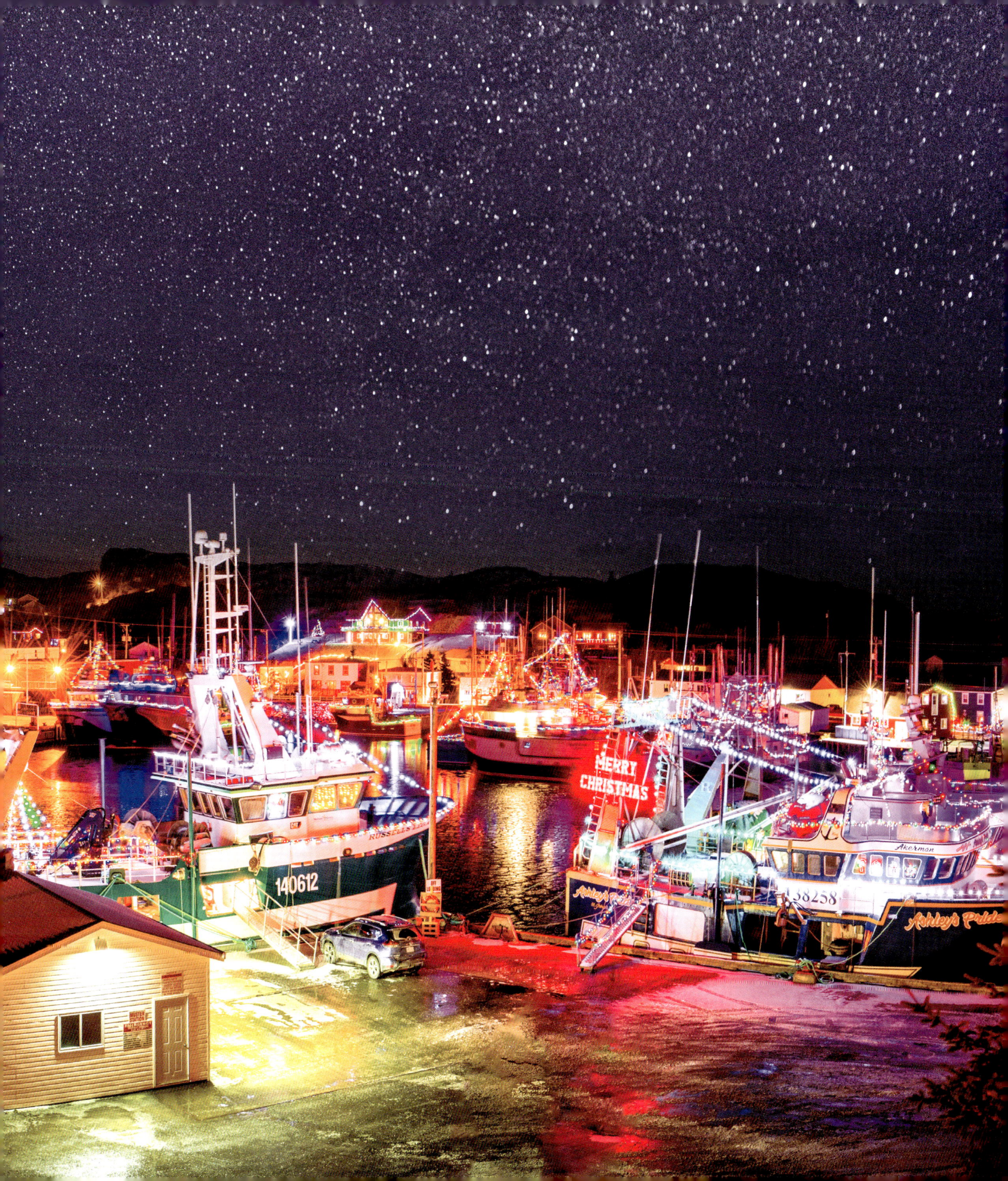
MERRY CHRISTMAS
140612
Ashley's Pride

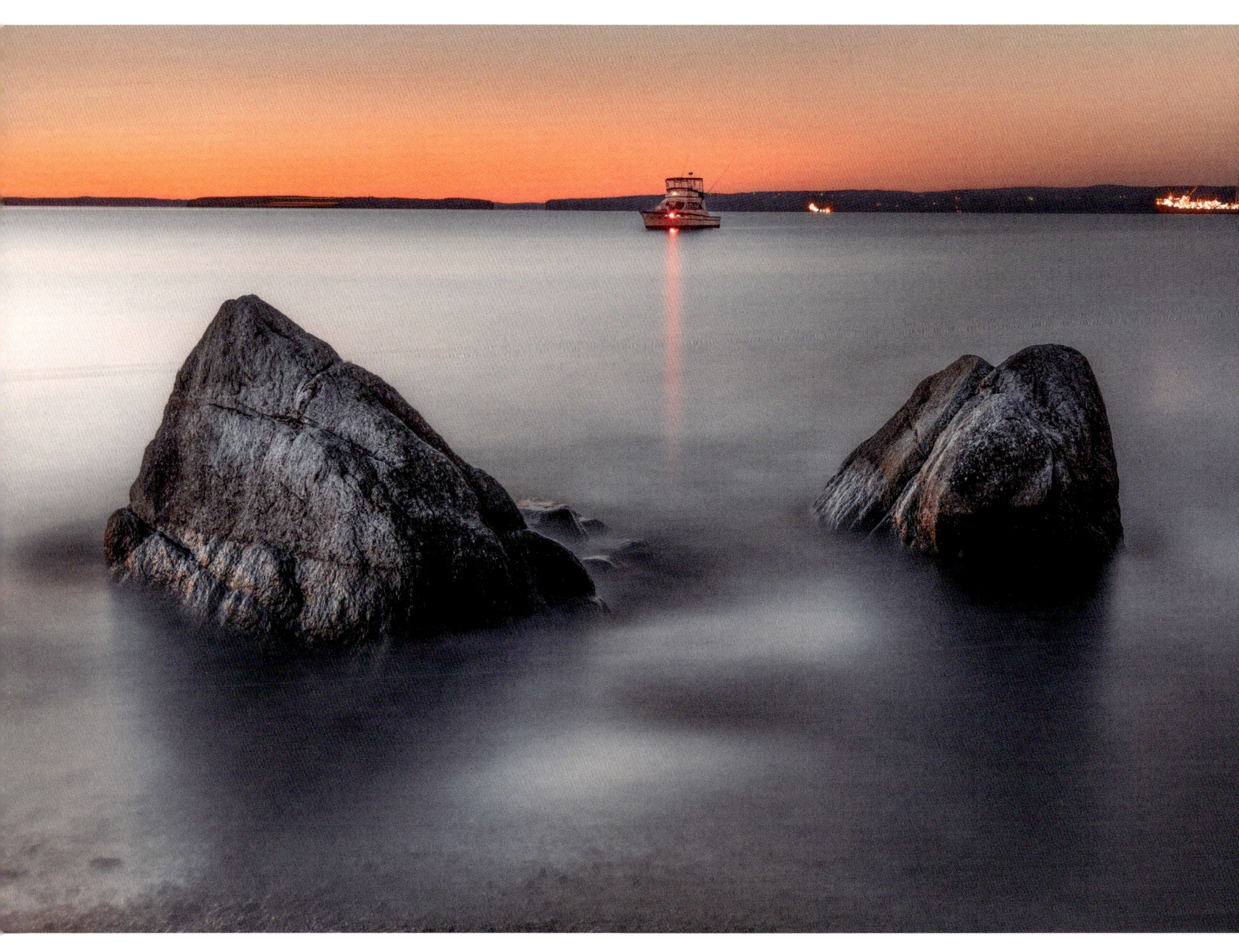

COMPANIONSHIP I love the two rocks at Topsail Beach. They must have kept each other's company for thousands of years.

YEAR: 2020

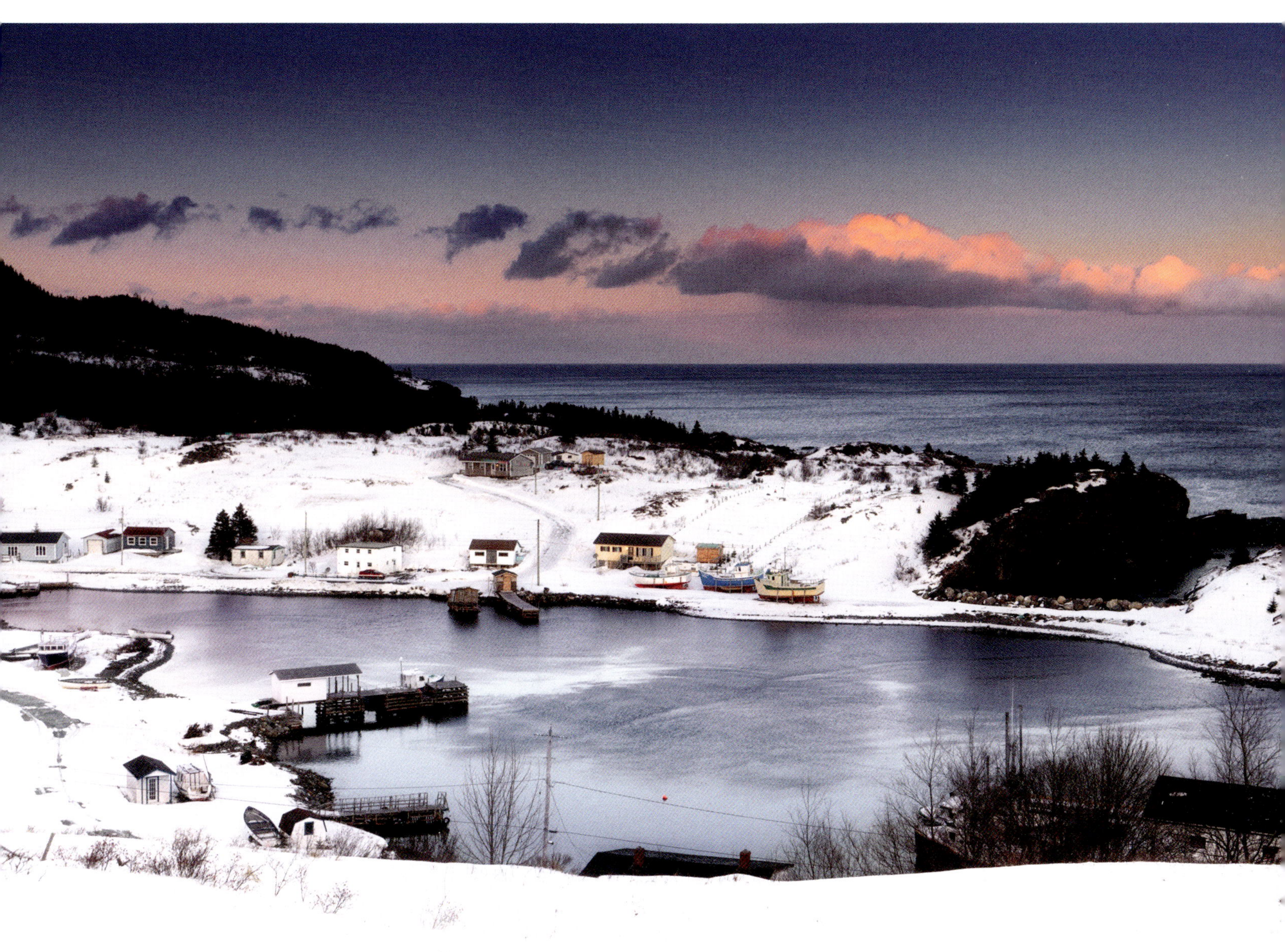

BRIGUS SOUTH EVENING A quiet evening in Brigus South. This small community is shrouded in dusk.

YEAR: 2020

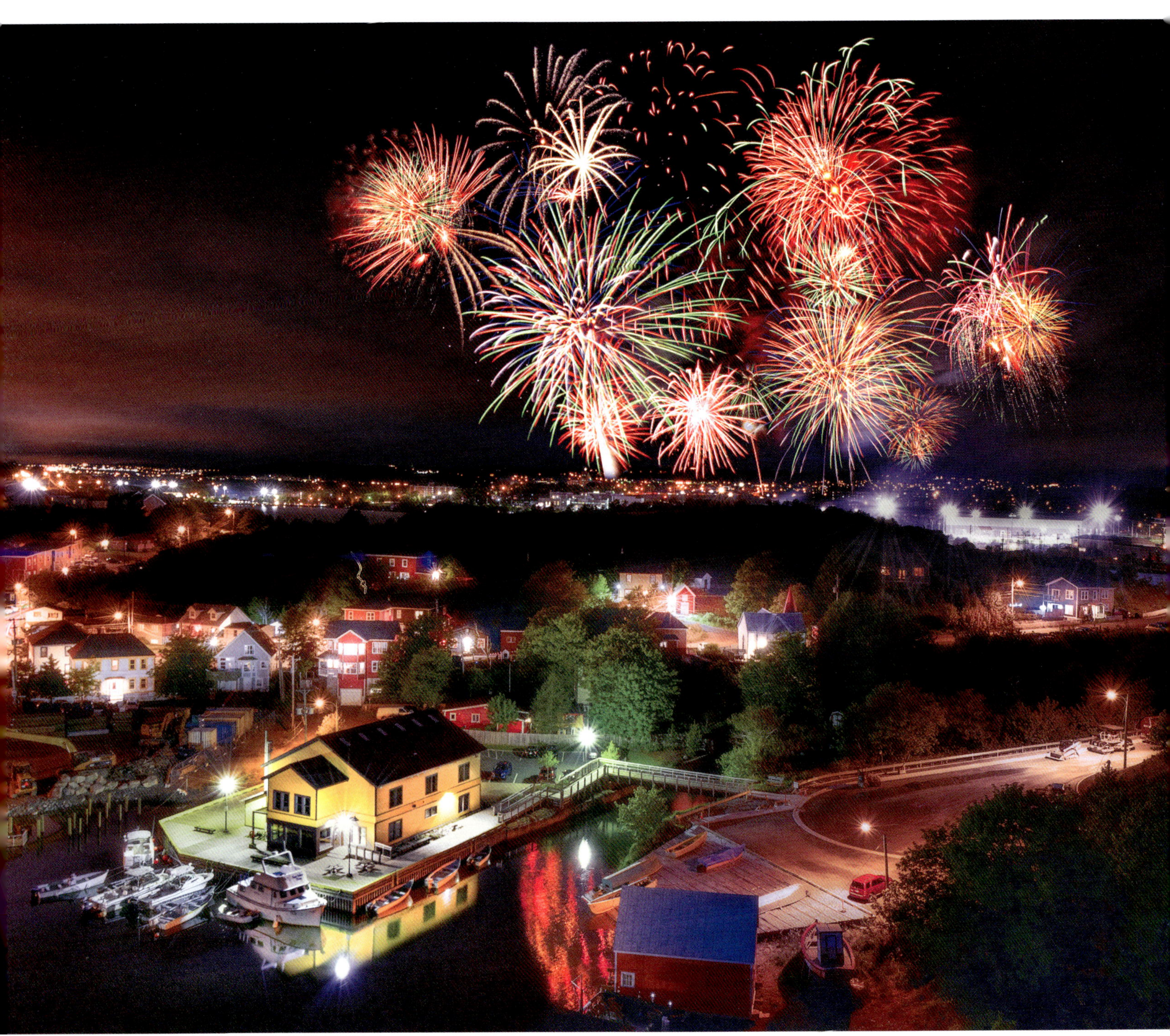

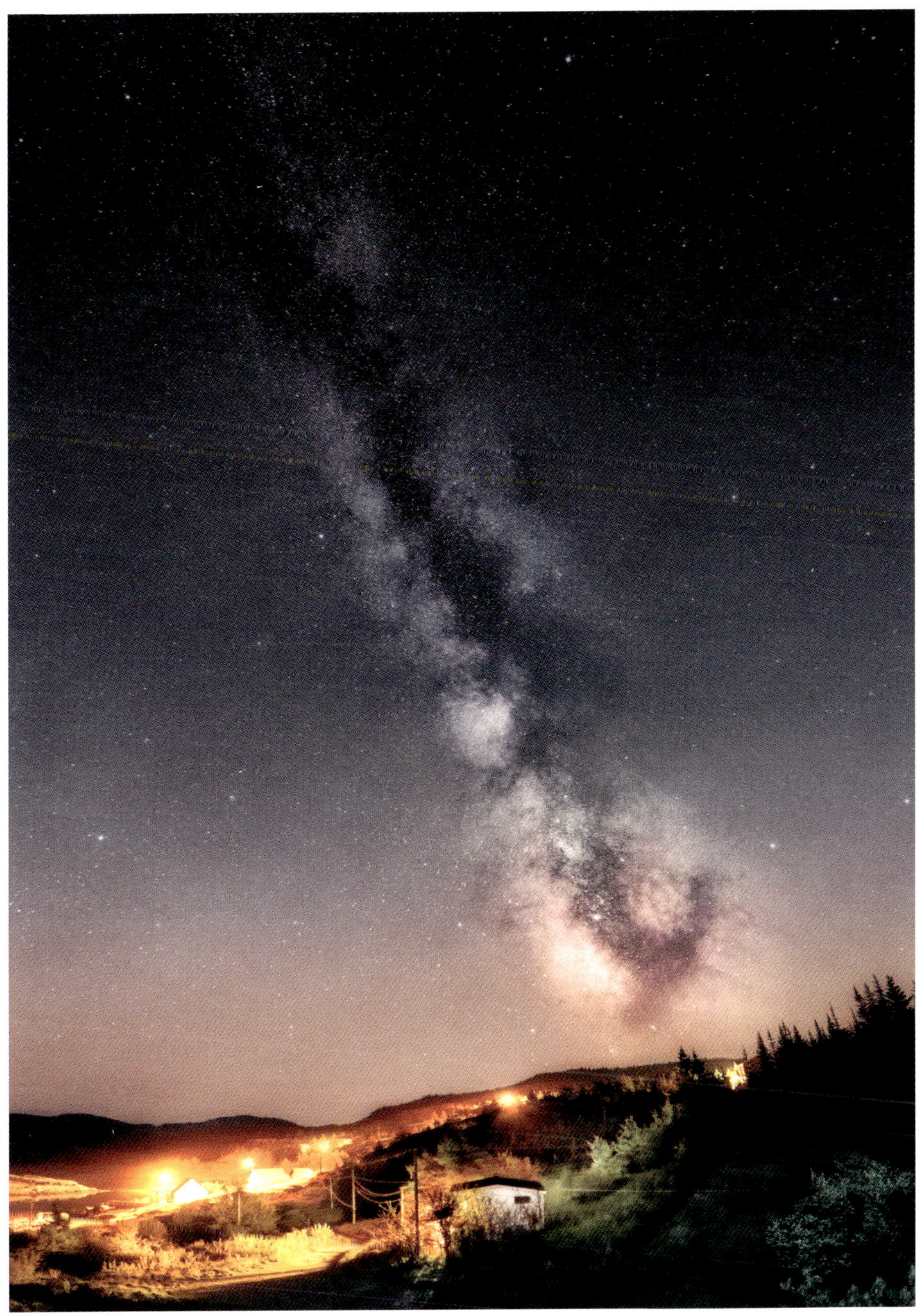

OPPOSITE

CANADA DAY FIREWORKS AT QUIDI VIDI Every year on Canada Day (July 1), the City of St. John's holds a popular fireworks celebration at Quidi Vidi Village. The rich colours of the fireworks and the festive atmosphere bring people a lot of joy.

YEAR: 2019

LEFT

THE MILKY WAY ABOVE BRIGUS SOUTH Above the sky of Brigus South, there is the Milky Way, over a century-old house that belonged to Robert's grandmother. Houses like this have seen the Milky Way rising and setting thousands of times.

YEAR: 2021

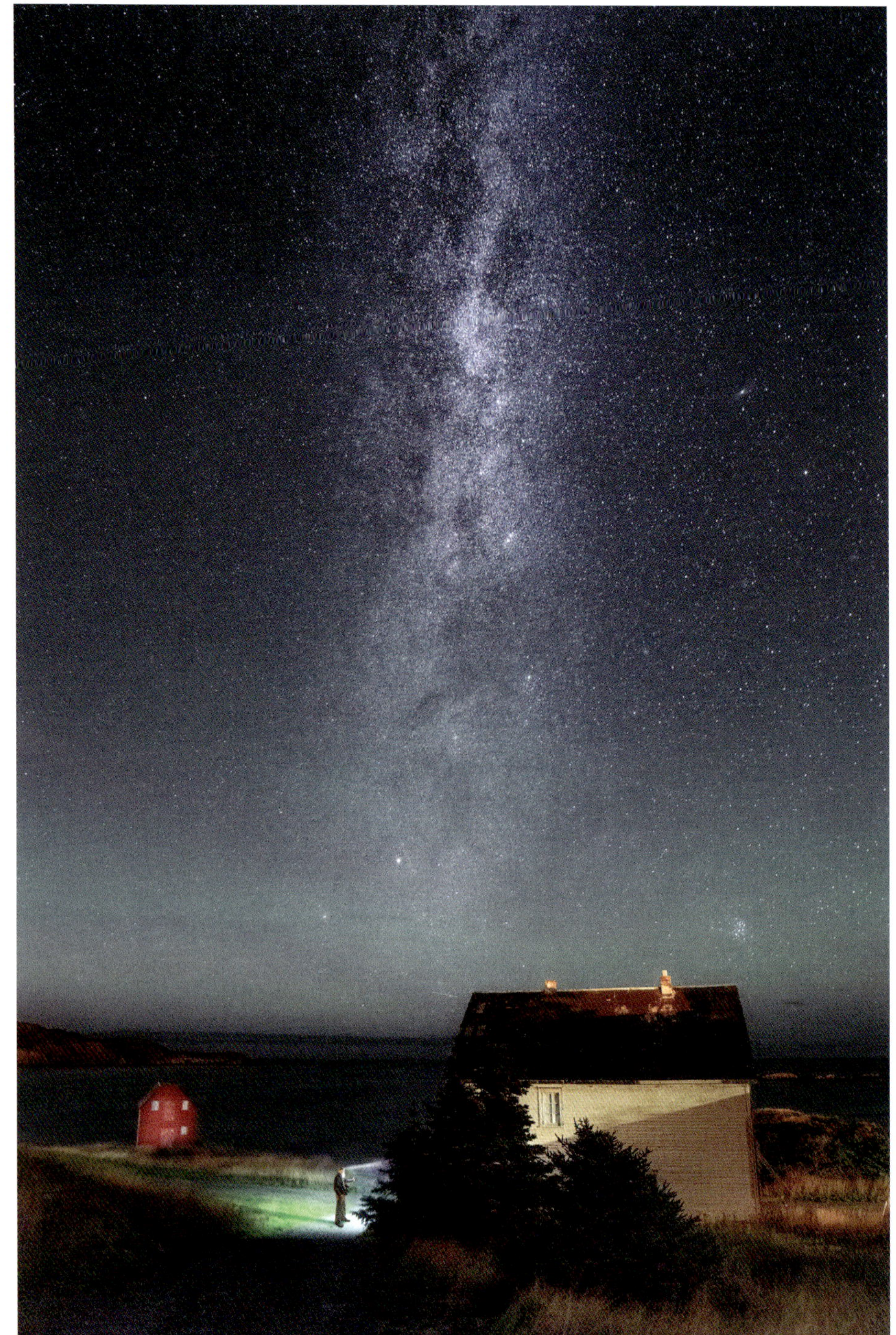

THE MILKY WAY ABOVE TILLEY HOUSE

The old man, the old house, and the Milky Way. Robert Tilley is standing beside the Tilley House, which was built by his great-great-grandfather in 1858 in Elliston. The Milky Way is shining, with some light clouds drifting below.

YEAR: 2021

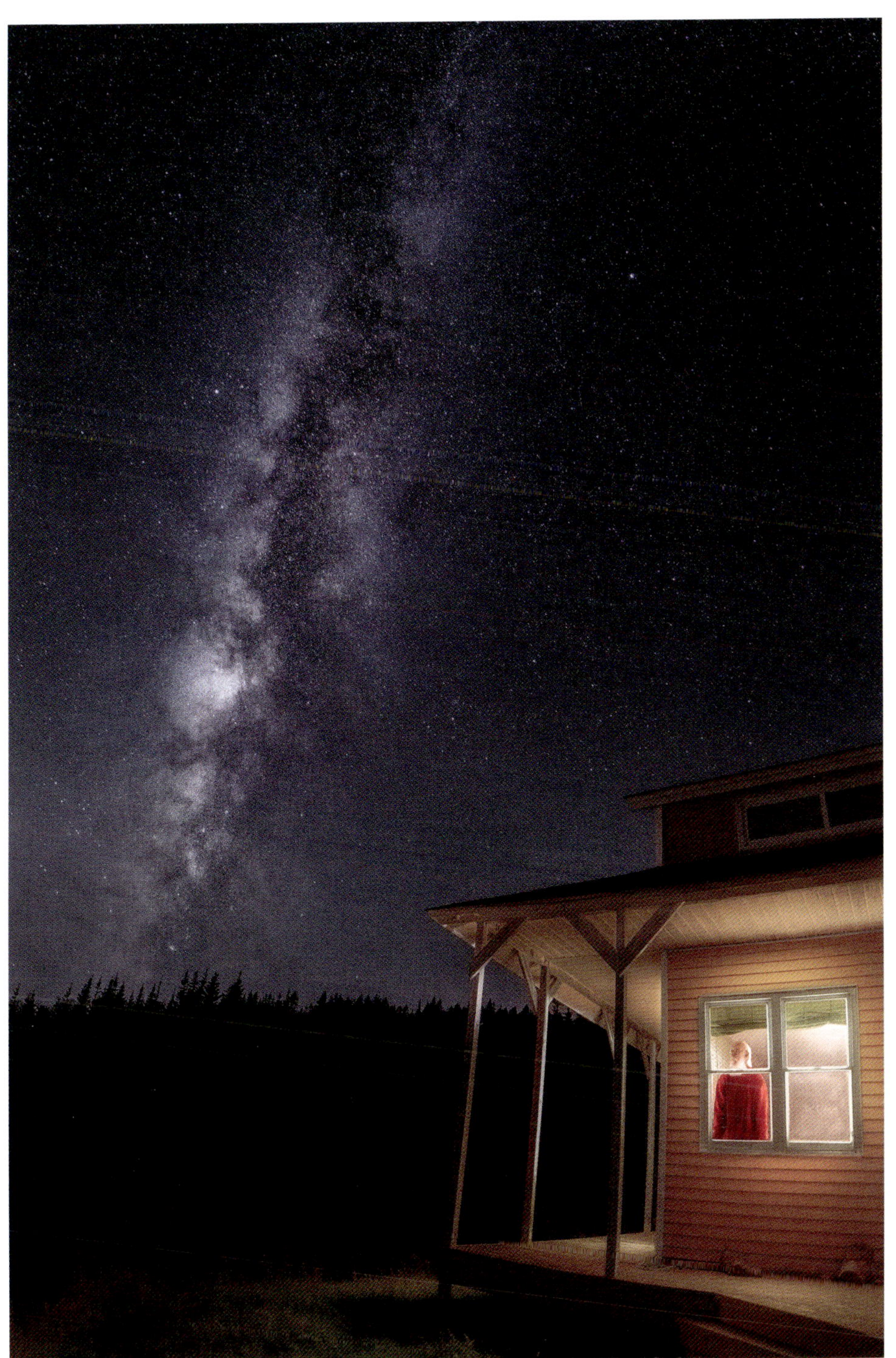

NIGHT IN BRIGUS SOUTH

A clear, quiet night in the fishing village of Brigus South. The Milky Way is shining in the sky. Its light mirrors the light from this house on the earth. Robert is standing beside the window of his house, which he built by himself more than forty years ago.

YEAR: 2021

SOUTH EAST BIGHT

Robert and I made an unforgettable trip to South East Bight, a tiny community on the east side of Burin Peninsula. It is accessible only by the ferry from Petit Forte. There are no cars in South East Bight. The main means of transportation is ATVs and, of course, your feet. We spent one night there and were lucky to see the Milky Way. I took this picture in front of the house where we stayed. The Milky Way is shining over a barn.

YEAR: 2021

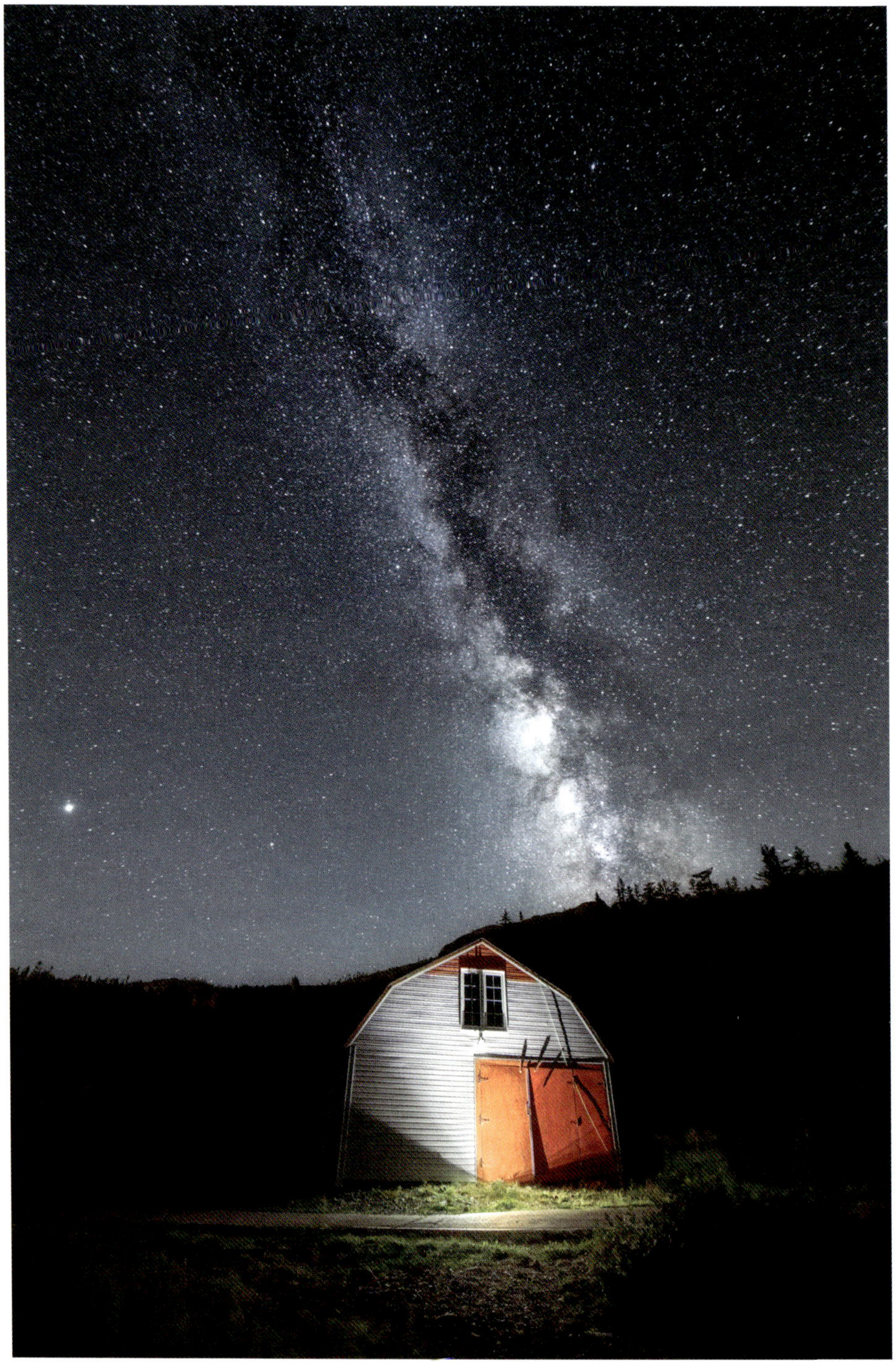

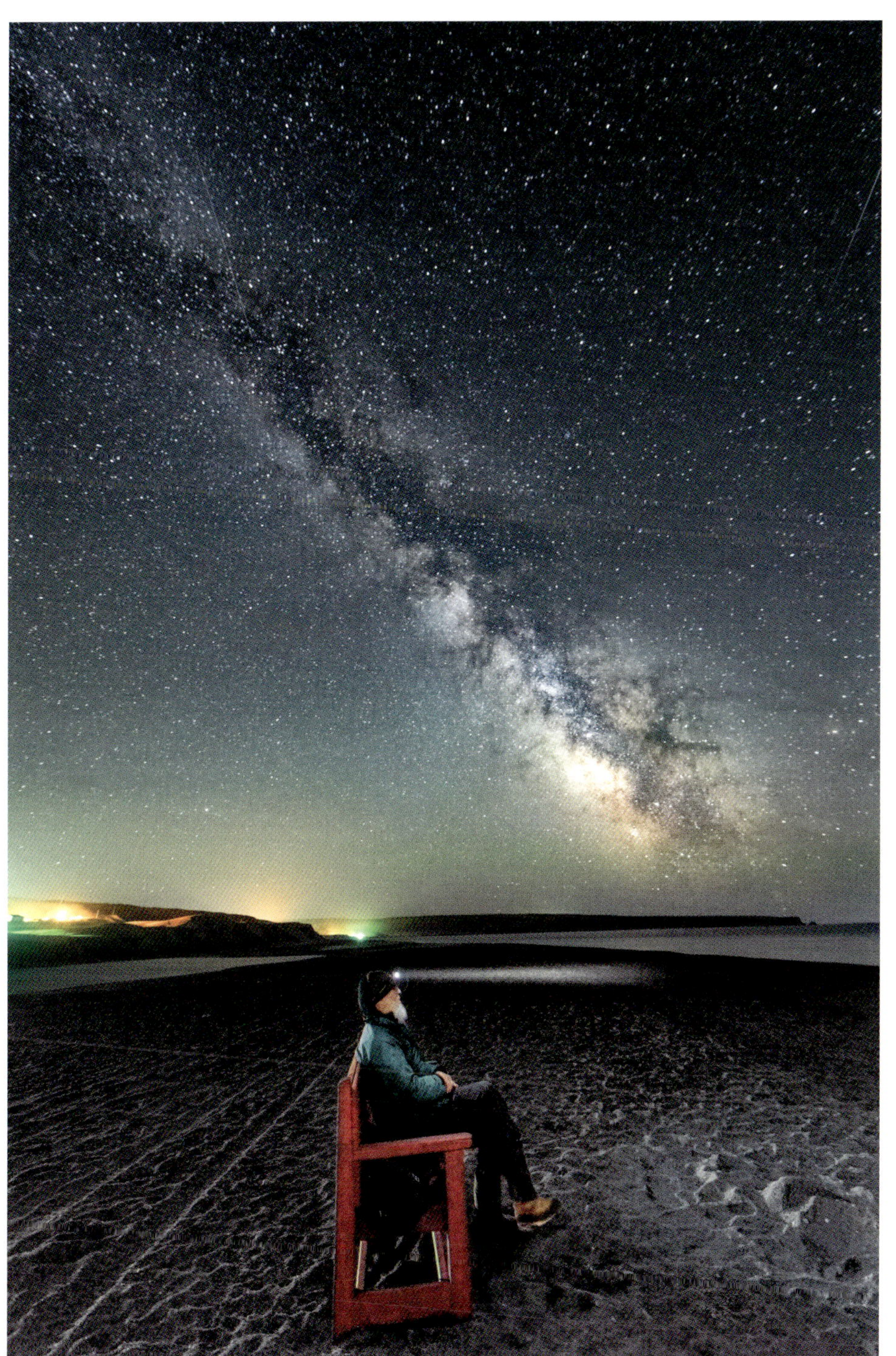

STARRY NIGHT AT ST. VINCENT'S

Robert and I were visiting a rocky Newfoundland beach at St. Vincent's on a starry night. We were lucky to see the Milky Way shining bright.

YEAR: 2021

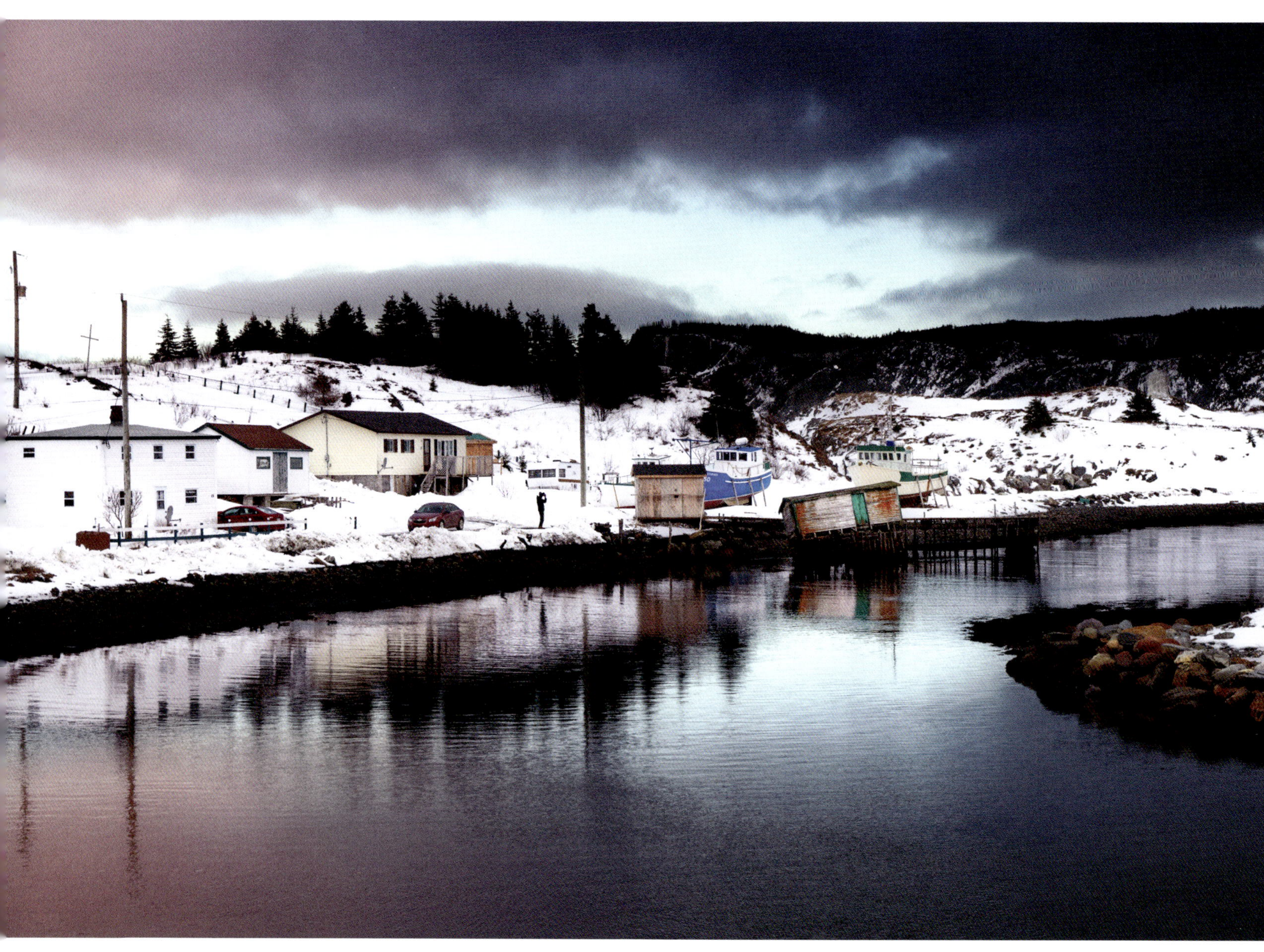

DUSK AT BRIGUS SOUTH Dusk in Brigus South. The tiny figure in this photo is Robert. He's taking photos of his favourite fishing stage, Francis Power Stage.

YEAR: 2020

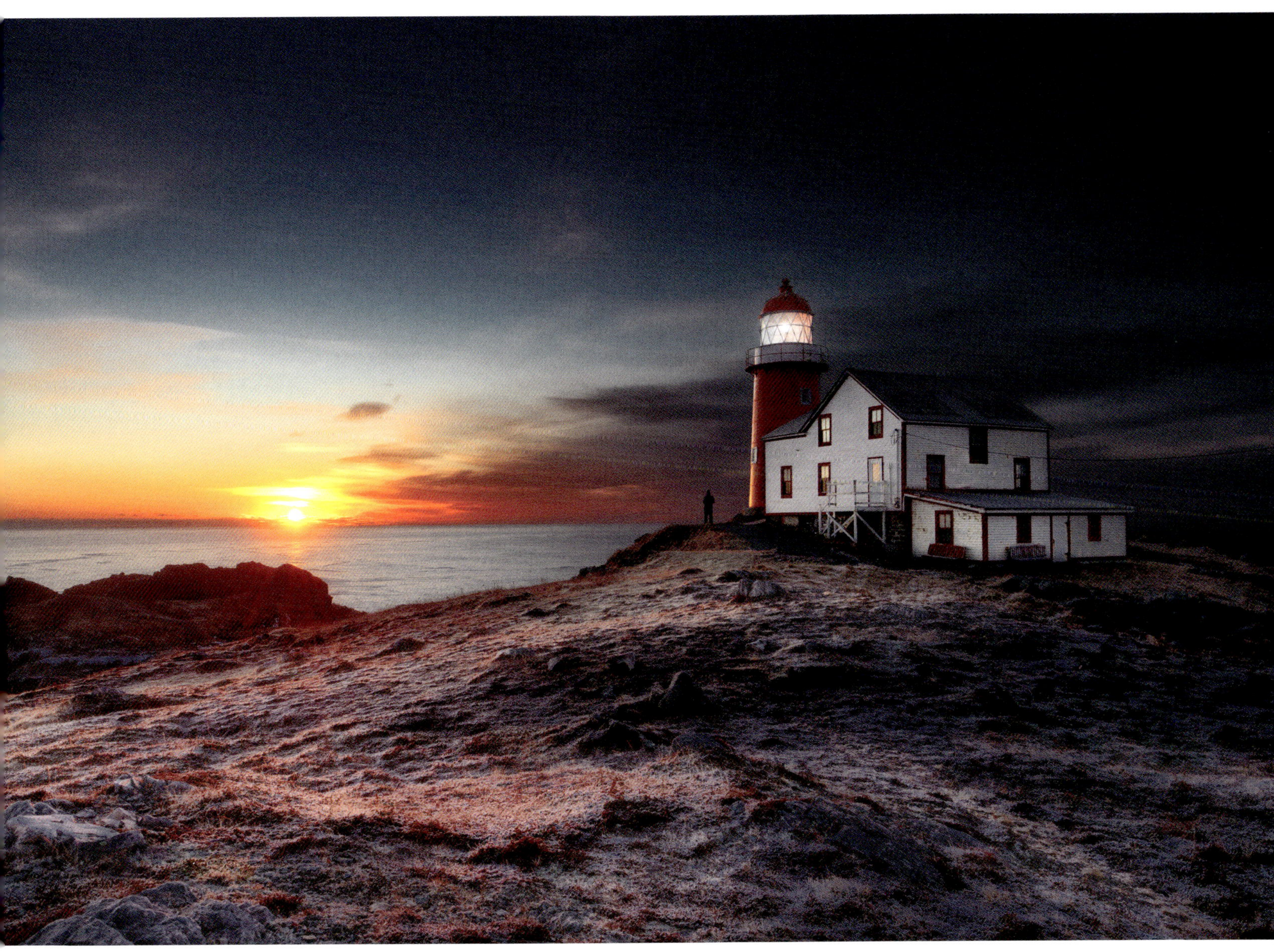

SUNRISE AT FERRYLAND LIGHTHOUSE Ferryland lighthouse is one of the province's magnificent historic sites. On the early morning of December 23, known as Tibb's Eve in Newfoundland, Robert and I hiked to Ferryland lighthouse. I took this photo while Robert stood in front of the lighthouse watching the sunrise.

YEAR: 2019

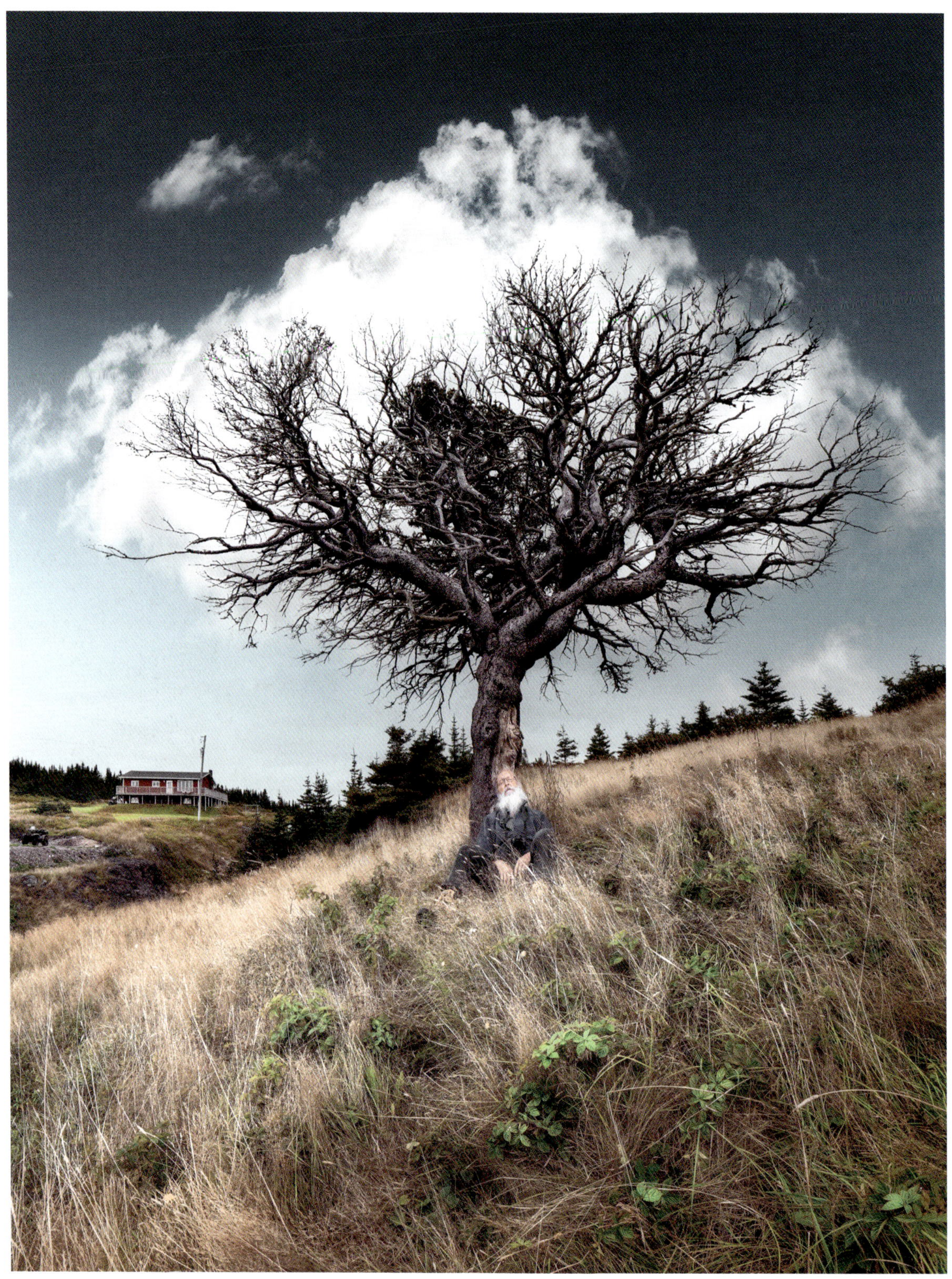

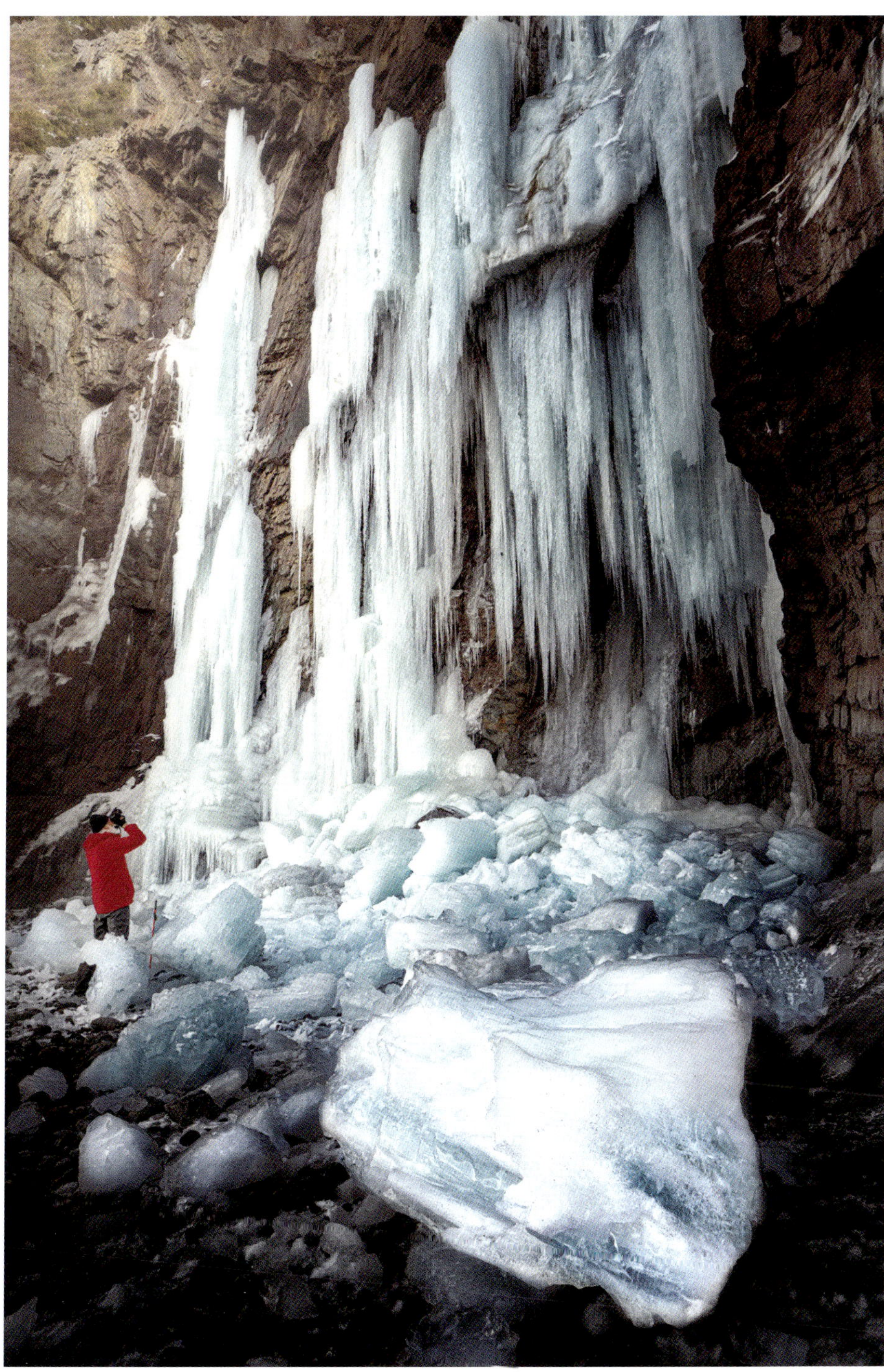

OPPOSITE

RESTING UNDER AN OLD SPRUCE Robert and I found this century-old spruce in St. Lawrence, a small community on the Burin Peninsula. They say that when spruce is old enough, clouds begin to grow on it. Robert napping under the tree looks just like Rip Van Winkle, a farmer in a folktale who wanders into the mountain and falls asleep for twenty years; when he wakes up, he has become an old man with a long white beard.

YEAR: 2021

LEFT

THE WORLD OF ICE
Middle Cove is famous for its giant icicles in winter. I took this photo when Robert was taking photos of the icicles.

YEAR: 2020

RIGHT

STARRY NIGHT AT COOK'S HARBOUR The Milky Way and its reflections at Cook's Harbour, the north end of the Northern Peninsula. Robert and I arrived there when it was getting dark and we were lucky to find a puddle with perfect reflections of the starry sky.

YEAR: 2020

OPPOSITE

THROWING A STONE You are never too old to throw a stone in the water. Robert was throwing a big stone into the water for fun at Ferryland, a community on the Southern Shore of Newfoundland.

YEAR: 2021

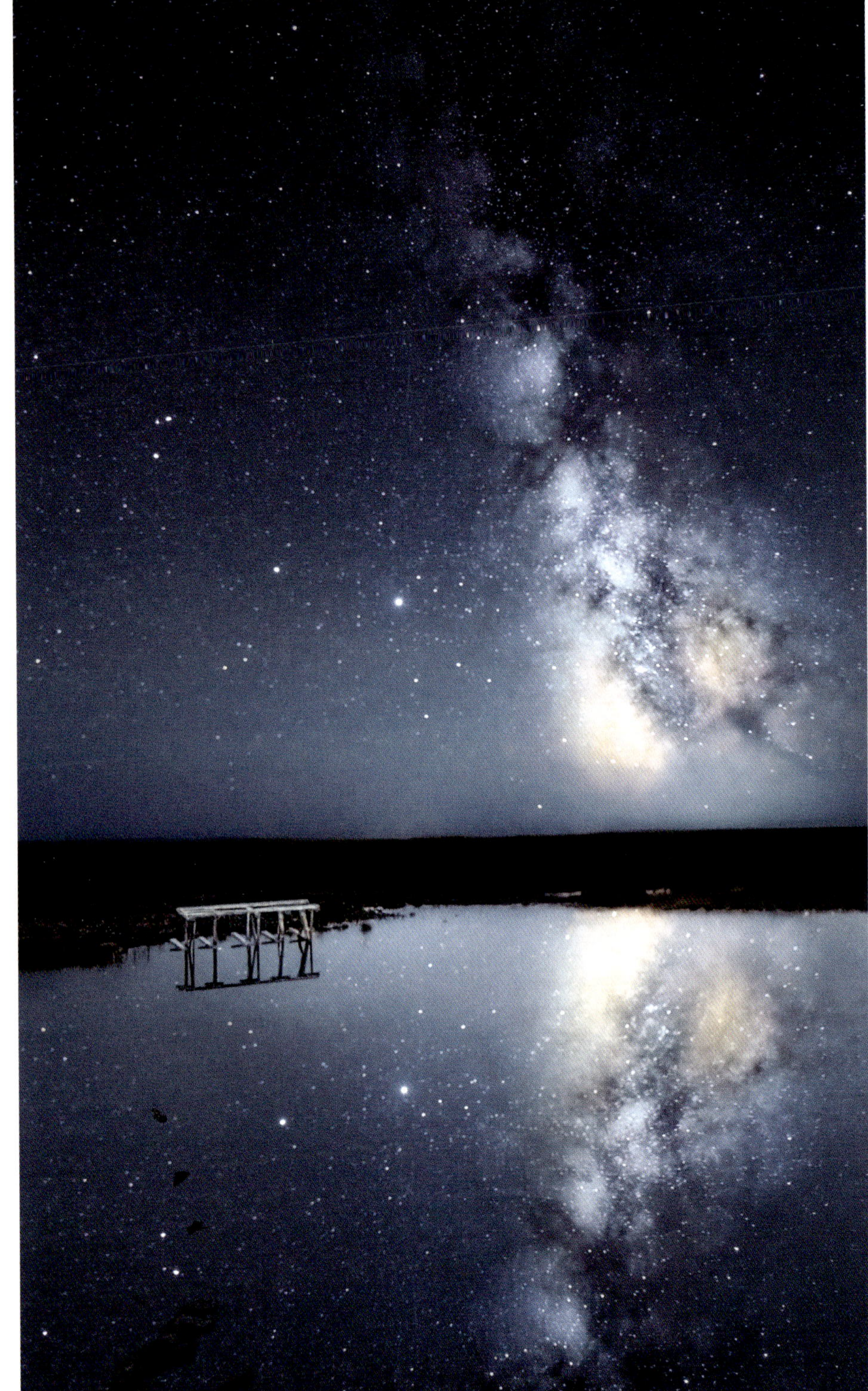

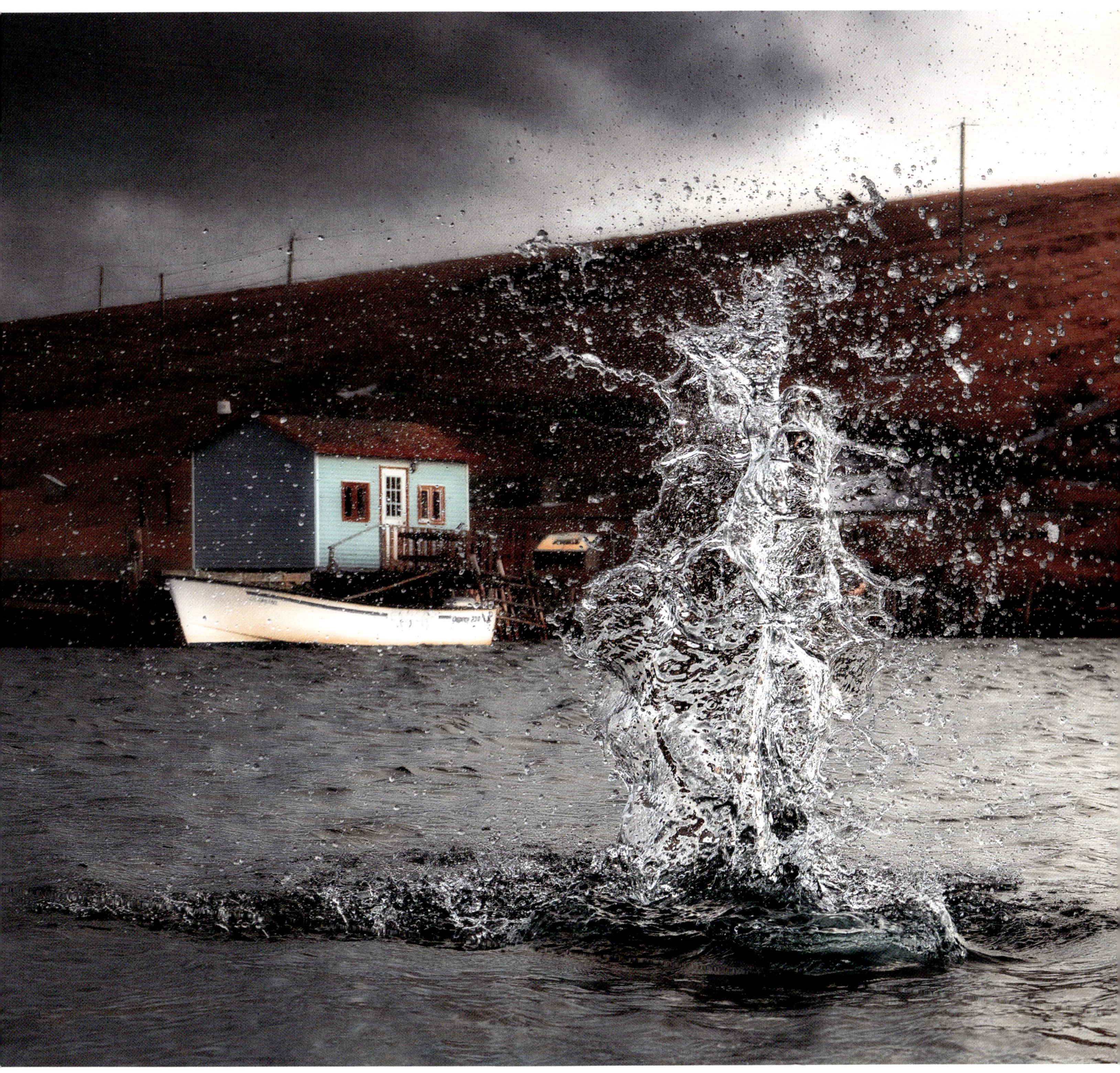

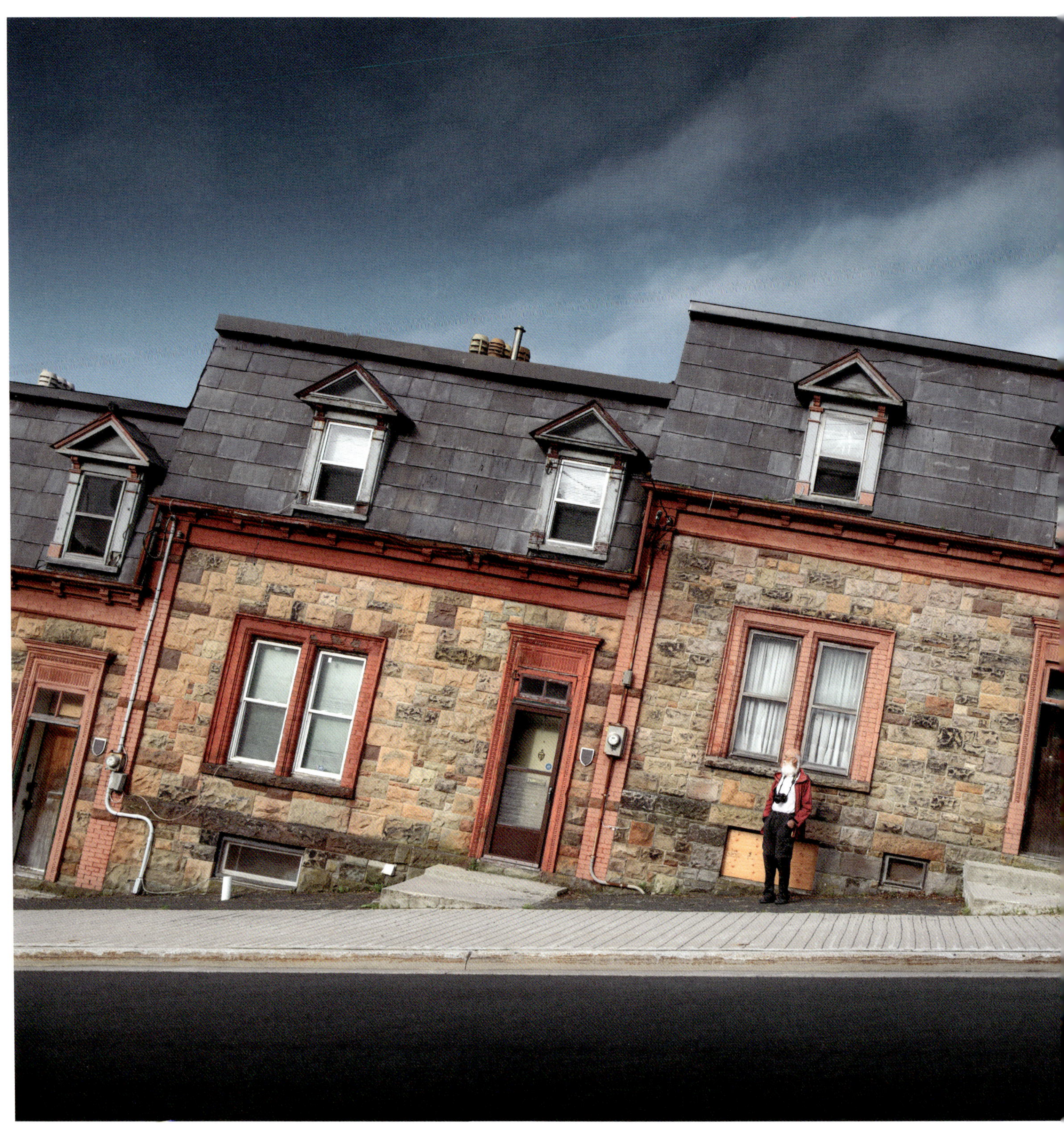

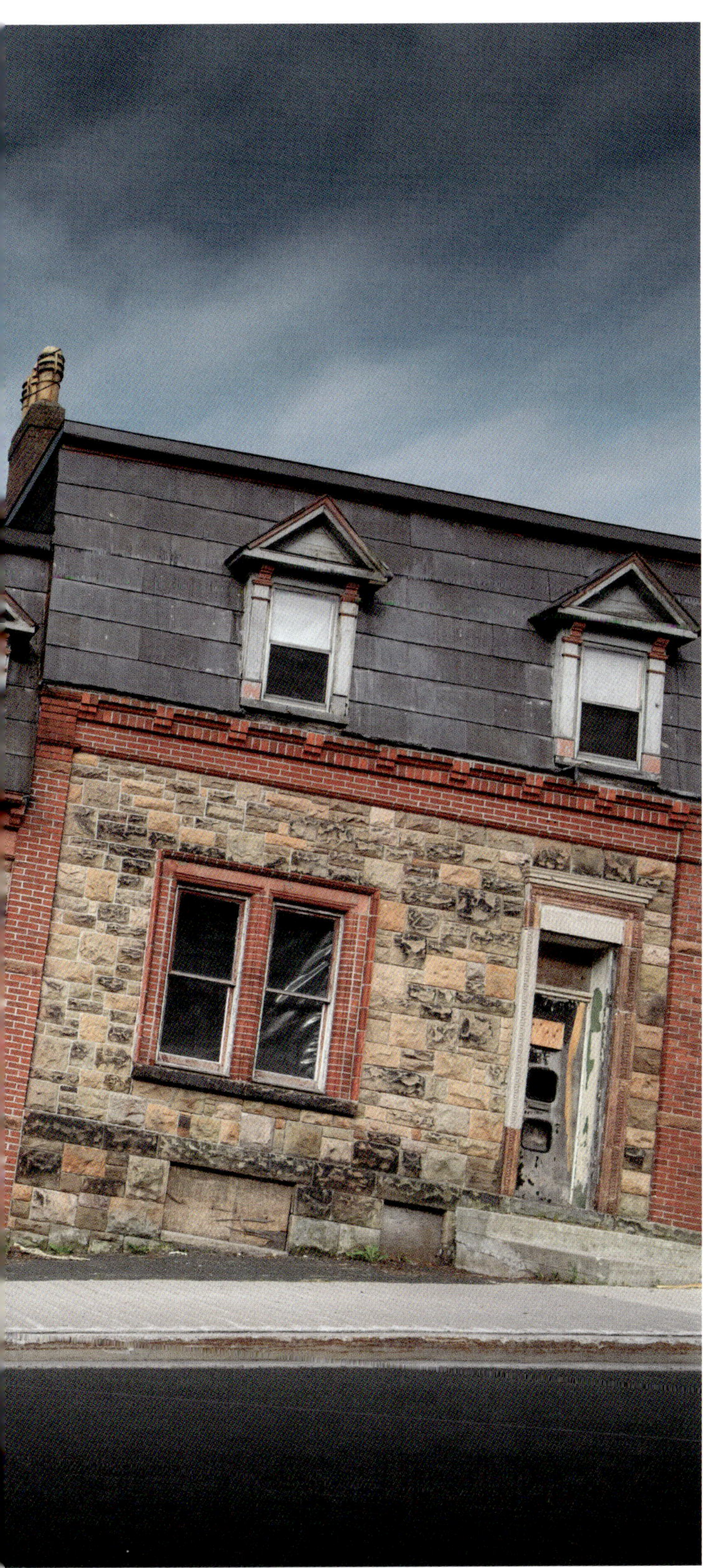

TILTING The Four Sisters in St. John's are a series of three-storey stone row houses. They were built in the late nineteenth century by Samuel Garrett, a prominent Newfoundland stonemason, as wedding gifts for his daughters. The Four Sisters were designated as Registered Heritage Structures by the Heritage Foundation of Newfoundland and Labrador in 1988. They are built on a hill that slopes steeply down toward St. John's harbour; that is why, if you make the ground horizontal, the houses seem to tilt. In this photo, Robert is standing in front of the houses.

YEAR: 2020

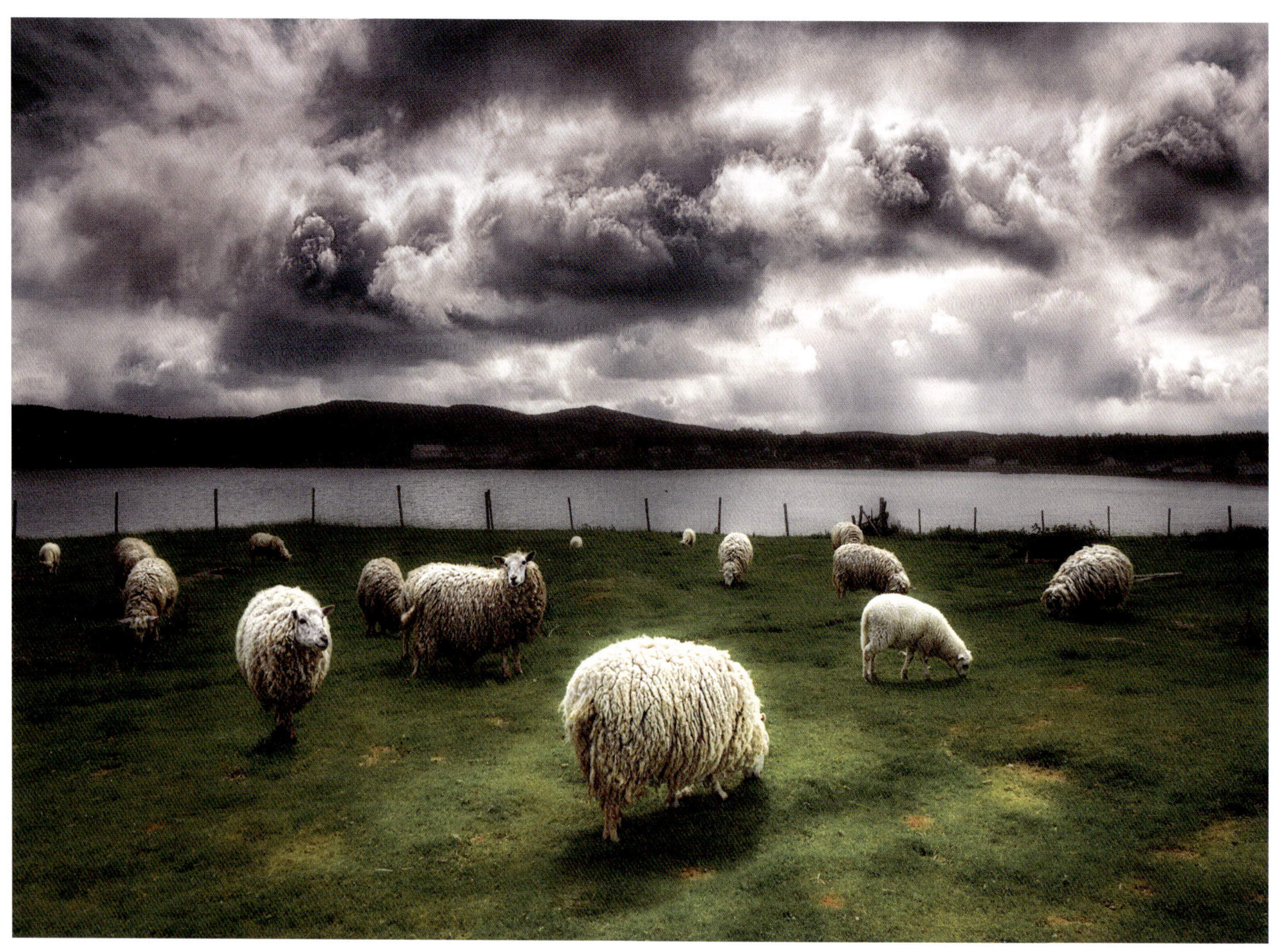

HEAVEN PASTURE On our road trip, we stopped by a farm in the village of Laurenceton, Newfoundland. A few sheep were grazing on the green pasture, some of them looking at us with curiosity. Suddenly the weather changed and the clouds in the sky began to swirl and gather, which made them look like a flock of sheep with curly fur. Maybe there is a pasture in heaven.

YEAR: 2020

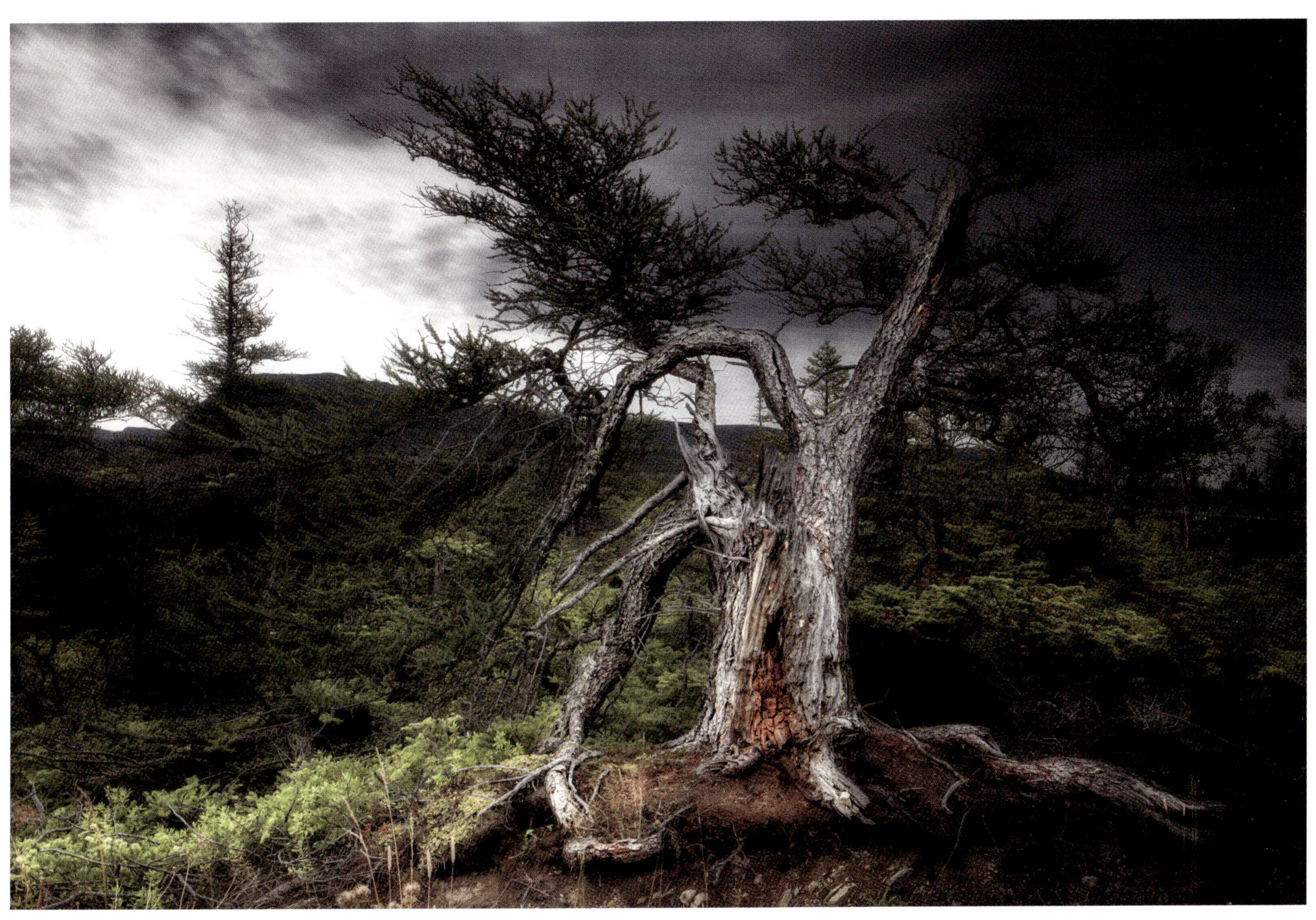

A WARRIOR A tree at Western Brook, Gros Morne. Its branches are twisted and half of its body has been cracked, but still it is struggling to live. A warrior.

YEAR: 2020

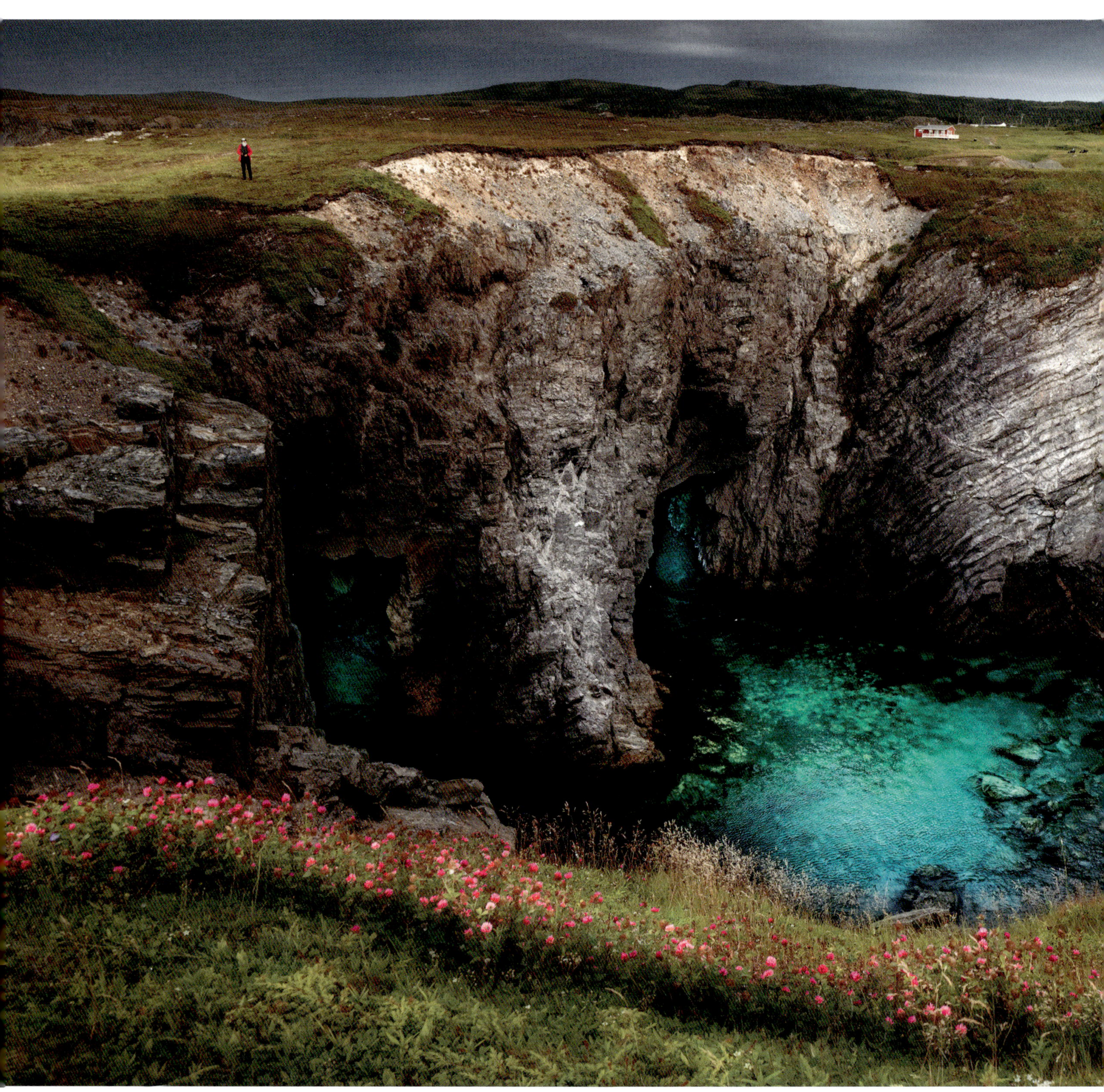

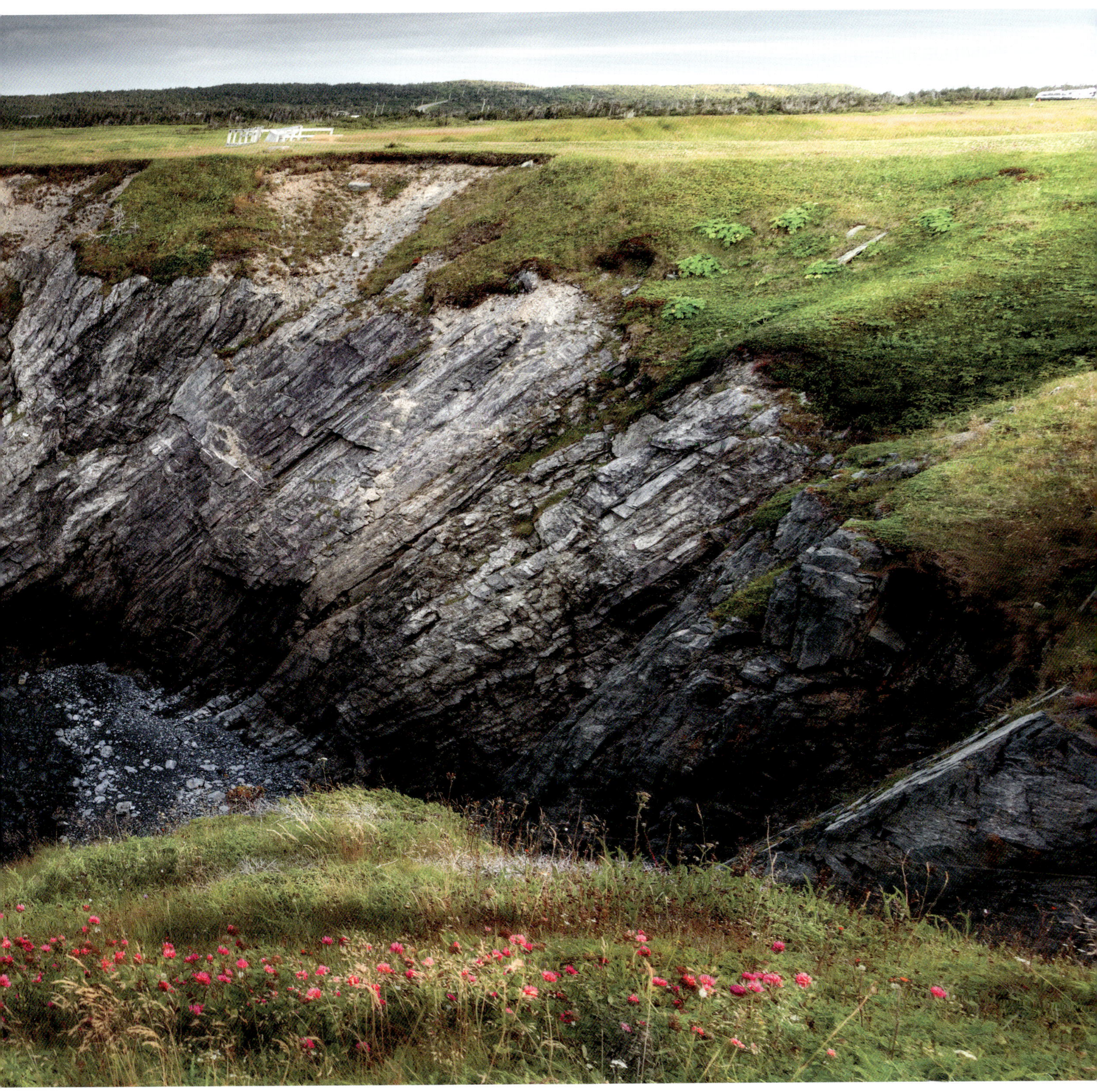

PREVIOUS

THE EYE OF THE EARTH This is a panorama view of the Dungeon in Bonavista, Newfoundland. The Atlantic Ocean sculpted a huge cave and two giant arches out of the rocks during the past tens of thousands of years. The glowing blue sea water in the Dungeon looks like an eyeball, and the rocks and ground around it look like the eyelids. This is the Eye of the Earth, which has been gazing for eons. Robert is standing in the upper left corner as a reference to show how big the Dungeon is. His ancestors began to settle in this area in the early nineteenth century.

YEAR: 2020

RIGHT

OCEAN HEART The huge cave and the giant arches in the rock were sculpted by running sea water over tens of thousands of years. The Dungeon looks like a glowing blue diamond heart of the ocean when the sea water is still.

YEAR: 2020

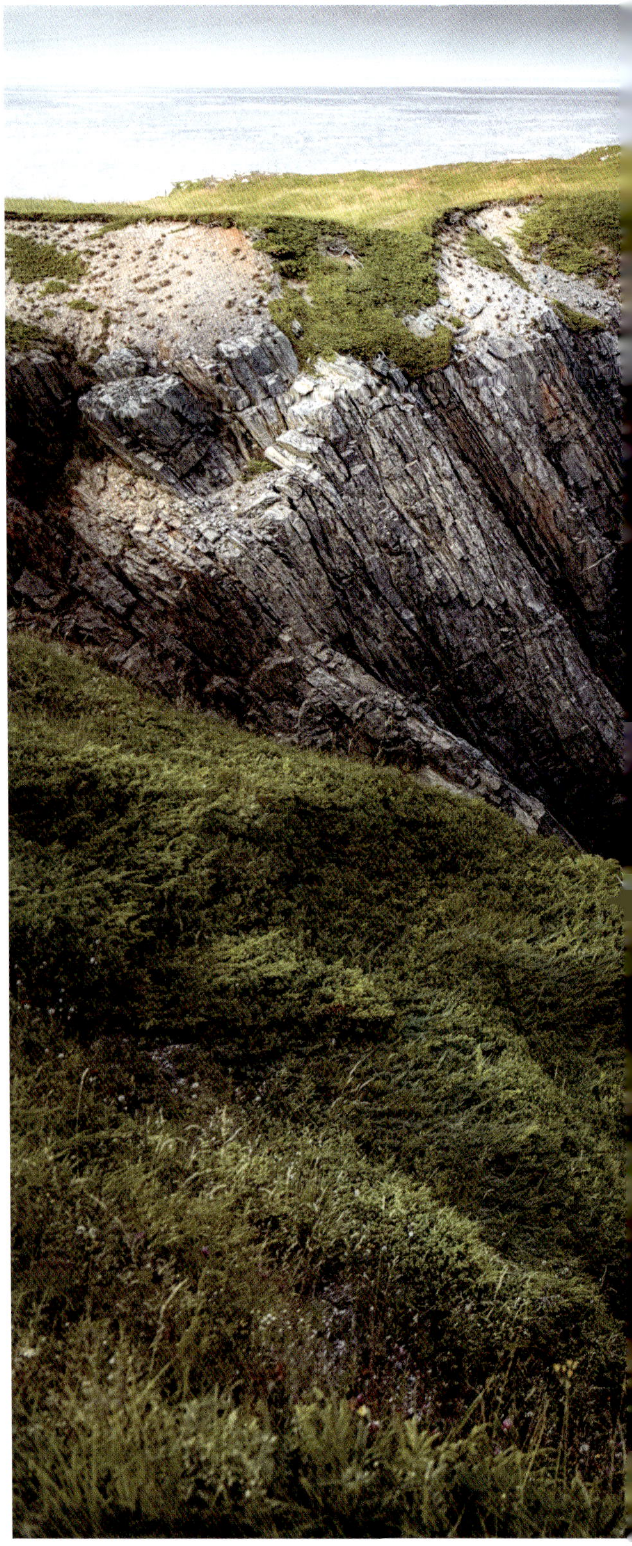

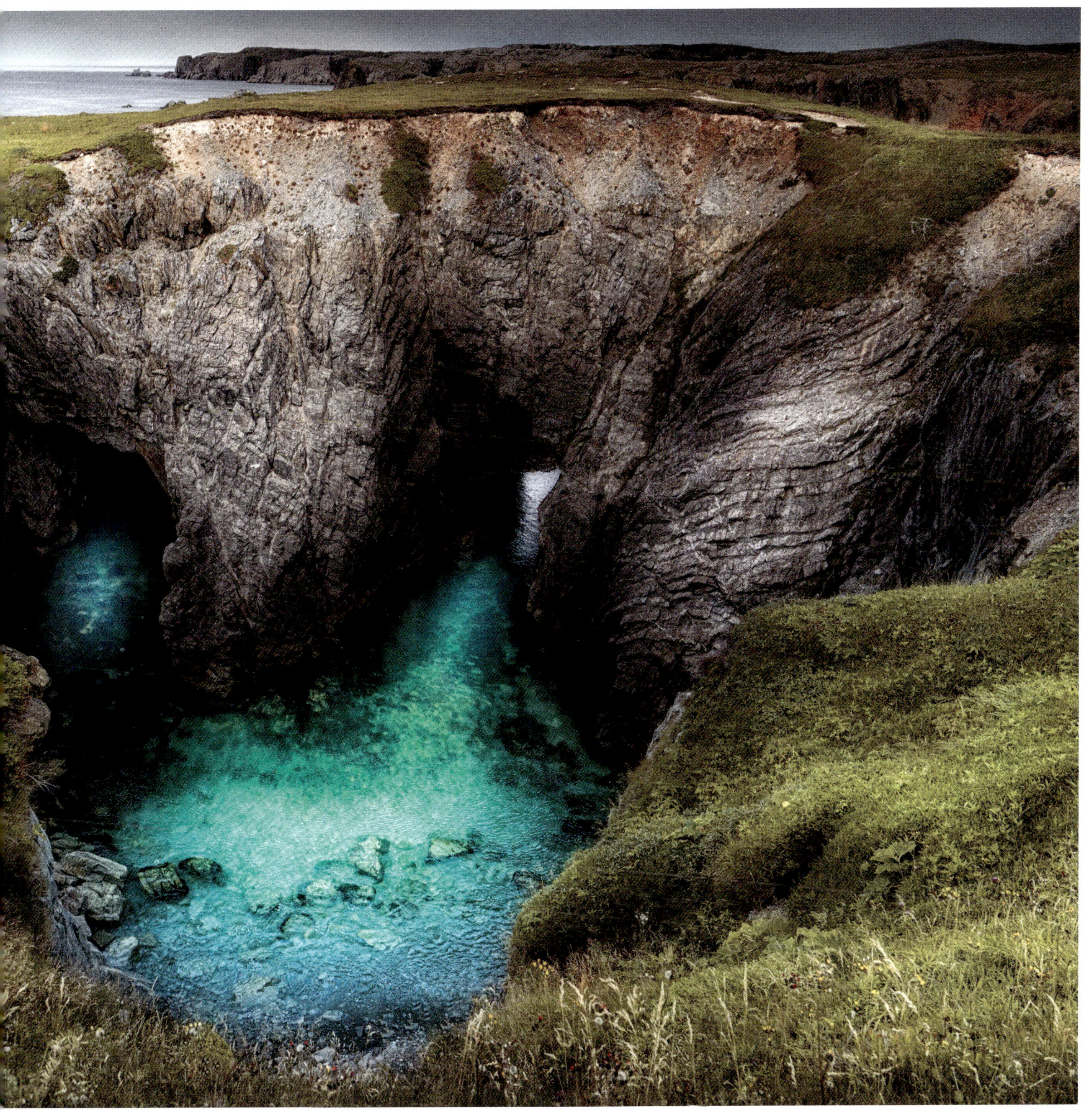

RIGHT

THE LONE FISHING STAGE

We visited Grand Beach, a small town on the Burin Peninsula, in the summer of 2021. Grand Beach is true to its name. It does have a long stone beach, and also a lone fishing stage. Robert crawled to the end of the old stage and sat there to watch the view.

YEAR: 2021

OPPOSITE

DANCING WATER SPIRITS

Robert and I visited Cape Spear on an early morning after days of rain. A big puddle had formed in front of the lighthouse. Robert threw stones into the puddle while I took photos. We captured the dancing water spirits.

YEAR: 2021

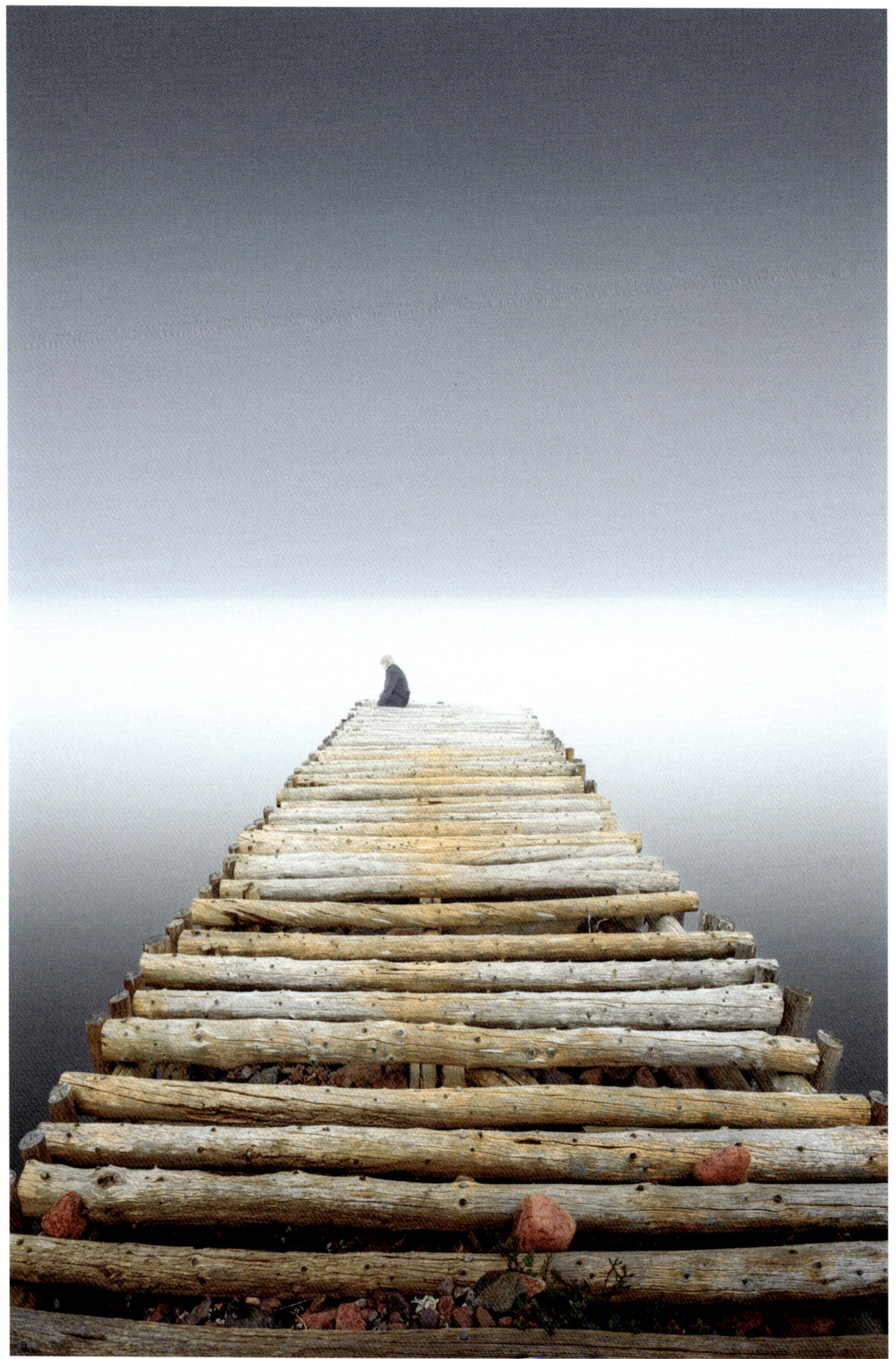

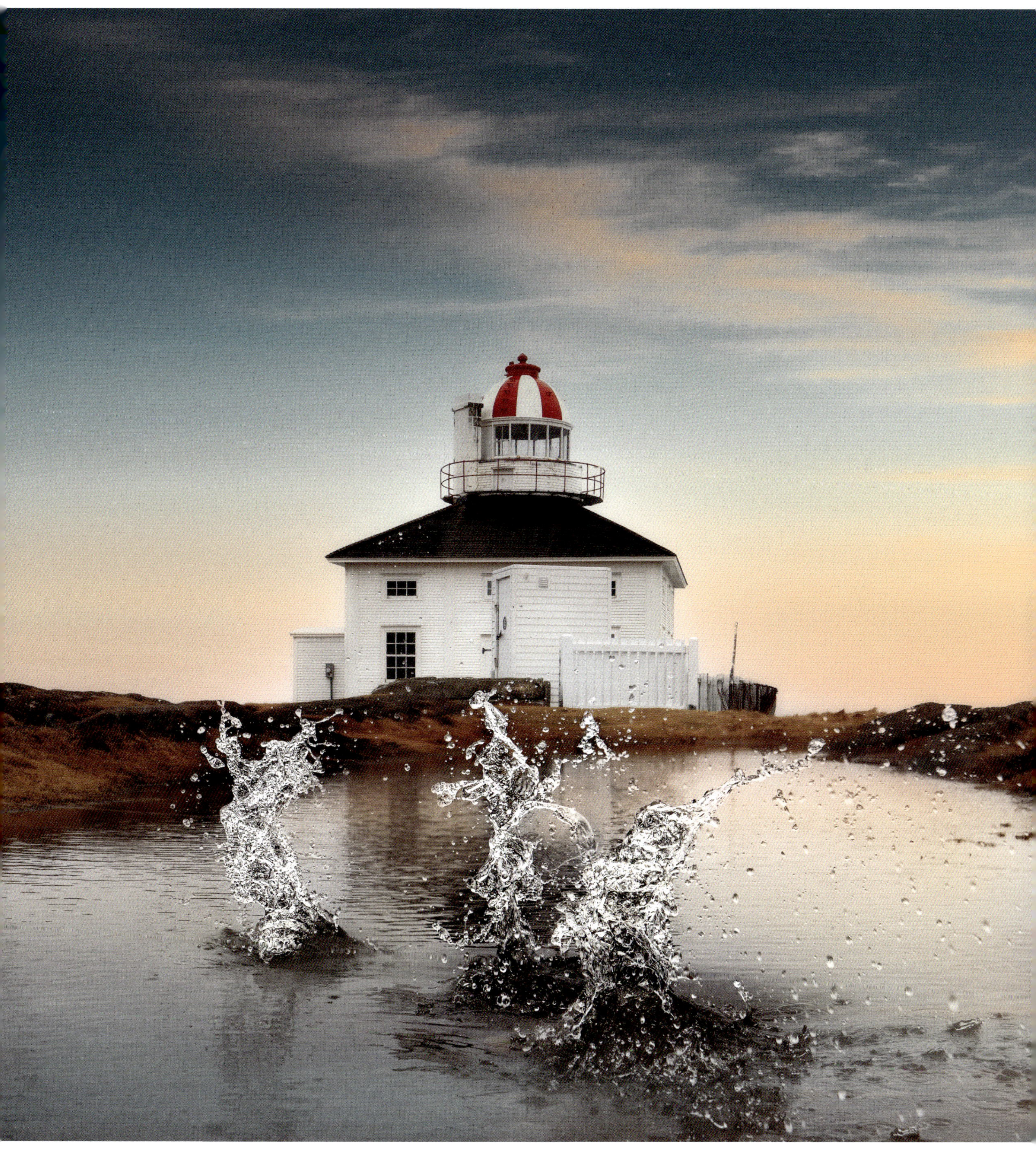

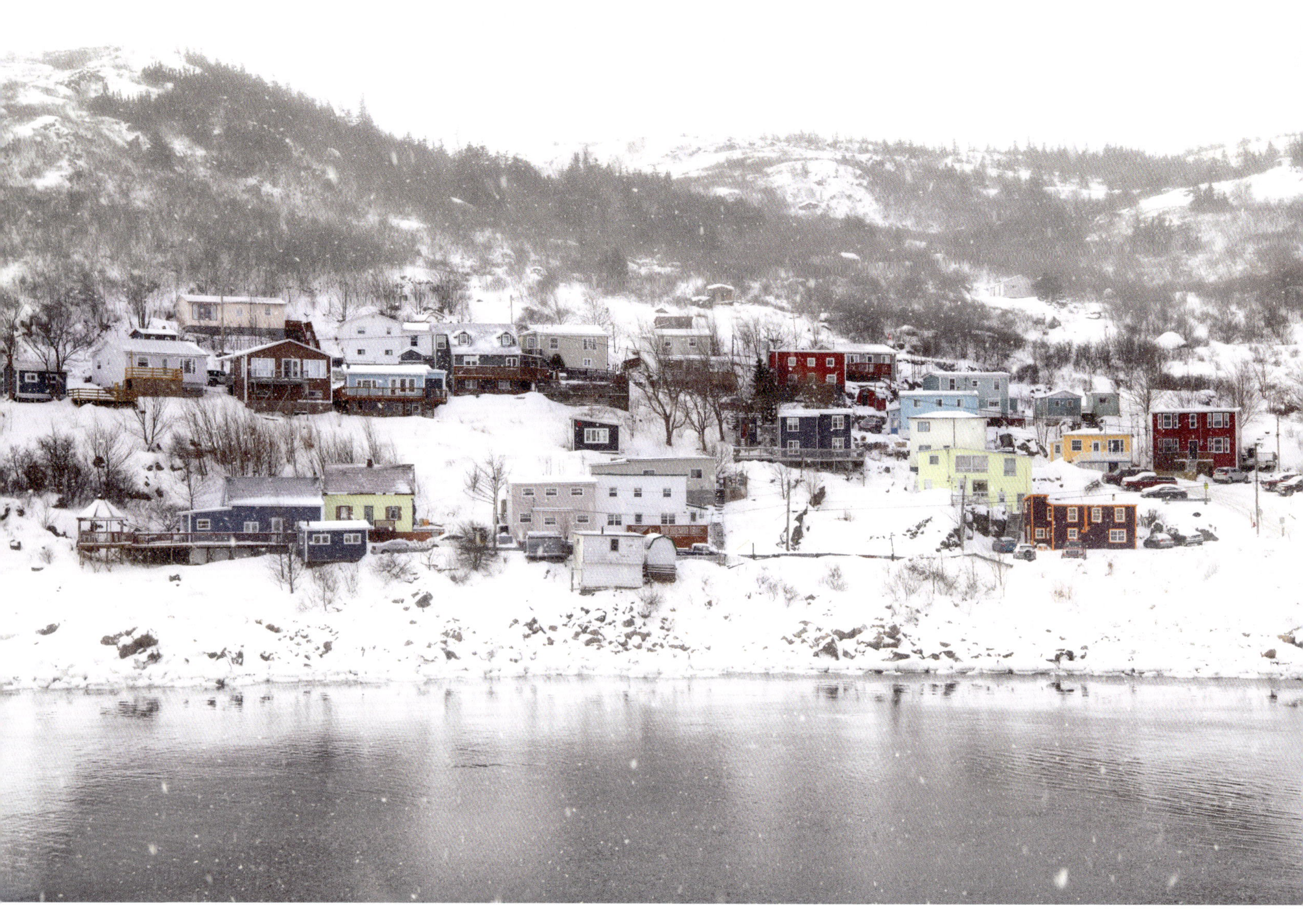

THE WINTER COLOURS OF PETTY HARBOUR The houses at Petty Harbour stand in the white snow. This is a typical colourful winter scene in a fishing village in Newfoundland.

YEAR: 2019

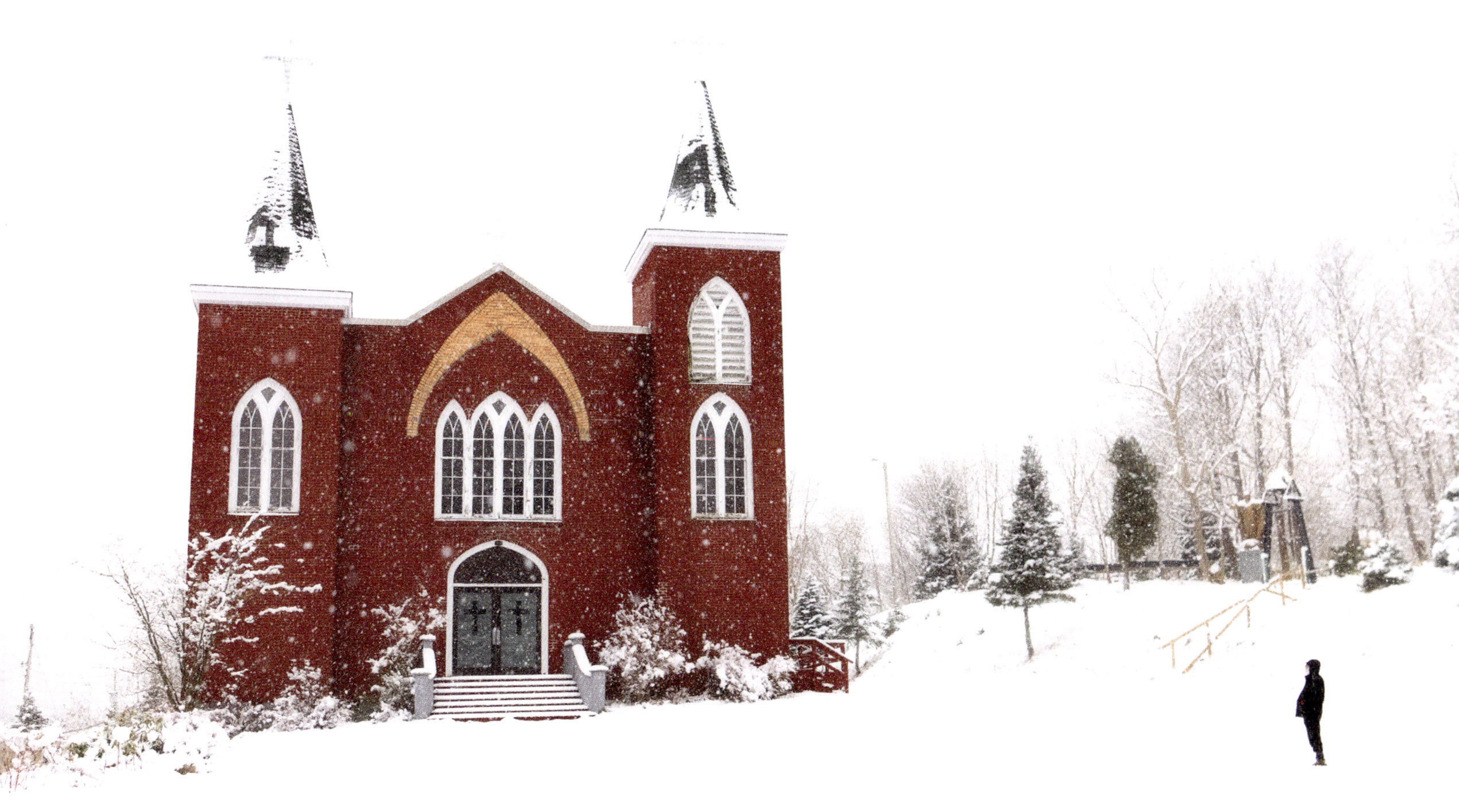

IN THE SNOW Immaculate Conception Church is a historic structure in Cape Broyle, a small fishing community in Newfoundland. This church plays an important role there. I took this photo when the snow had just started. Robert is standing beside the church. It seems as if this is happening in a snow globe.

YEAR: 2021

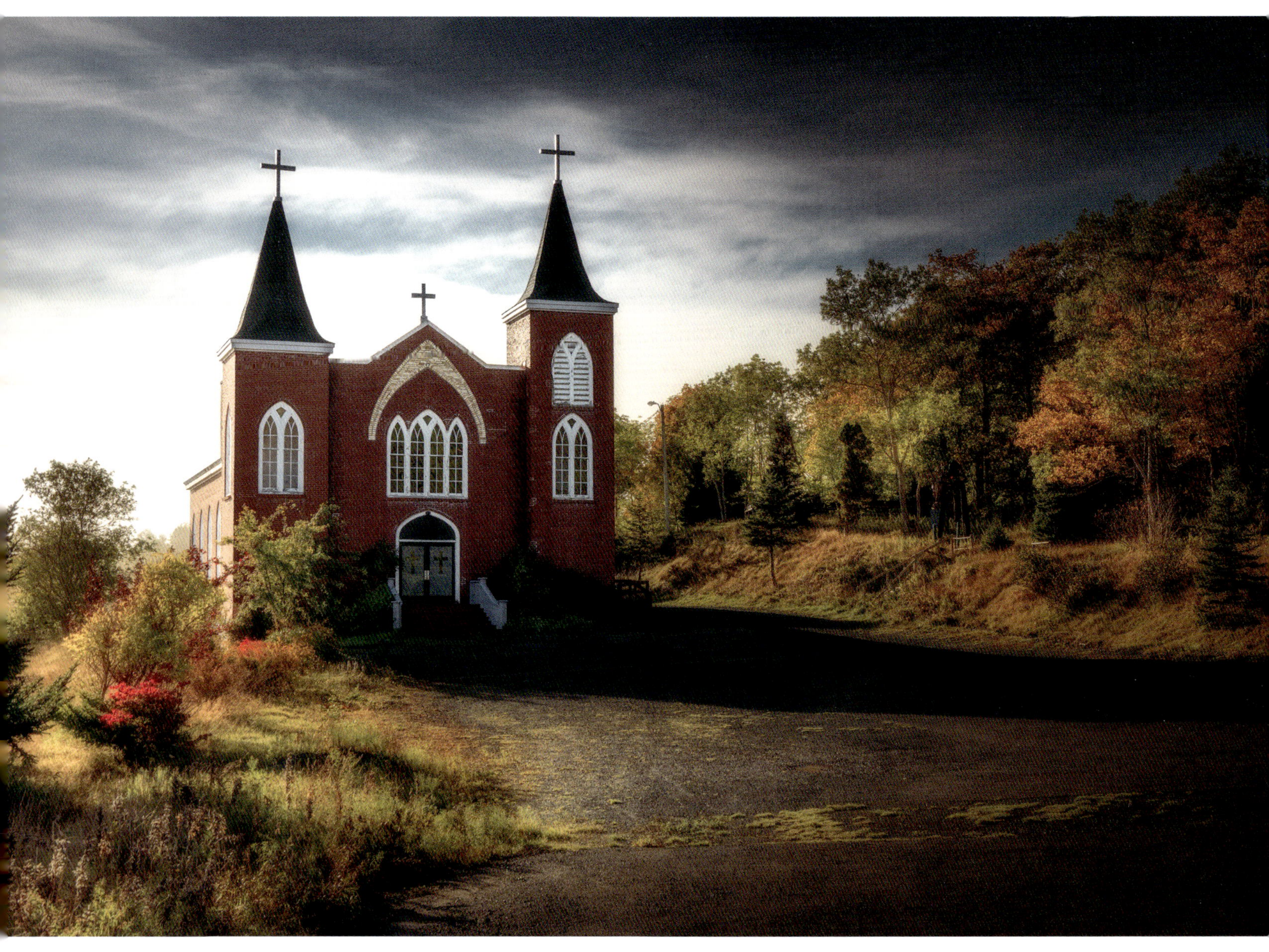

CAPE BROYLE AUTUMN Immaculate Conception Church: I took this photo when the church was surrounded by autumn colours.

YEAR: 2020

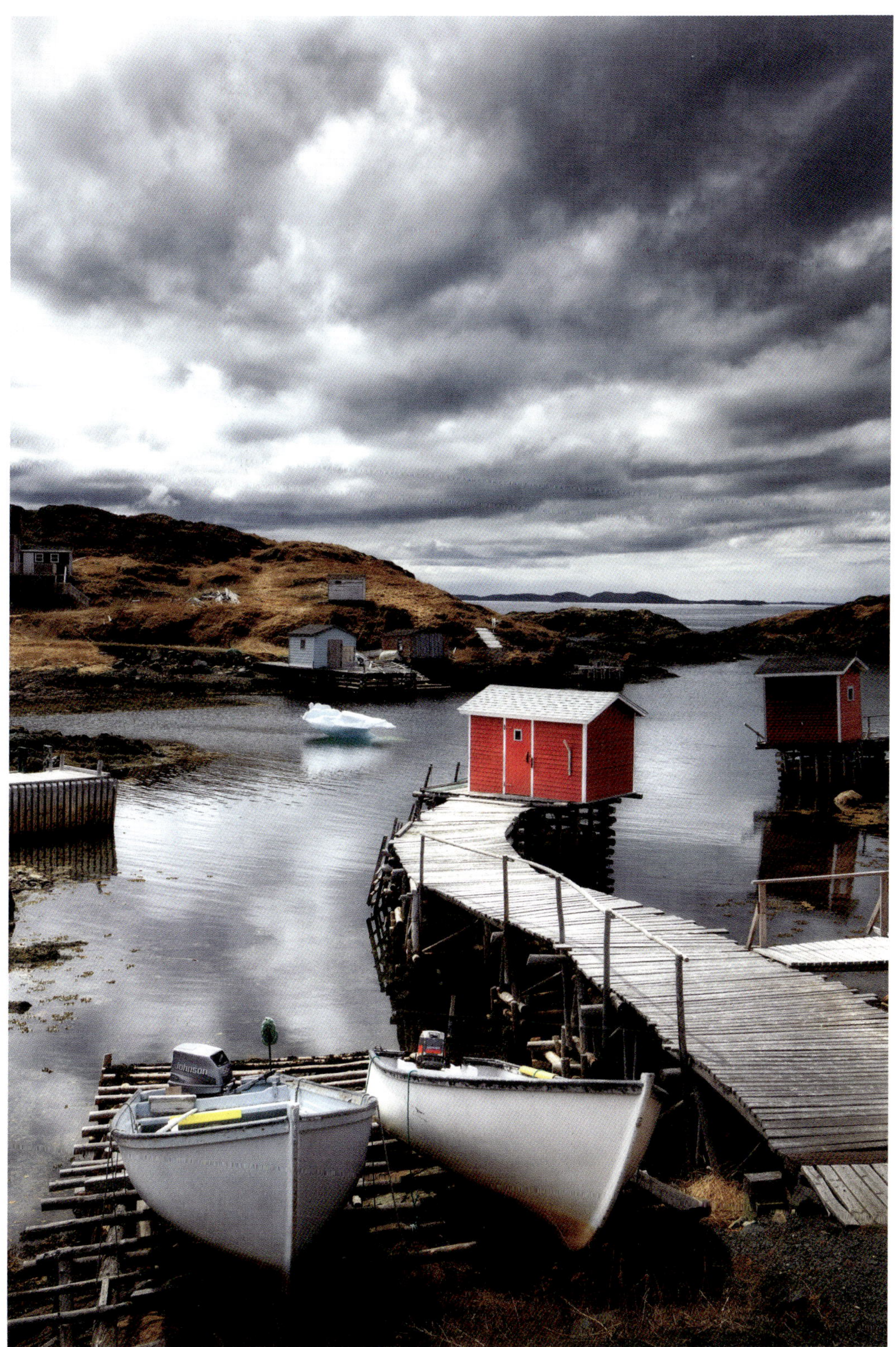

CHANGE ISLANDS

A lovely small harbour on Change Islands.

YEAR: 2019

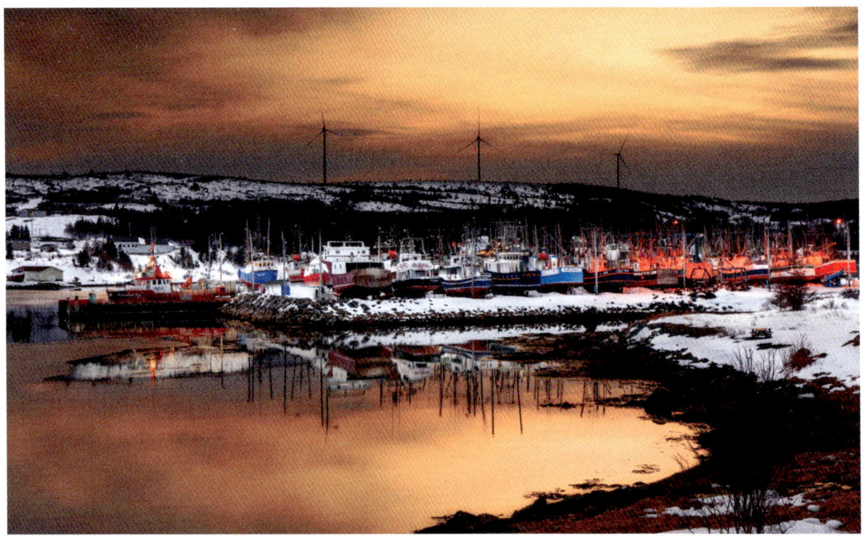

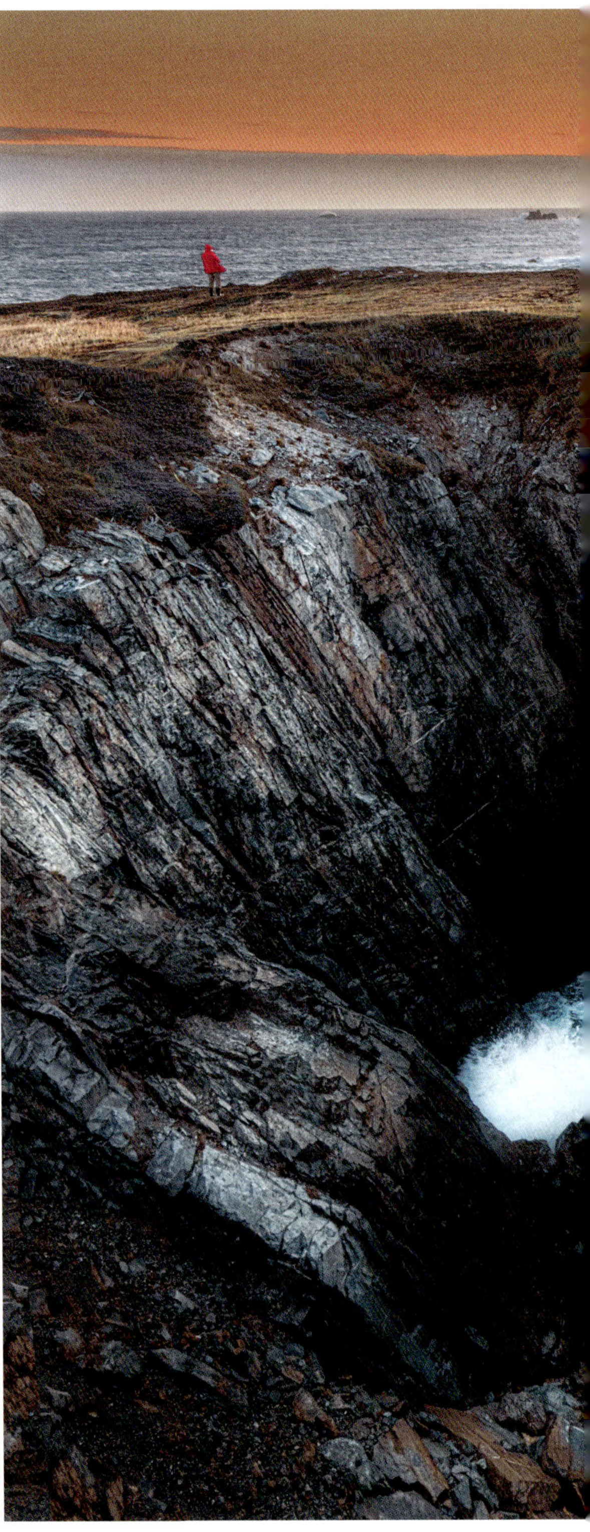

ABOVE

THE GOLDEN POND A golden sunset and golden pond in Fermeuse.

YEAR: 2020

RIGHT

SUNRISE AT DUNGEON SEA ARCHES

Roaring seawater has been coming through the arches for thousands of years. You can tell how huge the arches are by comparing them with Robert, in red, standing on top of the rock. It was a stunning experience to see the sunrise above this geographical wonder.

YEAR: 2019

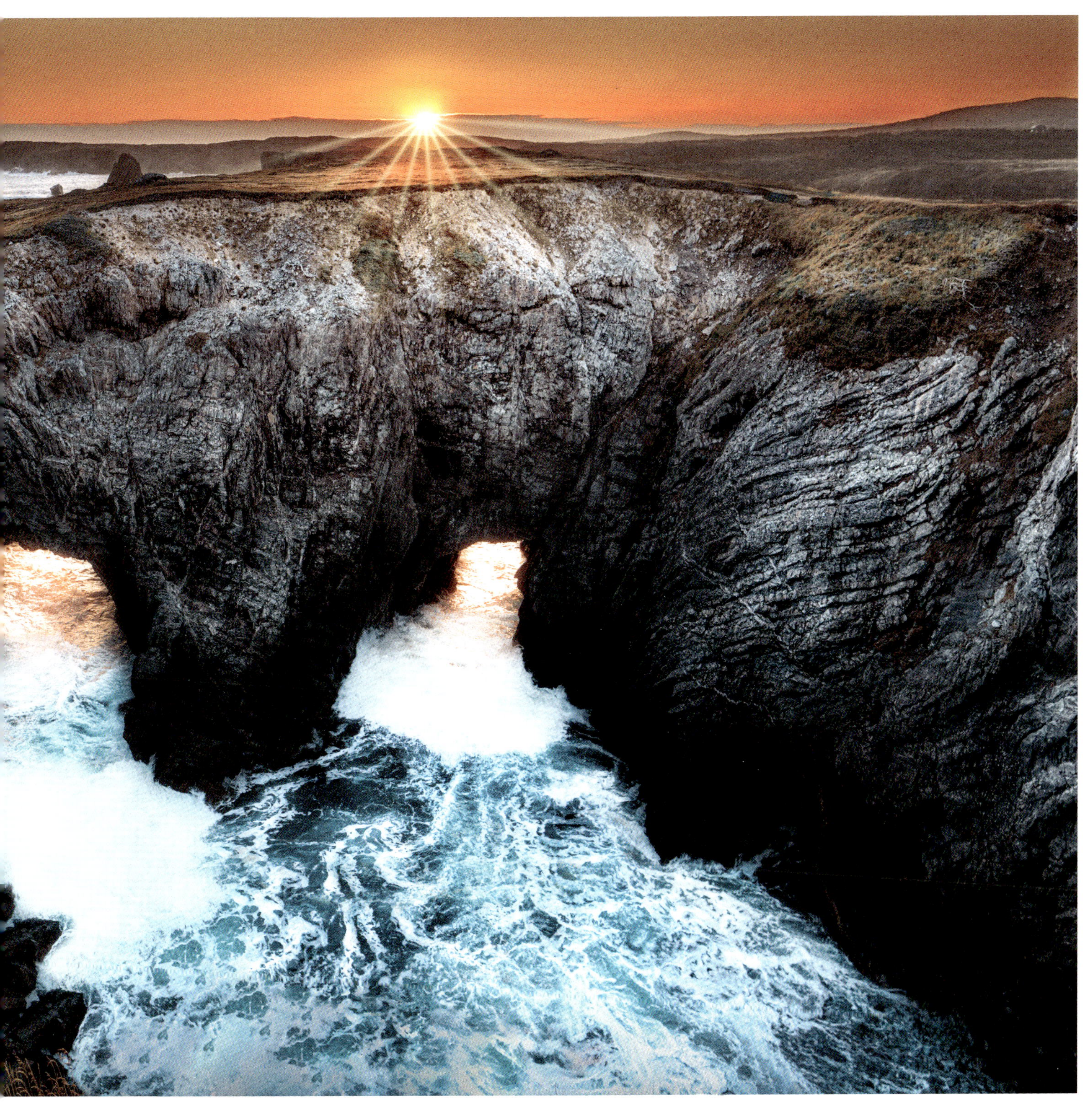

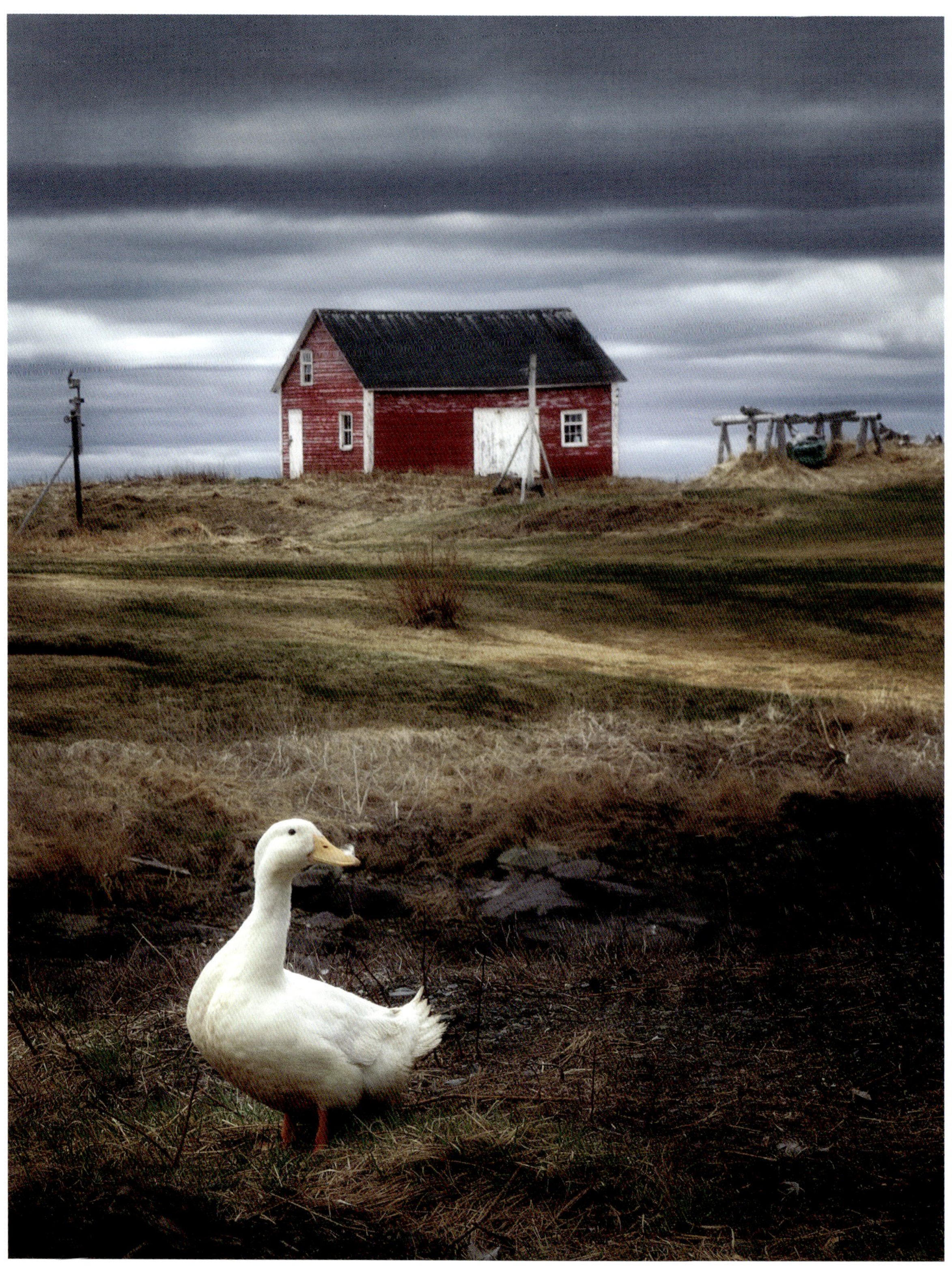

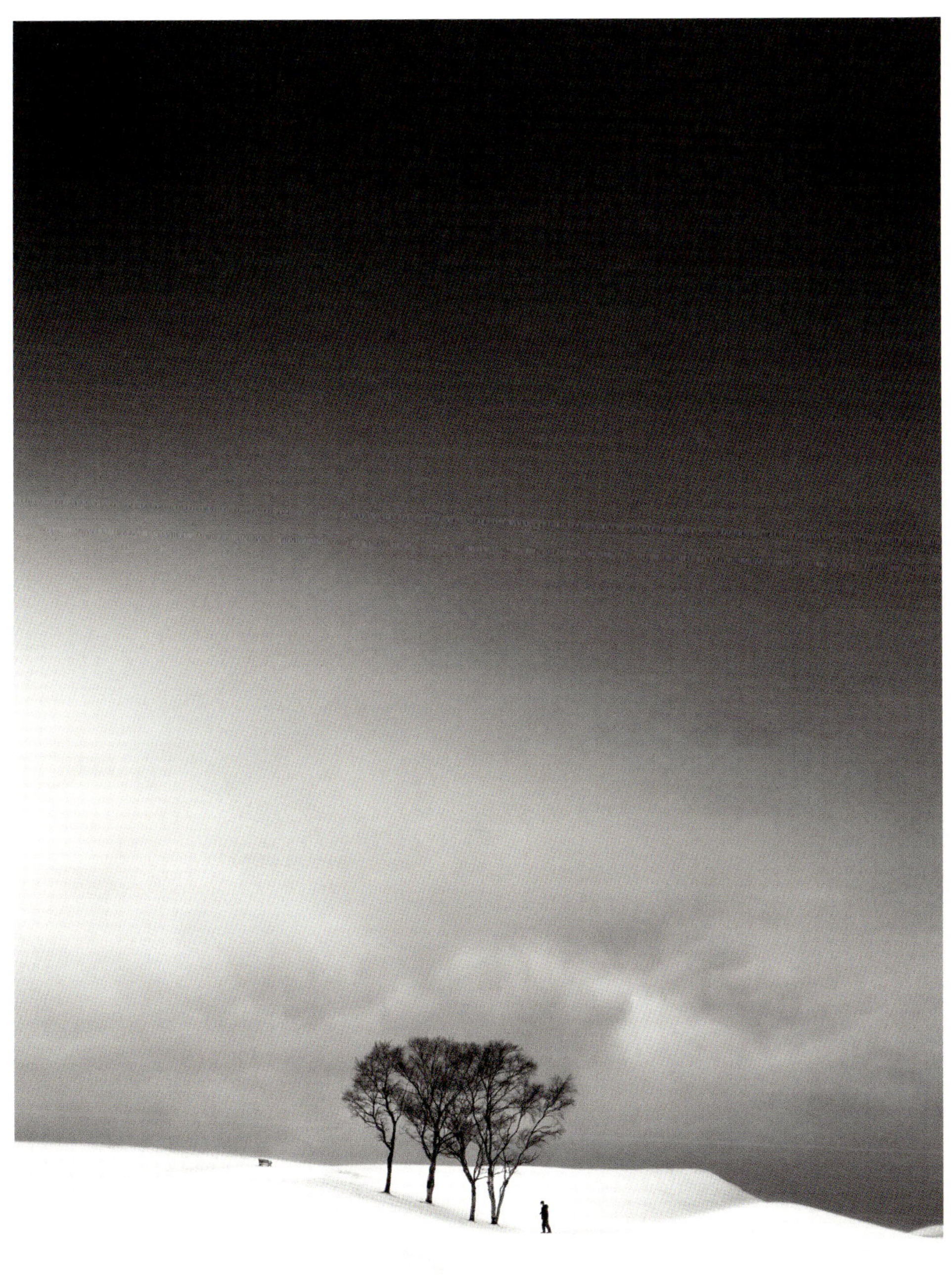

OPPOSITE

THE DUCK ON CHANGE ISLANDS When I visited a farm on Change Islands, a duck came to me and posed for me in front of a shed. Now I know Newfoundland has not only cute puffins but also cute ducks.

YEAR: 2019

LEFT

VASTNESS Robert was trying to climb a hill in Bowring Park that was covered by thick snow.

YEAR: 2021

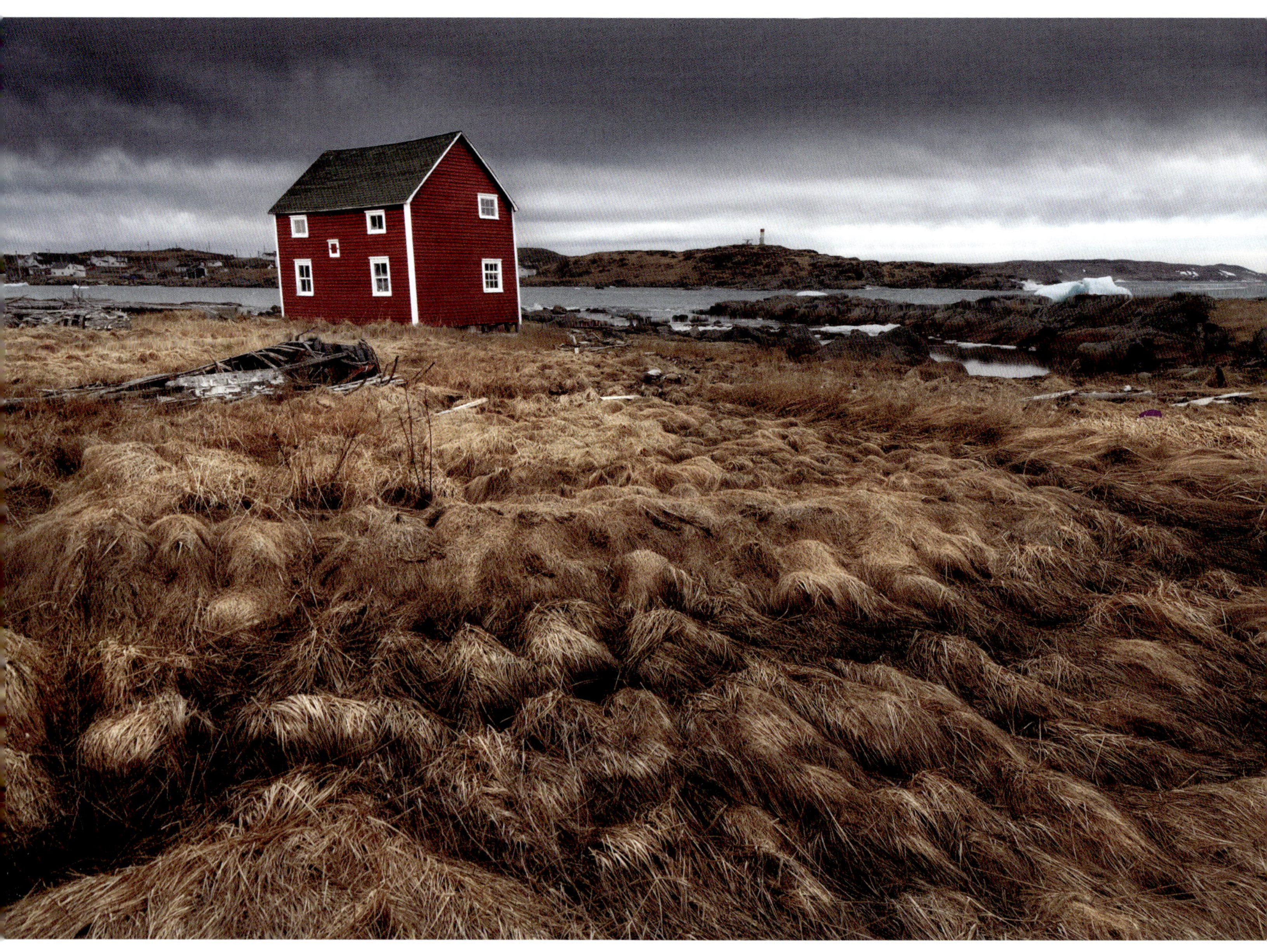

SPRING IN TILTING Spring in Greene's Point, Tilting, Fogo Island. Spring always comes late in Newfoundland; the grass hasn't turned green yet in May.

YEAR: 2019

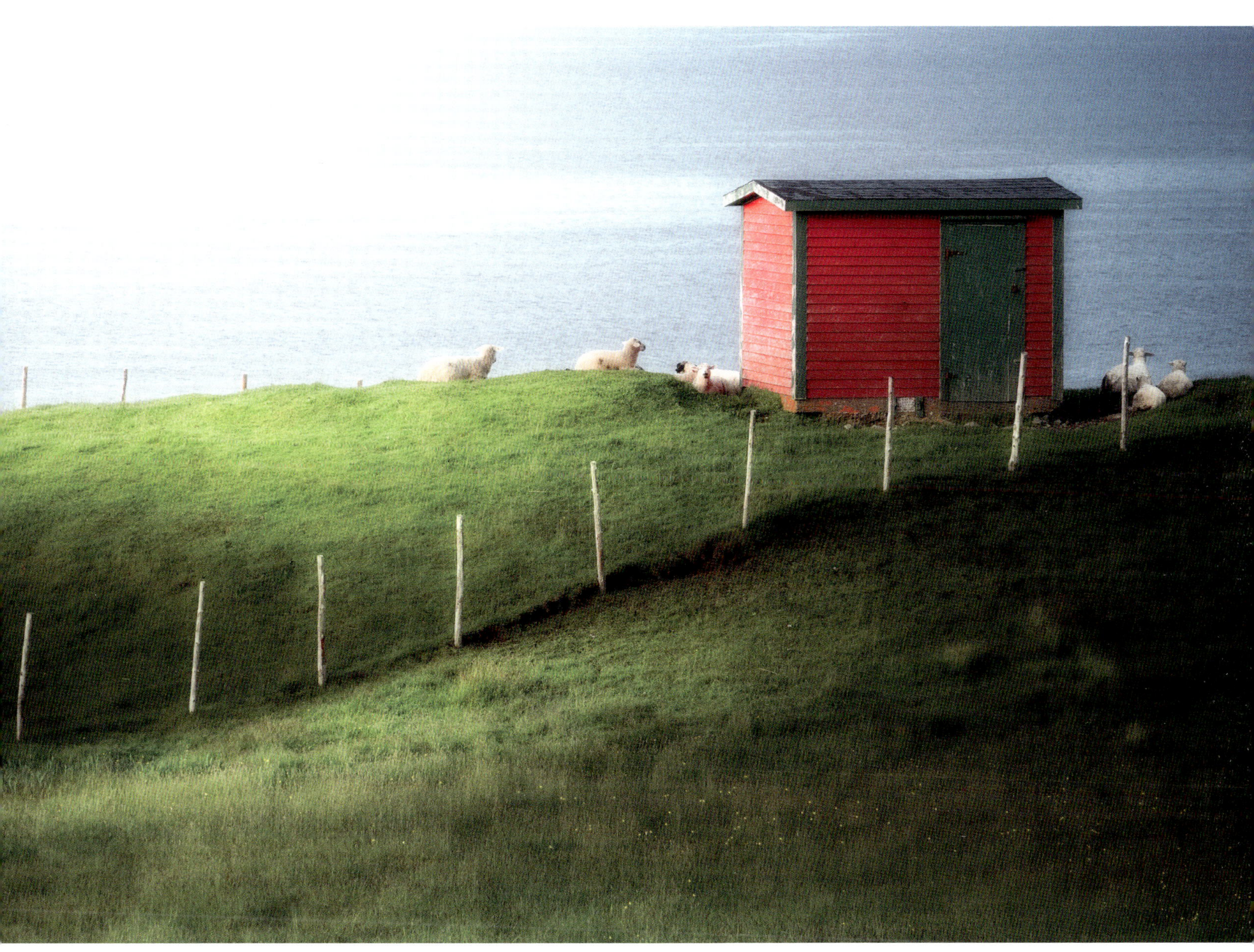

LIE DOWN IN GREEN PASTURES BESIDE QUIET WATERS I saw this peaceful scenery in St. Mary's Bay, in the early morning. A few sheep are grazing, resting on the green grass and enjoying the sea view.

YEAR: 2020

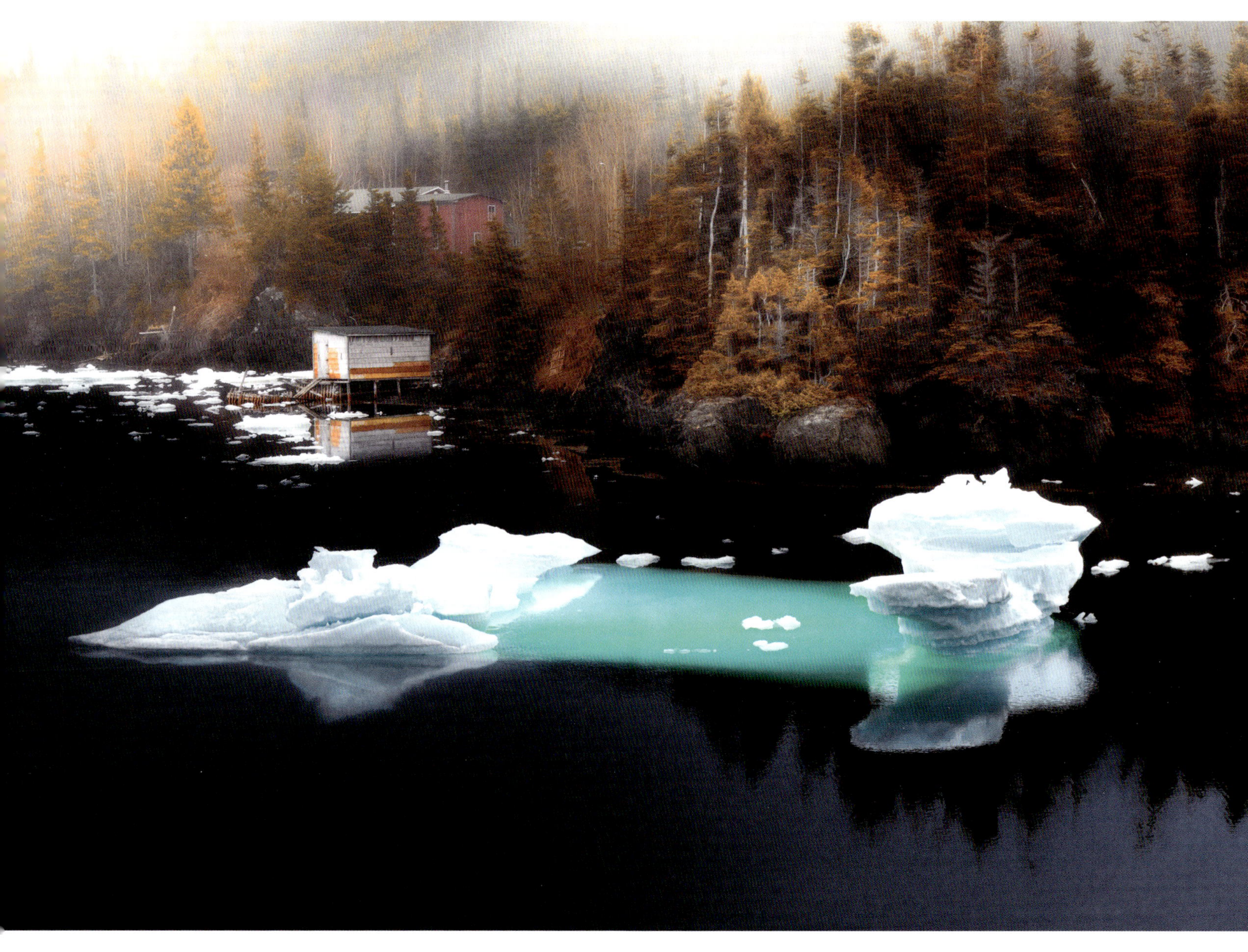

FLOATING A shed, the mist, and a huge piece of floating ice. I took this photo in Newville.

YEAR: 2019

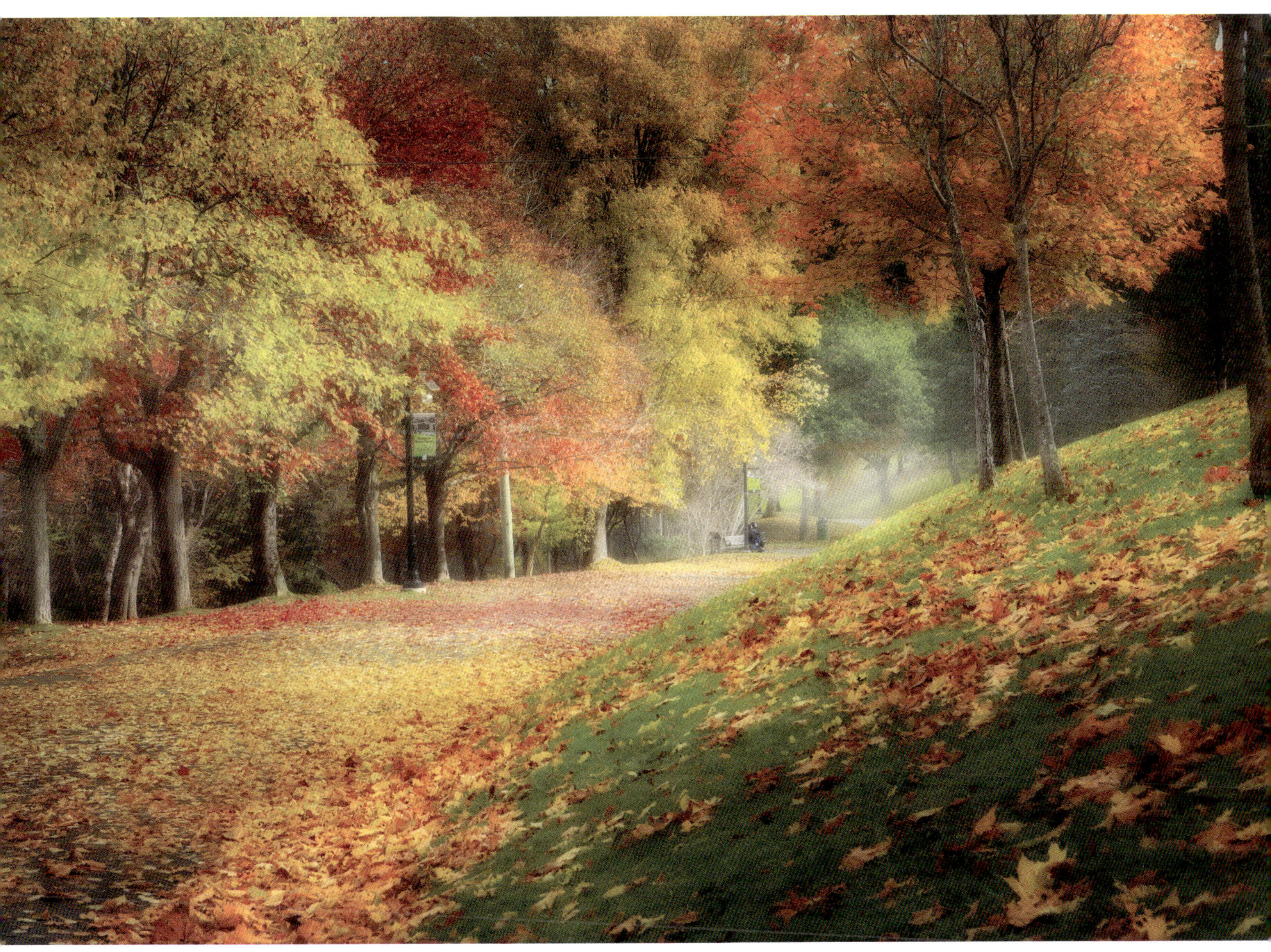

AUTUMN COLOURS IN BOWRING PARK Bowring Park in St. John's is a great place to visit, especially in the autumn; I was lucky to see these stunning colours in the fall of 2019.

YEAR: 2019

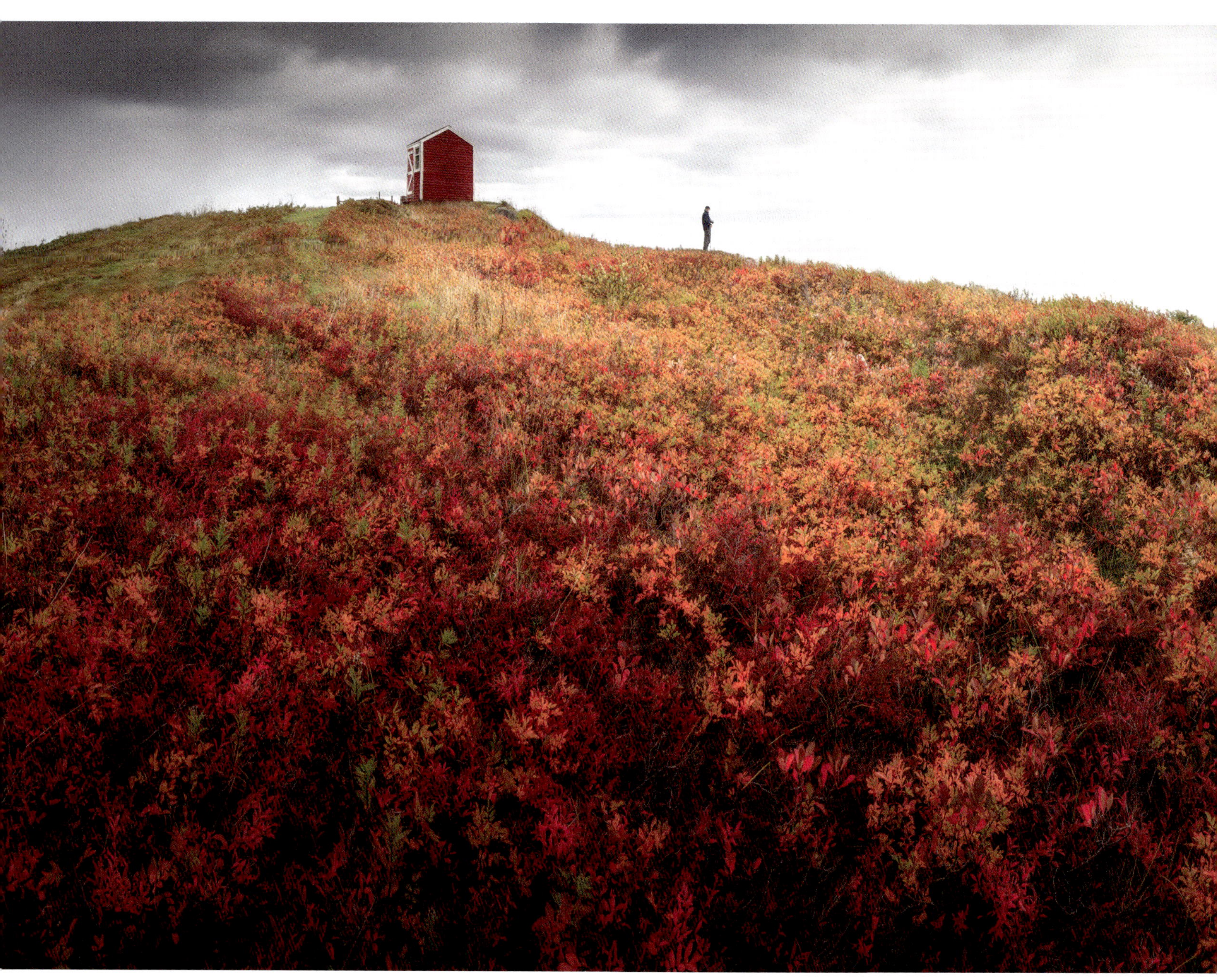

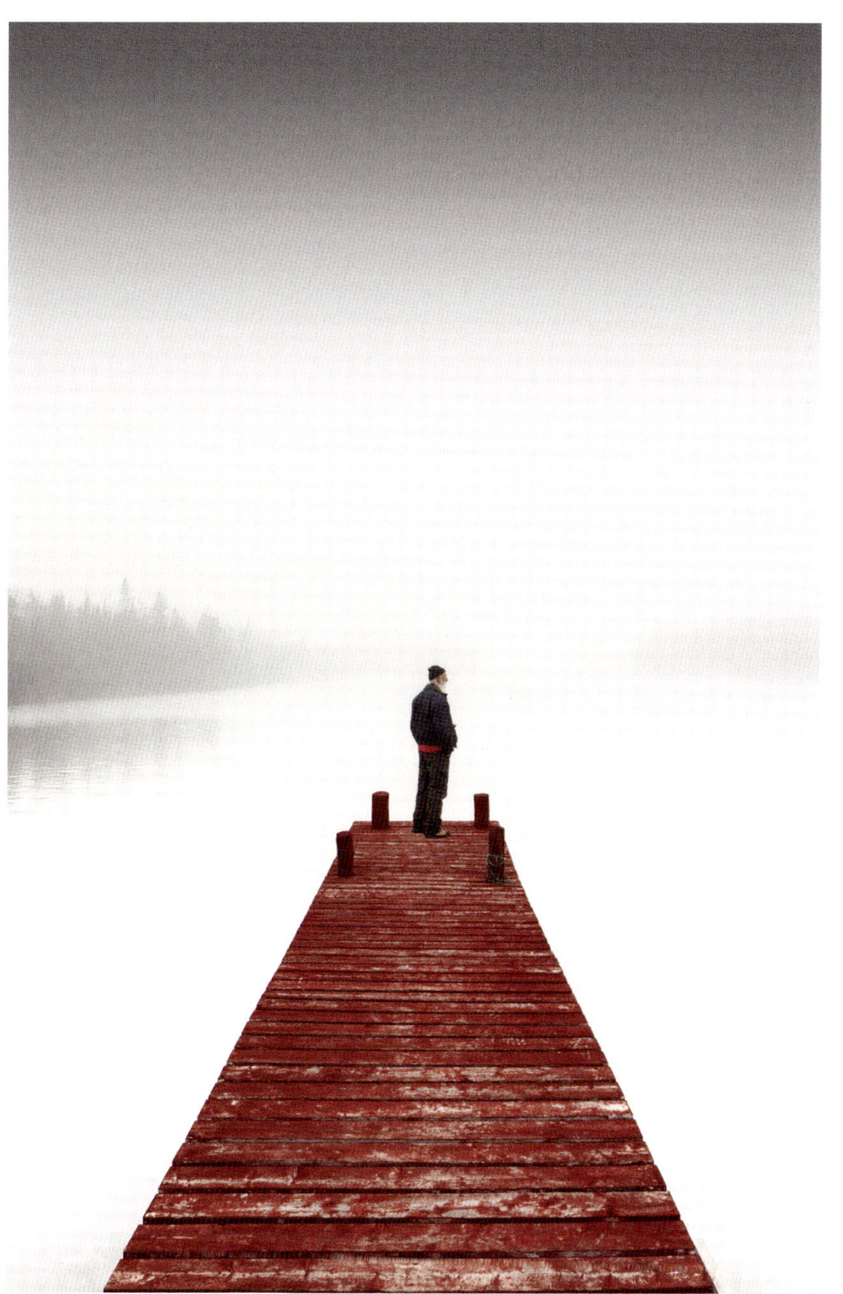

OPPOSITE

FLORA CARPET Nature weaves a floral carpet when the autumn comes. A Brigus South man—no surprise, it's Robert—is walking the red carpet on Turtle Island in Brigus South.

YEAR: 2021

LEFT

THE DOCK A foggy day at Brigus South. Robert was standing at the dock not far from his home.

YEAR: 2021

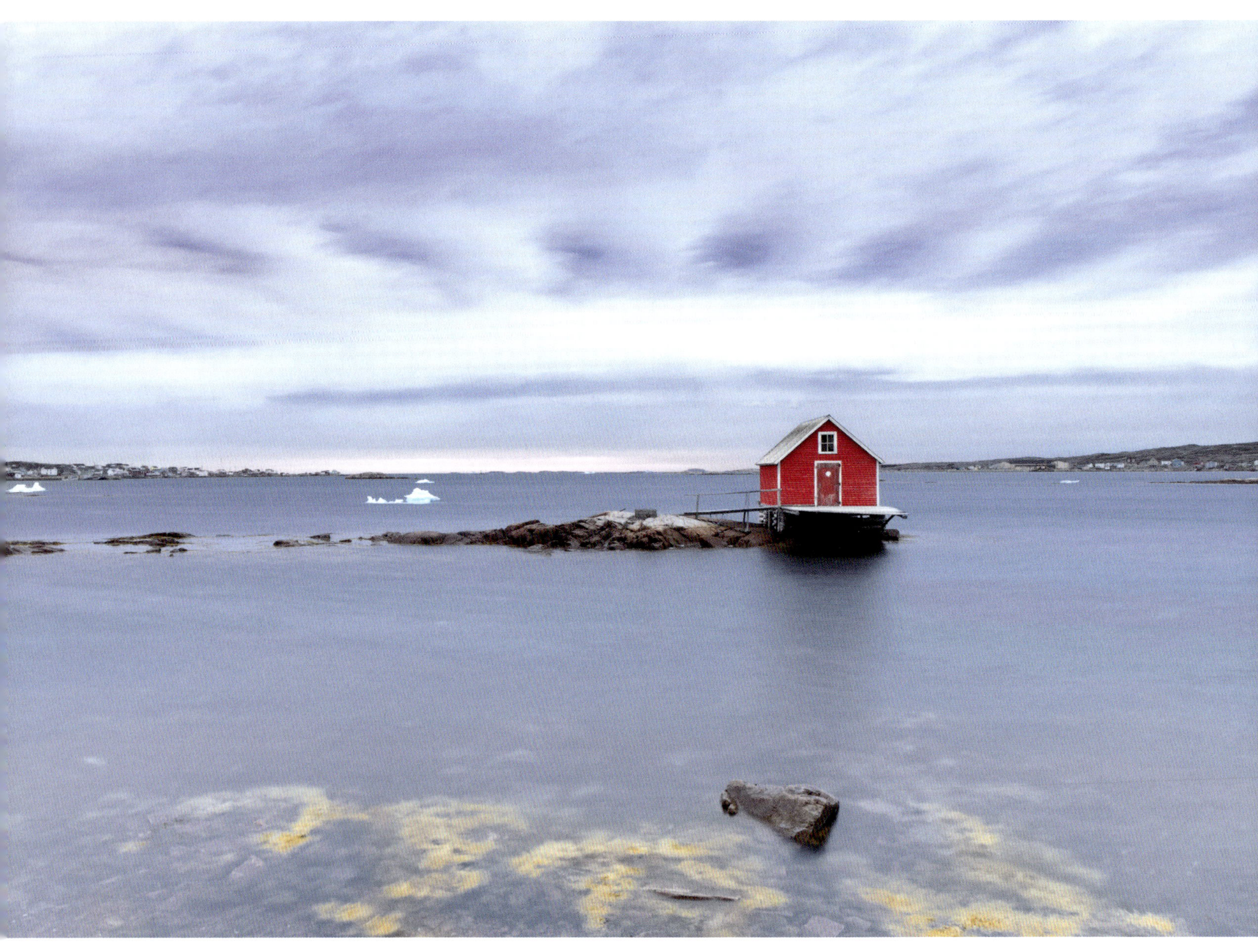

FOGO Fogo Island, the largest island off Newfoundland's coast, is famous for its fishing stages, a vernacular structure associated with the cod fishery. I took this photo of a fishing stage in Fogo Island when I visited in 2019. Spring is always late in Newfoundland, and you can still see an iceberg floating on the sea far away.

YEAR: 2019

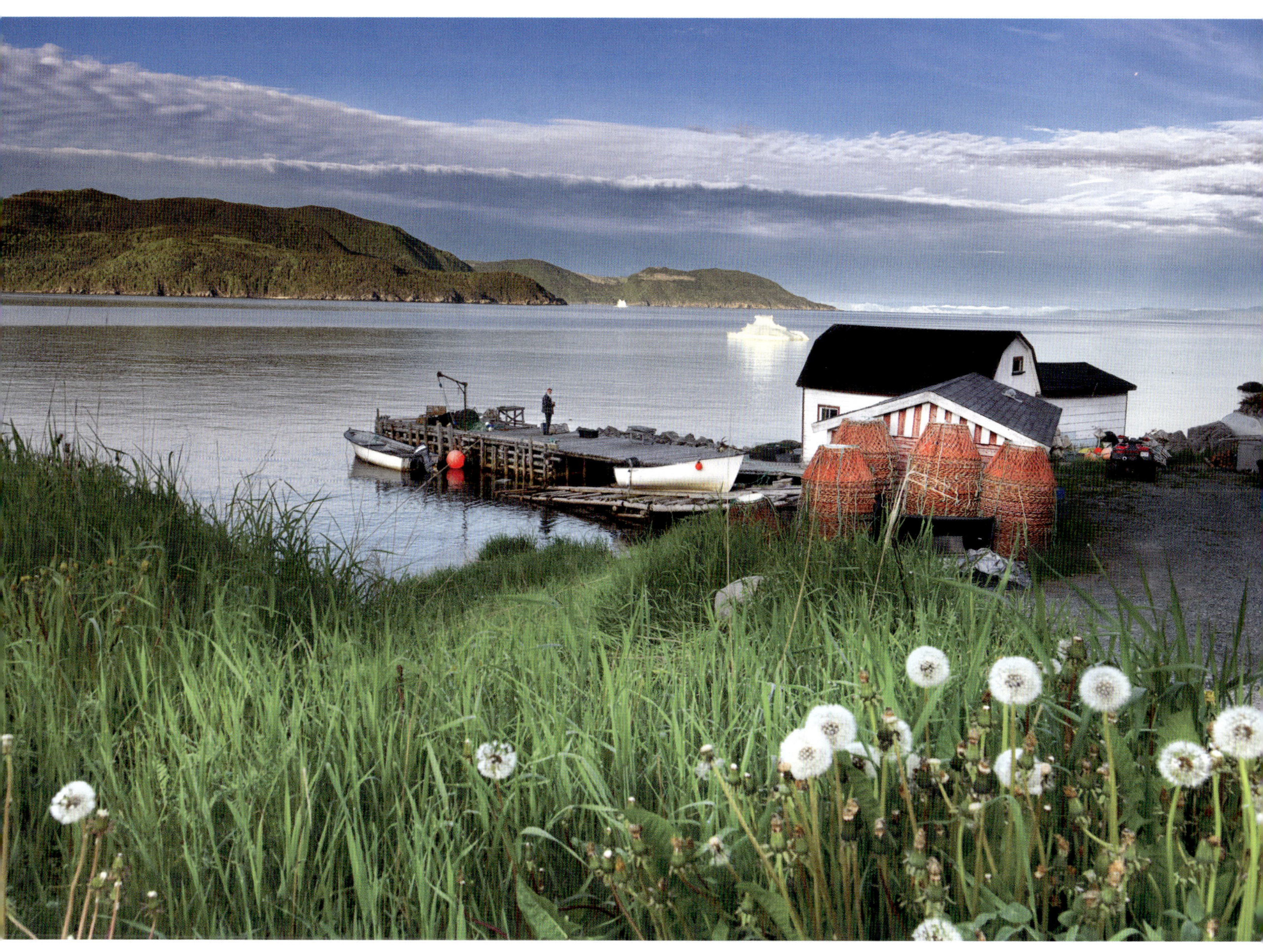

SEAL COVE MORNING Early morning in Seal Cove, a small fishing village located on the northwest coast of Newfoundland, near Baie Verte. A few dandelions near a quiet wharf are swinging in the breeze. Robert is standing on the dock. An iceberg is floating far away.

YEAR: 2019

WALKING BY THE SEA Robert was walking along the beach by a calm sea.

YEAR: 2021

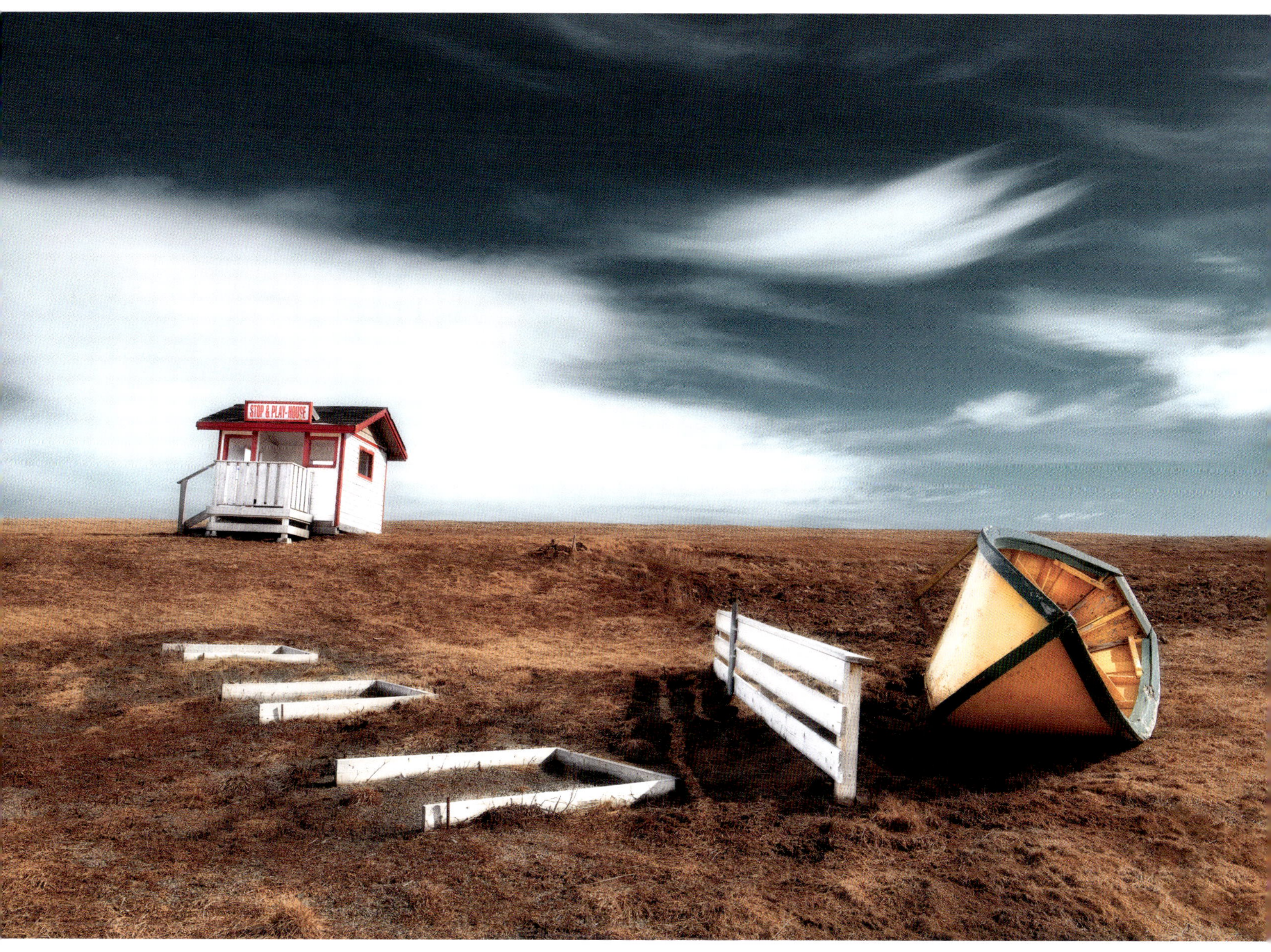

STOP AND PLAY I paid a short visit to Bell Island in March, and the grass had not yet turned green. I found this playhouse and the dory not far from the Bell Island lighthouse. There are free jigsaw puzzles in the house for children and adults, for tourists or local residents.

YEAR: 2019

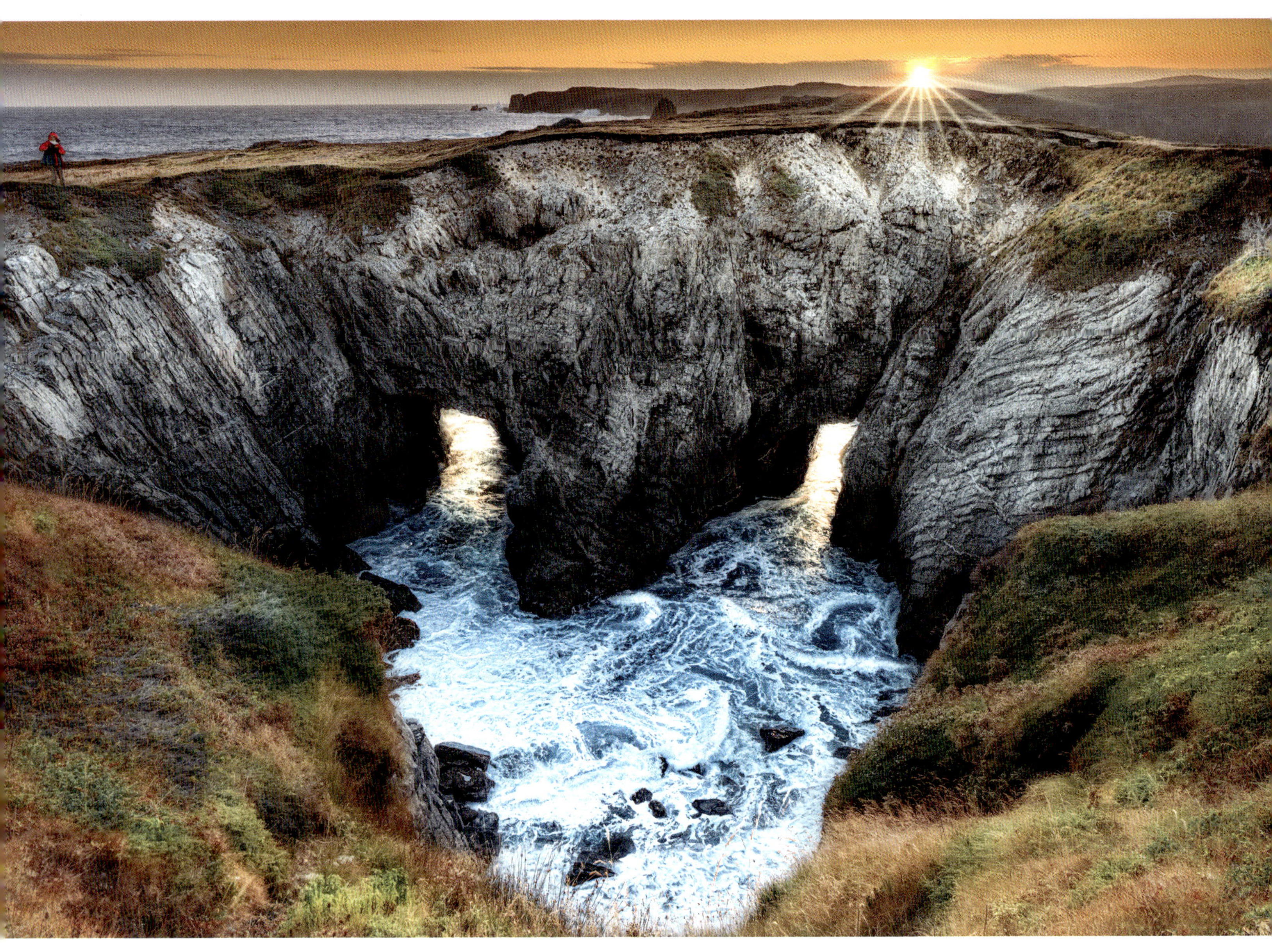

THE HEART OF THE OCEAN The Dungeon in Newfoundland is an impressive example of the power of the North Atlantic Ocean. You can tell how huge the arches are by comparing them with Robert in red standing on top of the rock. Robert is now in his seventies, but he can still vividly remember playing on top of Dungeon when he was a child.

YEAR: 2019

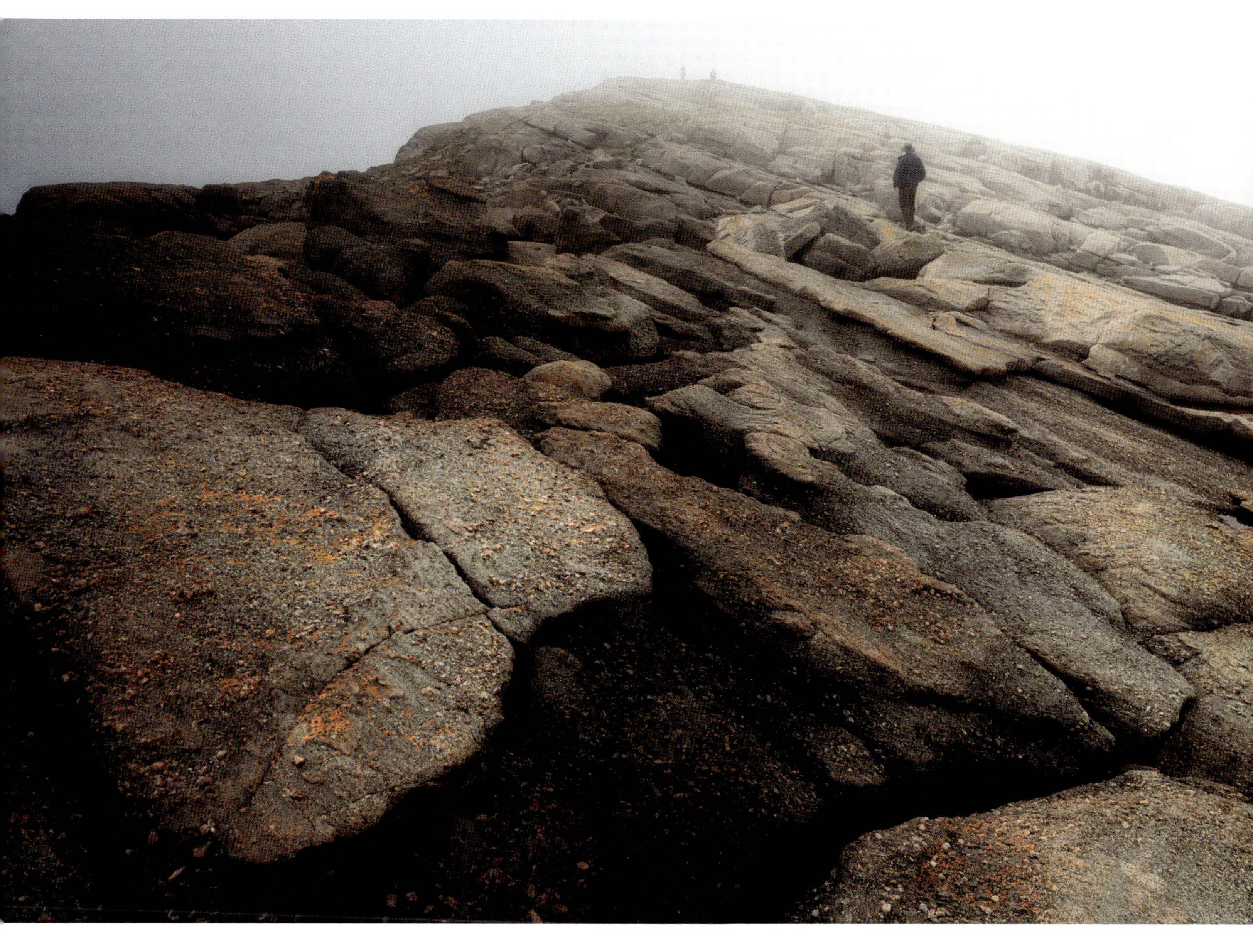

FLATROCK Robert is walking on the rocks at Flatrock when the fog is coming.

YEAR: 2021

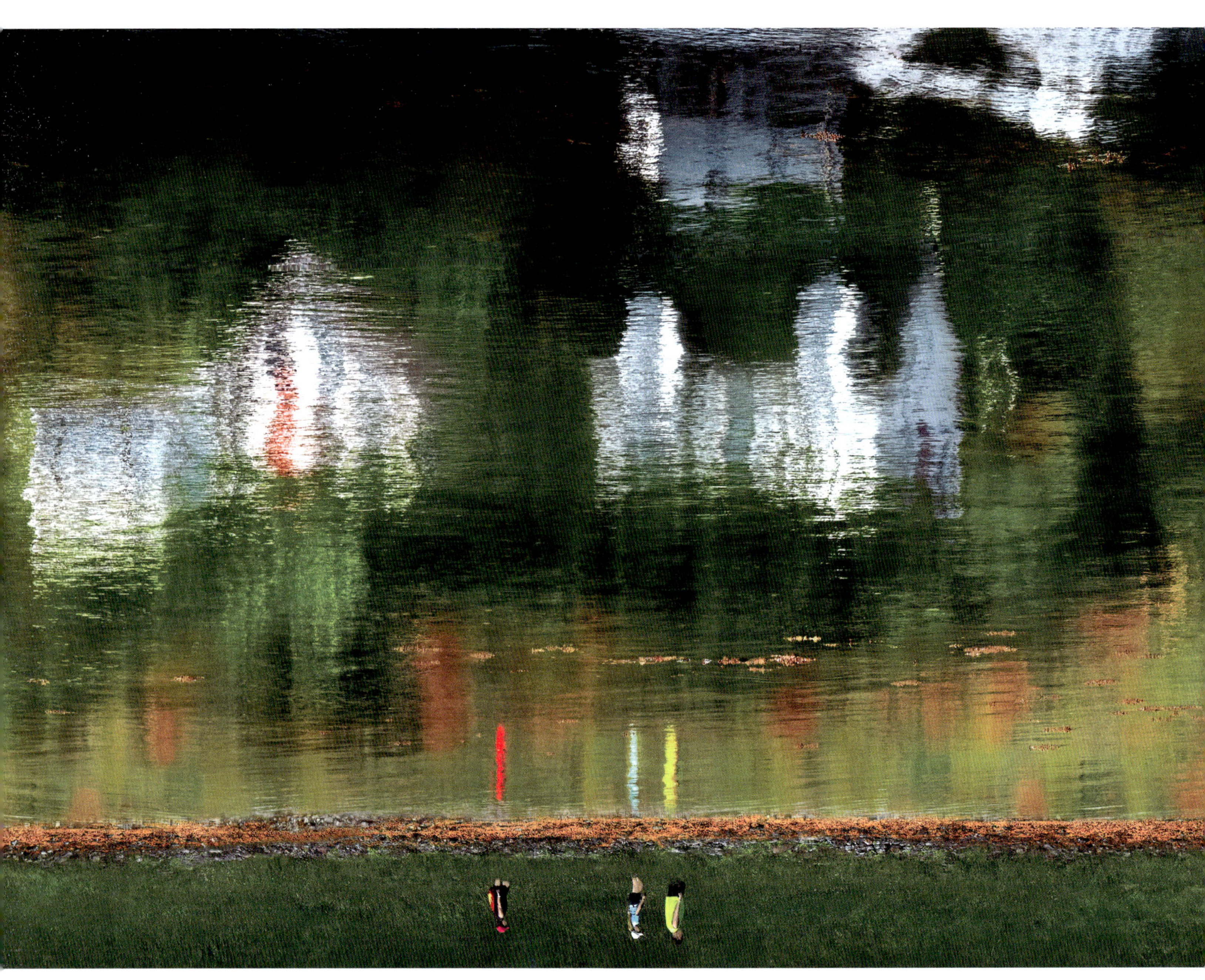

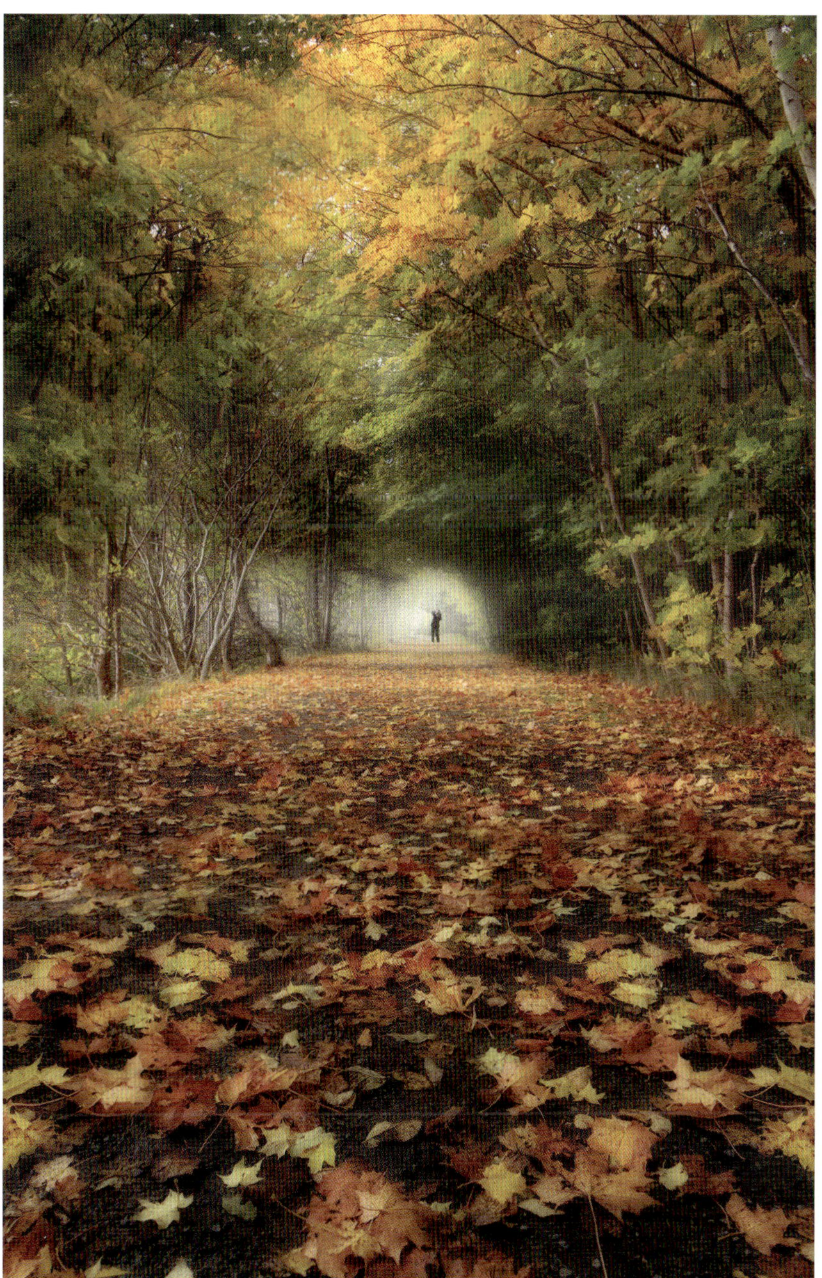

OPPOSITE

IMPRESSIONIST BRIGUS SOUTH

A beautiful day in Brigus South. The reflections of the sheds mirrored in the water look like a perfect Impressionist painting. Three people happened to walk by when I took this photo, and they became a lovely part of this image. (This image is upside down, in case you haven't realized it yet!)

YEAR: 2022

LEFT

FOLIAGE ARCH IN BOWRING PARK

Foliage arch in Bowring Park, St. John's. Robert is standing in the middle of the arch taking photos of me while I was taking photos of him. Bowring Park was officially opened to the public in 1914.

YEAR: 2019

FOLLOWING

SUNRISE AT PETTY HARBOUR

Robert watches the sunrise at Petty Harbour.

YEAR: 2020

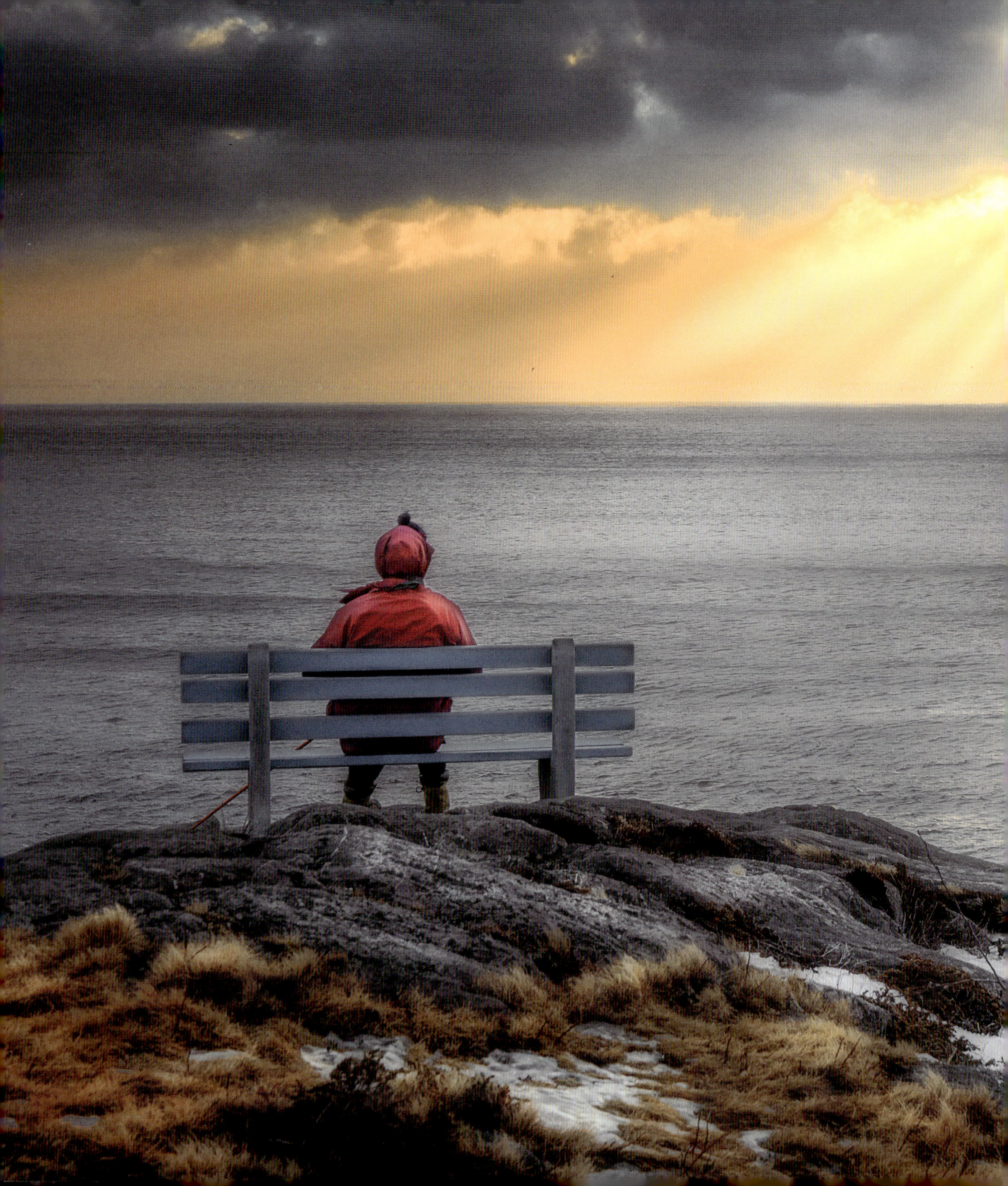

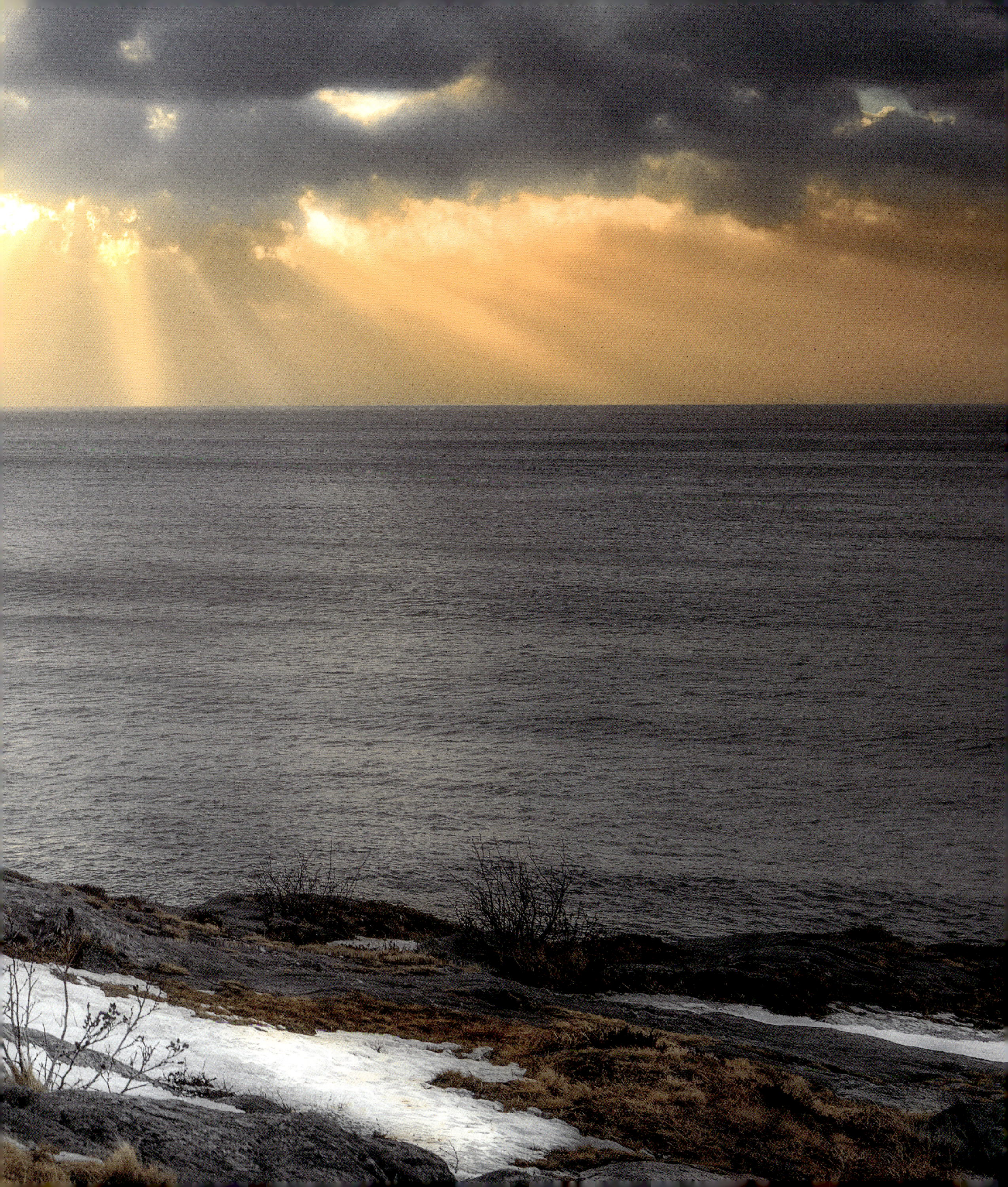

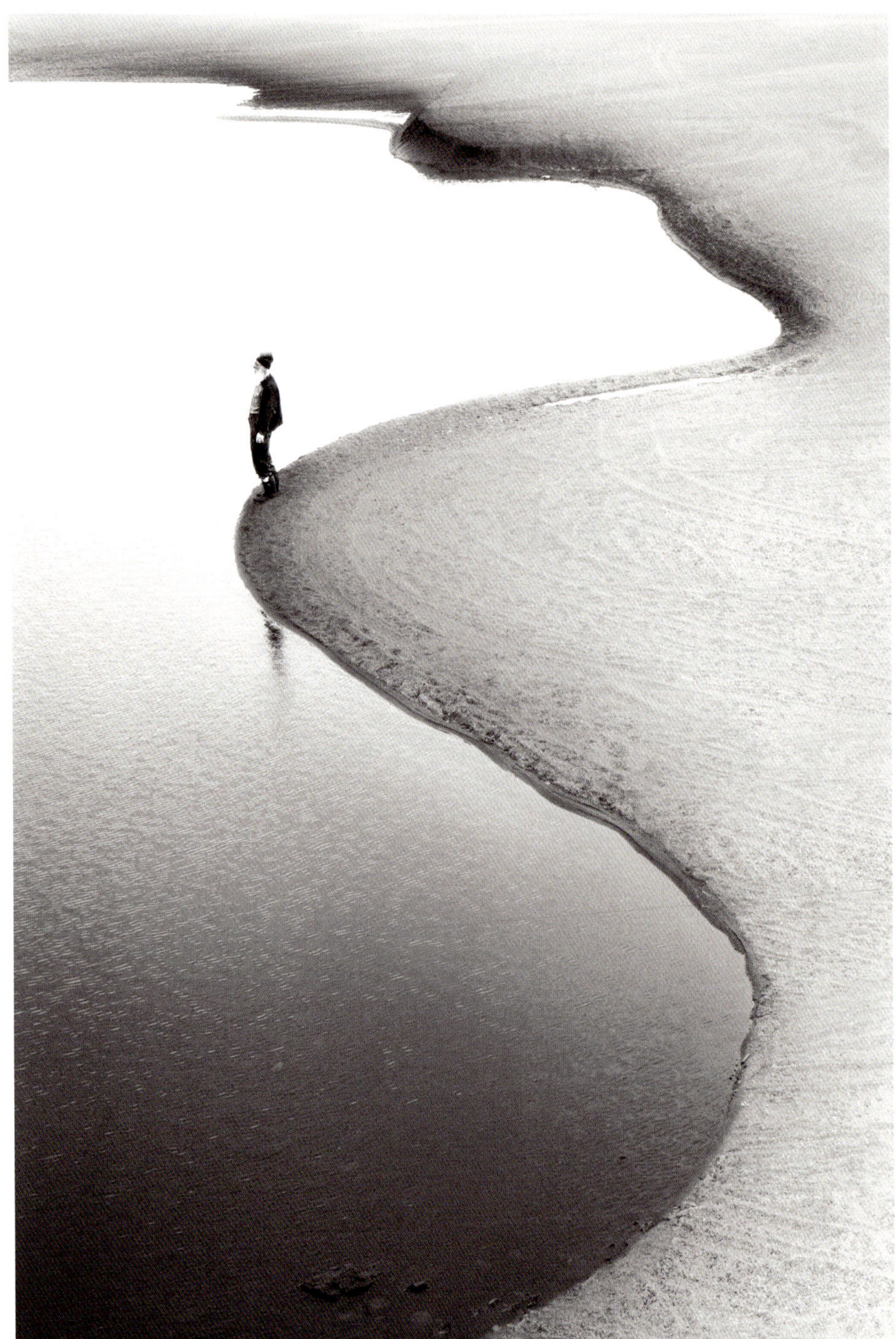

SERENITY IN ST. VINCENT'S

Robert was standing on the edge of the sandy and curving shore of St. Vincent's, facing the calm water. The calm water in Newfoundland always reminds me of the place where I was born and raised. There is a big river in my hometown, and both the river there and the water here sometimes share the serenity.

YEAR: 2021

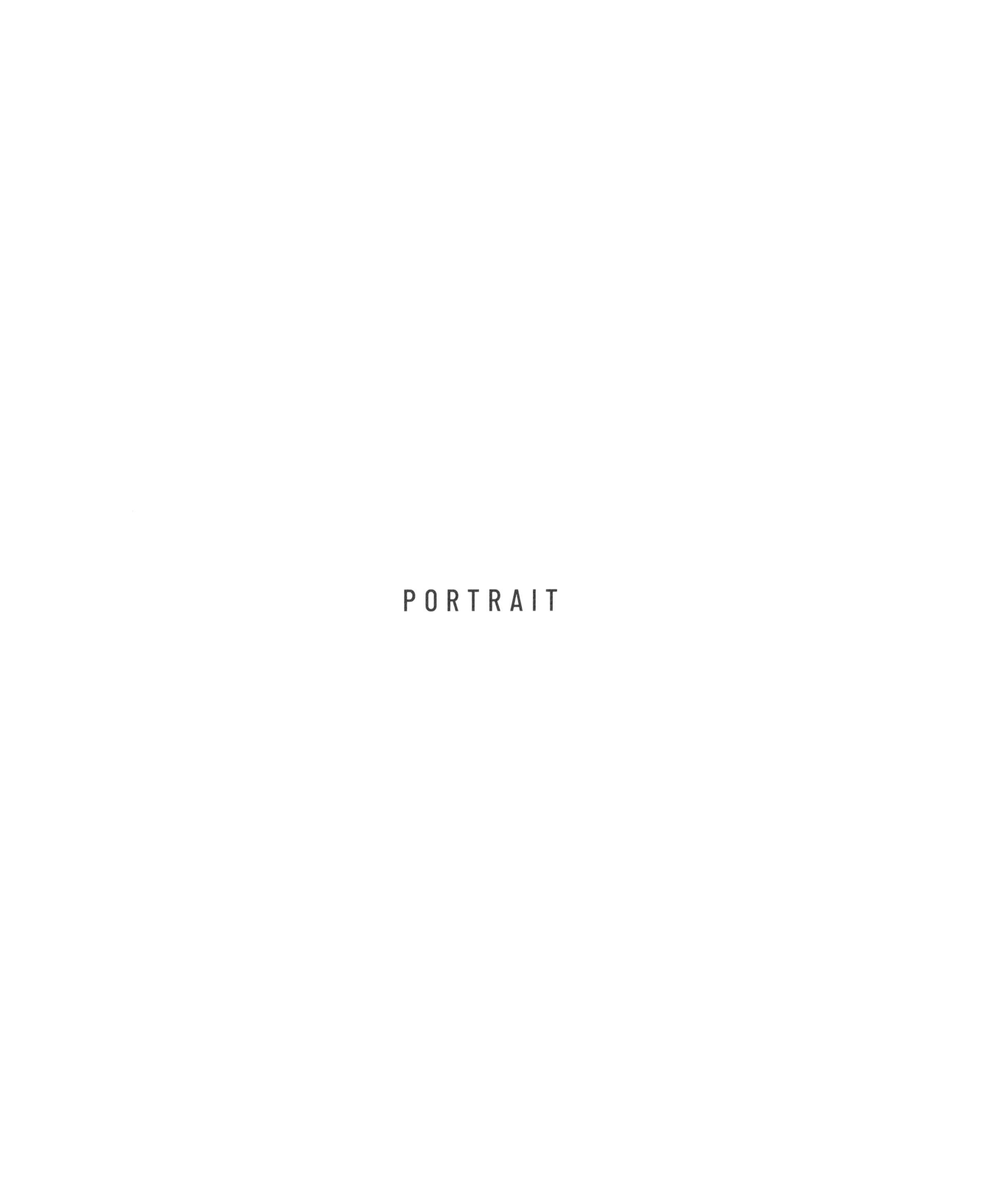

PORTRAIT

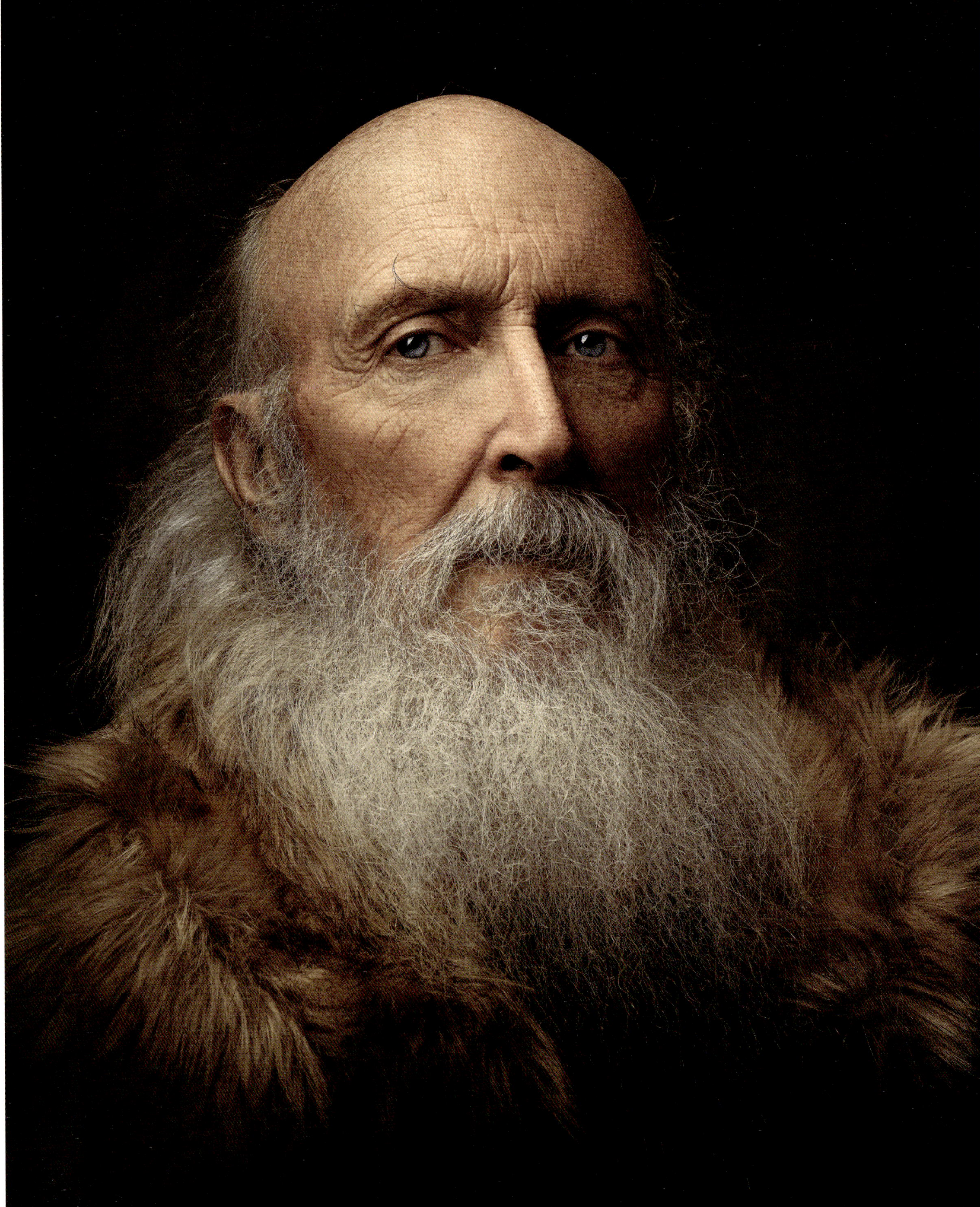

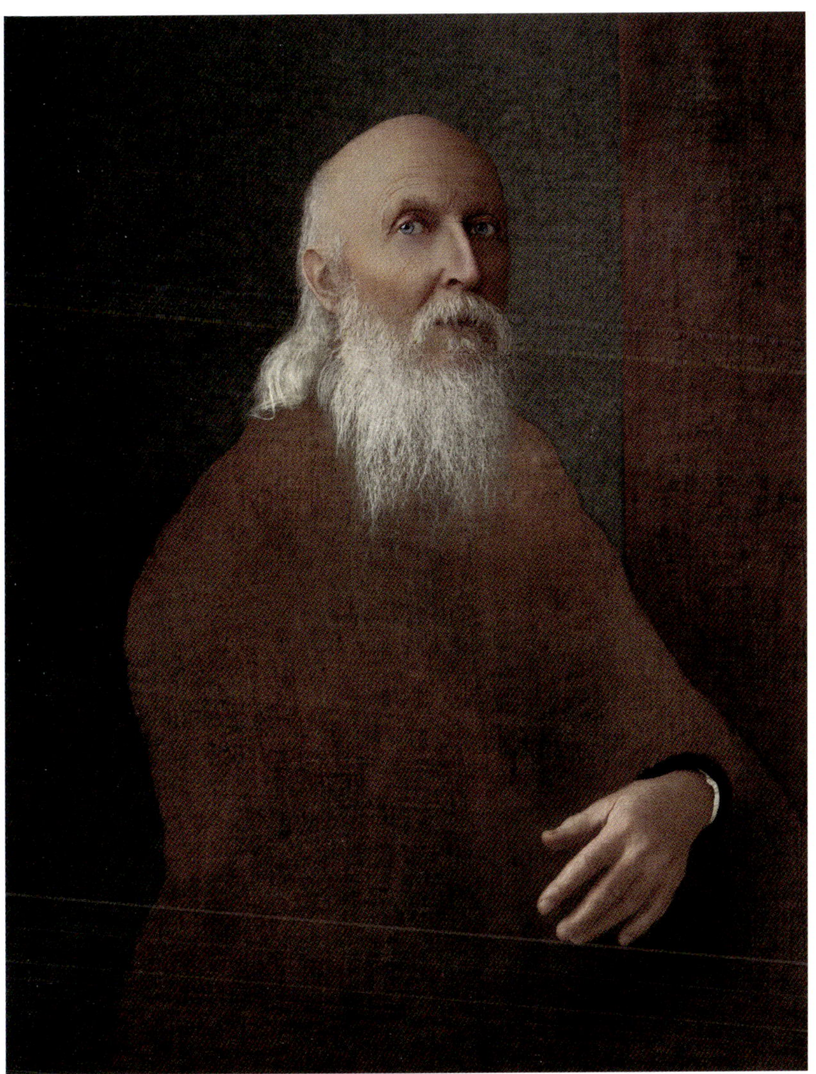

OPPOSITE

THE DUKE A portrait of Robert Tilley, the best friend I've made since I came to Canada in 2018 as an international student. I took this portrait one day before Robert turned seventy-three years old. Robert's grandfather, who was born in 1882 and lived a legendary life in the US and Canada, had the nickname "Duke," an abbreviation of his full name, William Marmaduke Tilley. The name Duke is perfect for this portrait. Robert made the vest he wears in the portrait more than forty years ago, when he worked in the cold of northern British Columbia.

YEAR: 2021

LEFT

UNFINISHED This artwork is inspired by and pays tribute to Daniele da Volterra's unfinished portrait of Michelangelo Buonarroti. The original portrait was probably painted in about 1545. Michelangelo's idea that "it is necessary to keep one's compass in one's eyes and not in the hand, for the hands execute, but the eye judges" is vividly embodied in this portrait. I painted the rest of the picture, except for Robert's head and hand.

YEAR: 2023

RIGHT

THE OLD MAN AND THE FLOWER

Flowers are too often associated with beauty and youth, but an old man also deserves a flower.

YEAR: 2021

OPPOSITE

I AND MYSELF IN ME

Human beings are complicated creatures with many layers in their personality. Everyone has an *I* and *myself* in *me*. The two overlapping faces of Robert are actually two different sides of his face. This overlapping/parallel profile portrait is inspired by *Jan de Bray's Portrait of the Artist's Parents, Salomon de Bray and Anna Westerbaen* (1664) and Peter Paul Rubens' *Agrippina and Germanicus* (c. 1614).

YEAR: 2023

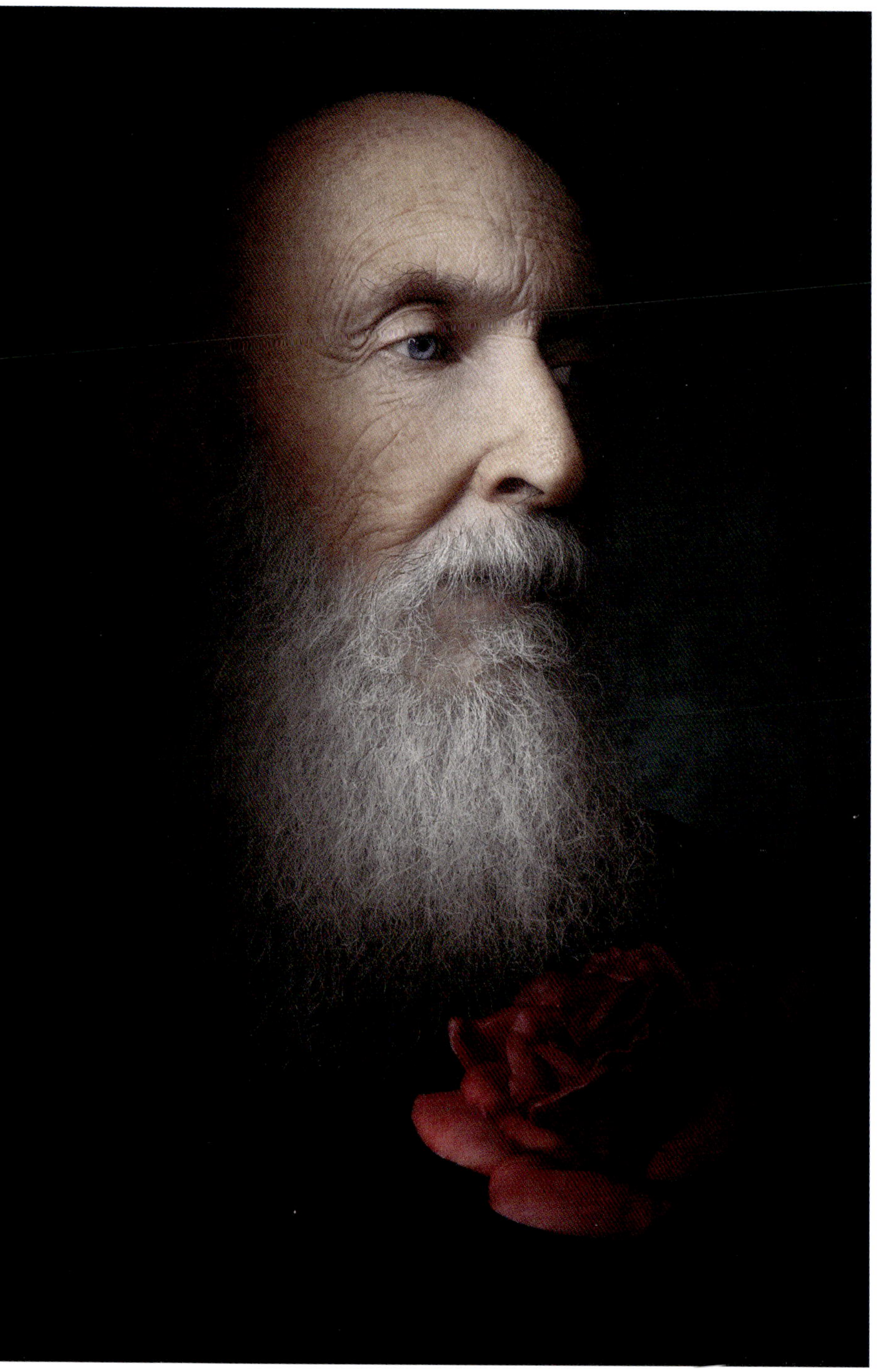

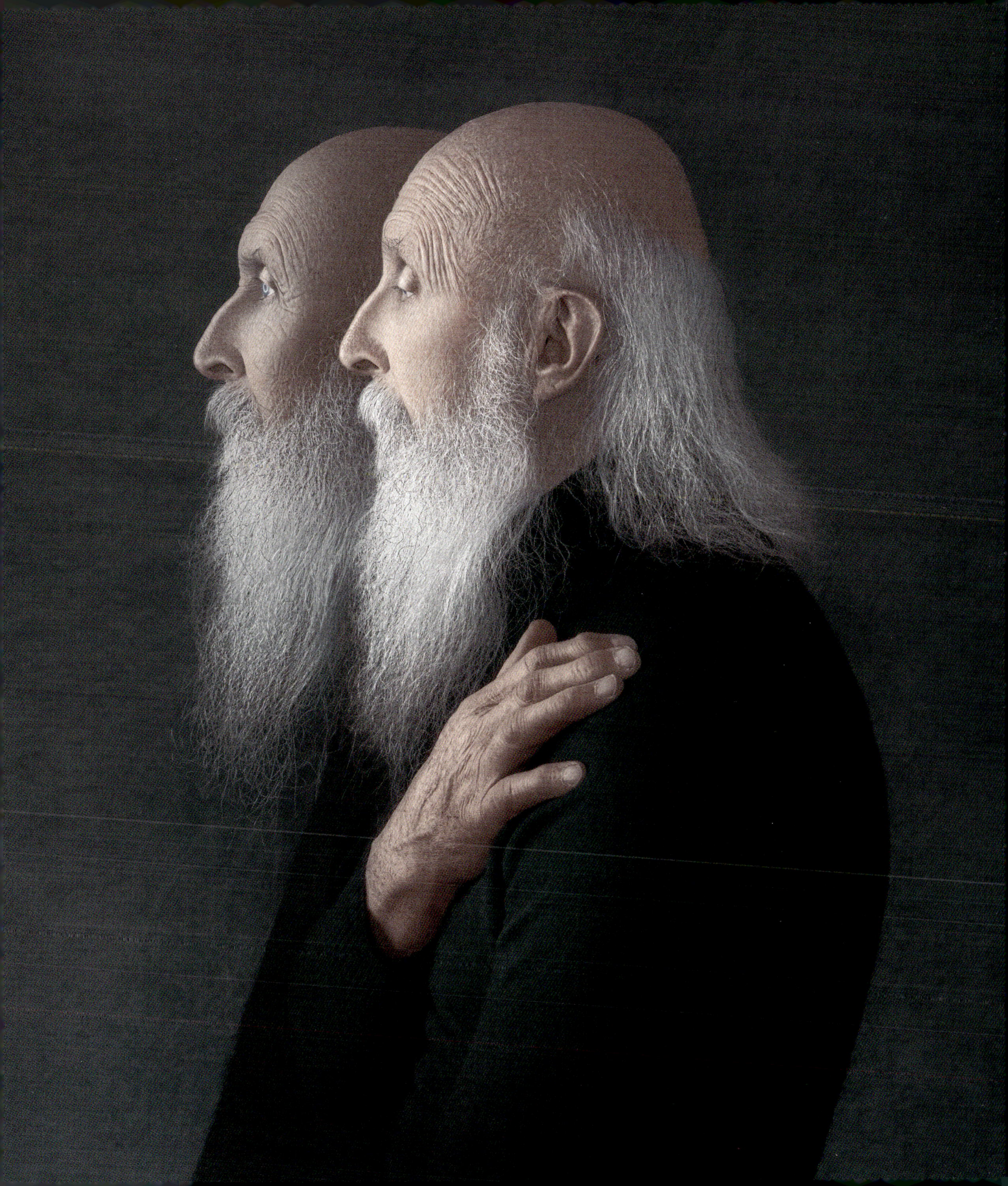

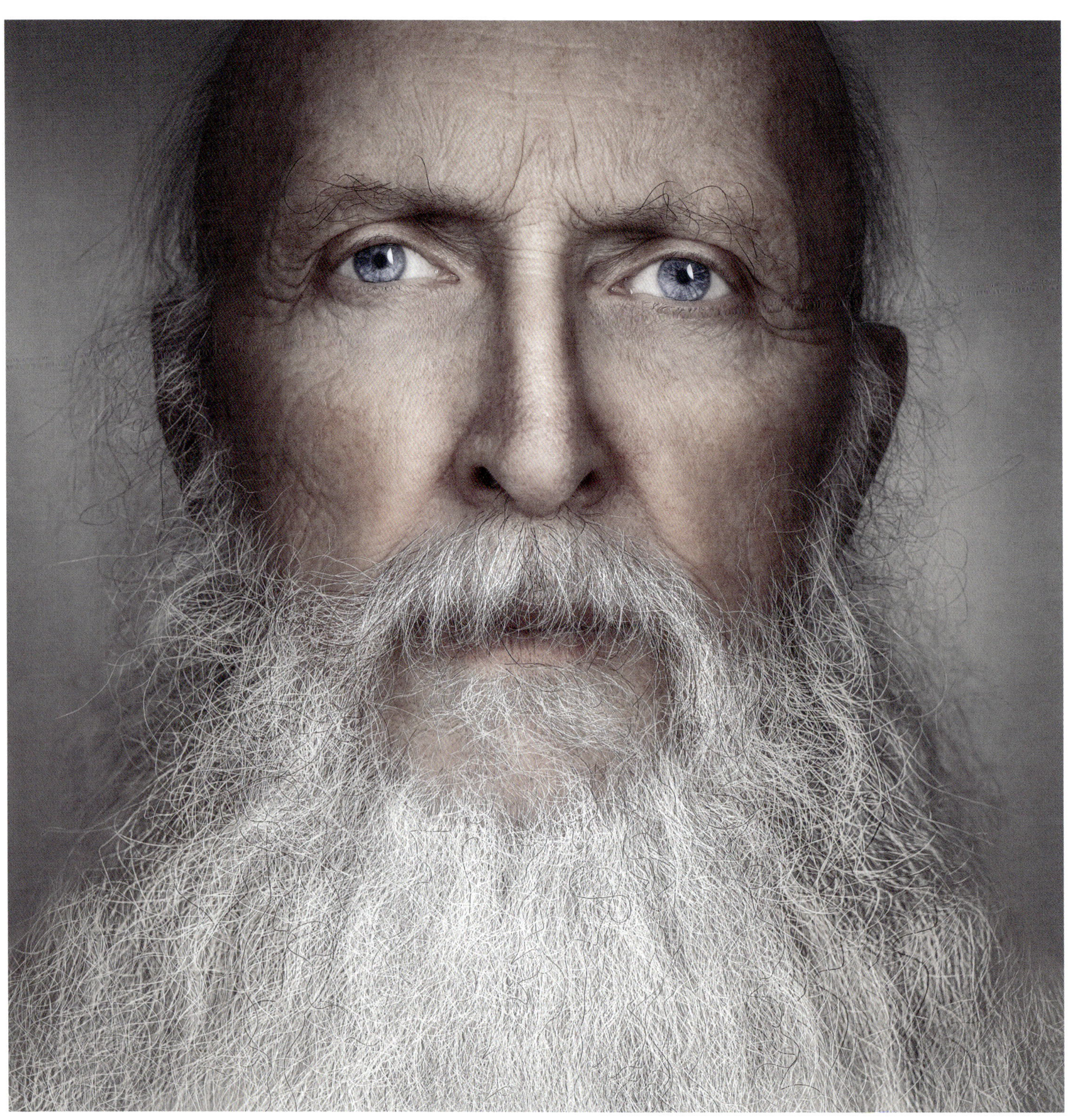

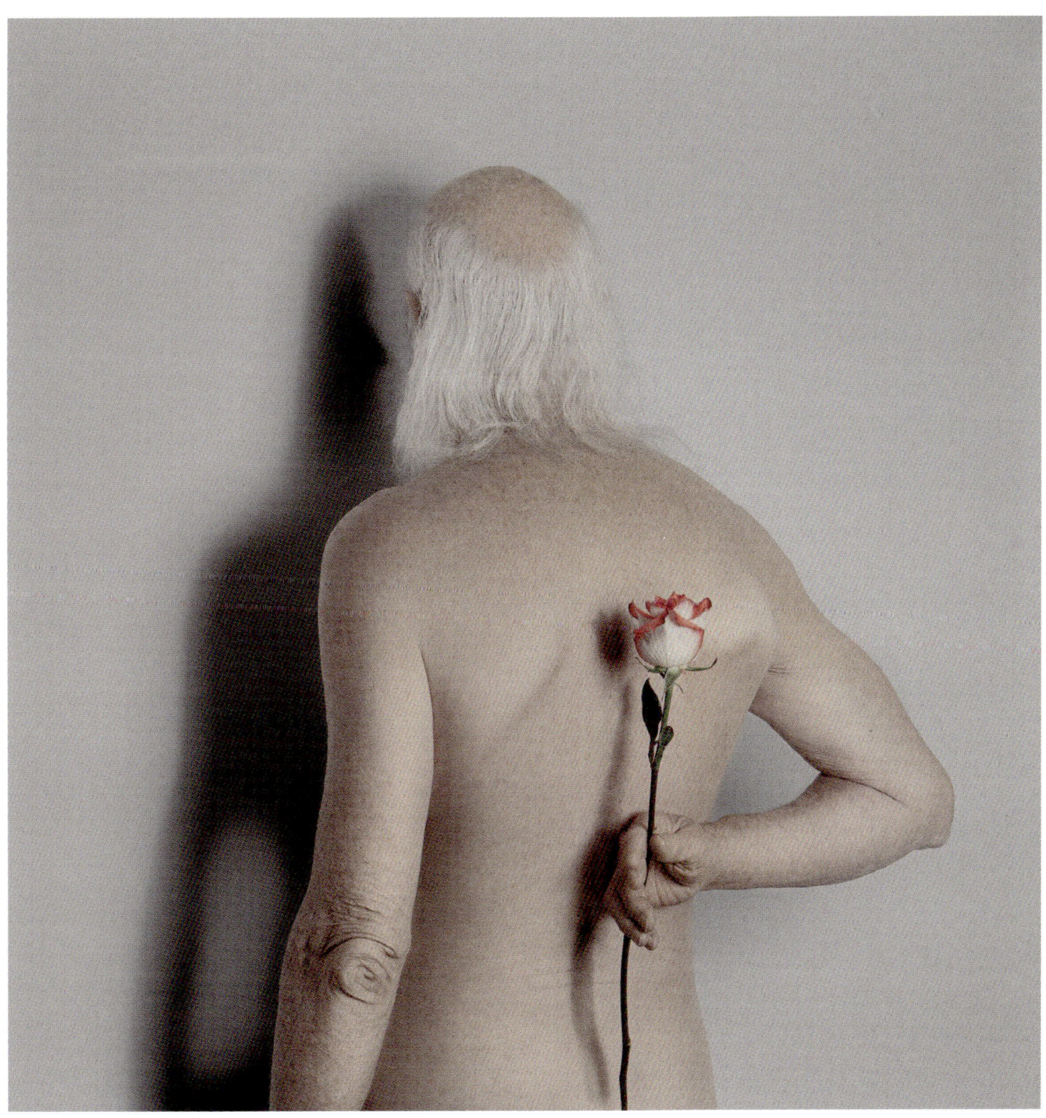

OPPOSITE

WHITE AND BLUE Robert's hair is white as snow, and his eyes are blue as the Atlantic Ocean. Snow is common in Newfoundland's winter, and this province lies in the arm of the Atlantic.

YEAR: 2022

ABOVE

GIVING A FLOWER TO YOURSELF
I give a flower to myself and my shadow. I love myself and embrace it.

YEAR: 2023

RIGHT

WEIGHT OF TIME

Time has weight. Every second that passes is lighter than a veil, lighter than a bubble. But when they accumulate, the weight of all the time you spend is the weight of your life. It is heavy enough to turn you from a young lad to an old man, heavy enough to turn your hair white.

YEAR: 2023

OPPOSITE

BUBBLED BLUE EYE

Some bubbles were flying across Robert's face, and I captured this moment when one flew right in front of his baby-blue eye. Because I don't have an assistant, I needed to set the camera on a timer and blow the bubbles myself. A few soap bubbles flew into Robert's eyes while we were shooting. I appreciate his patience!

YEAR: 2022

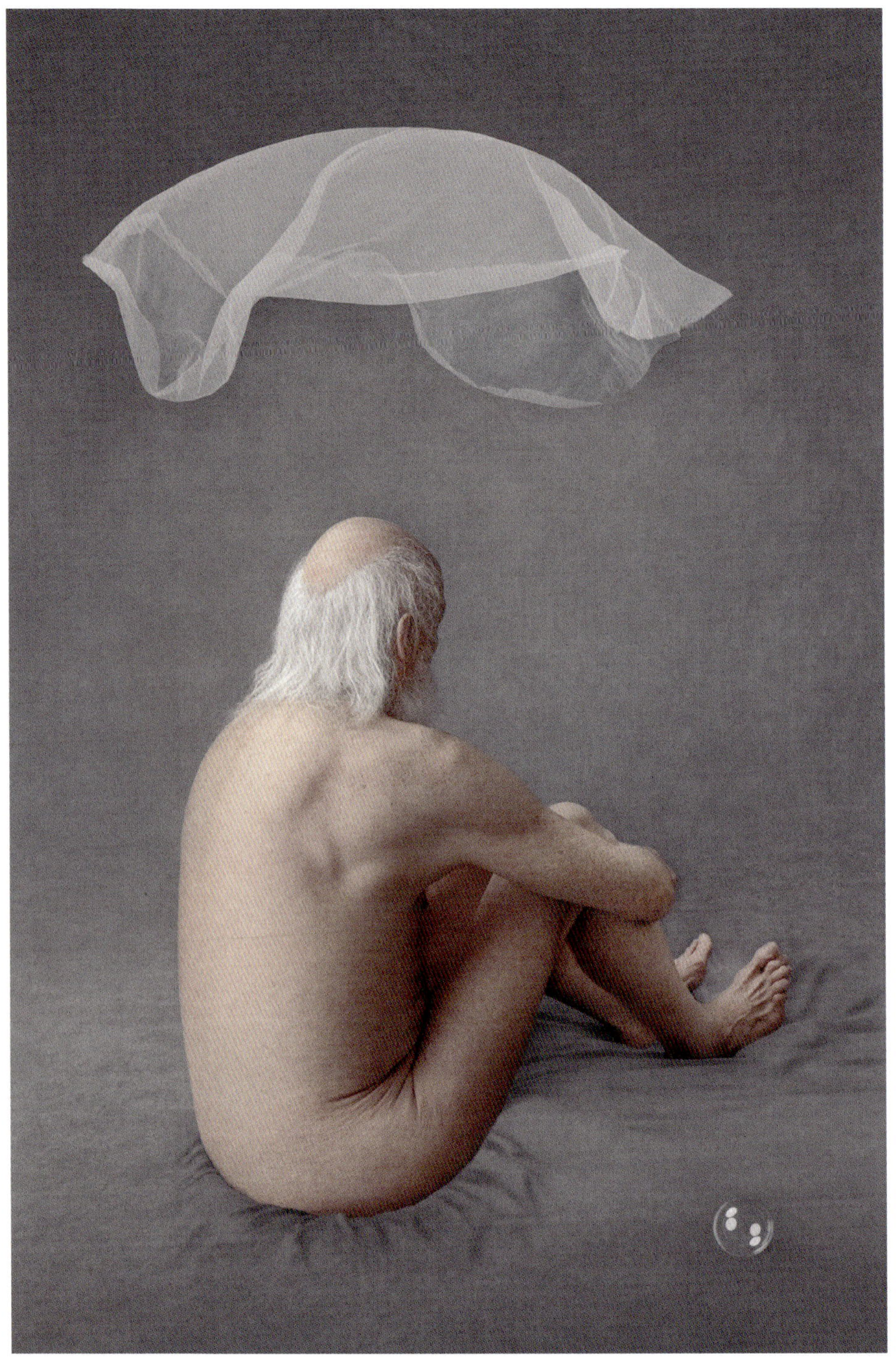

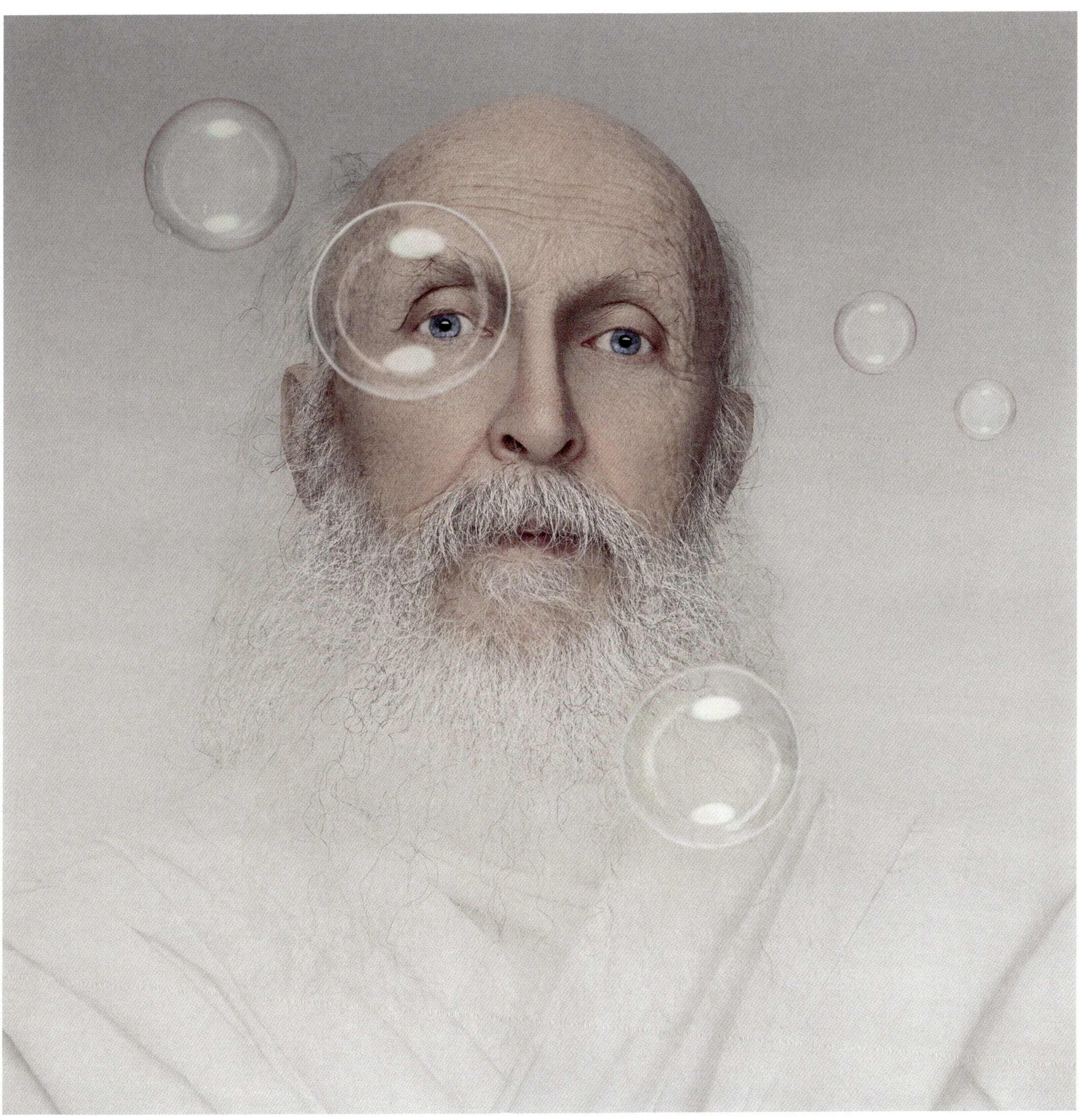

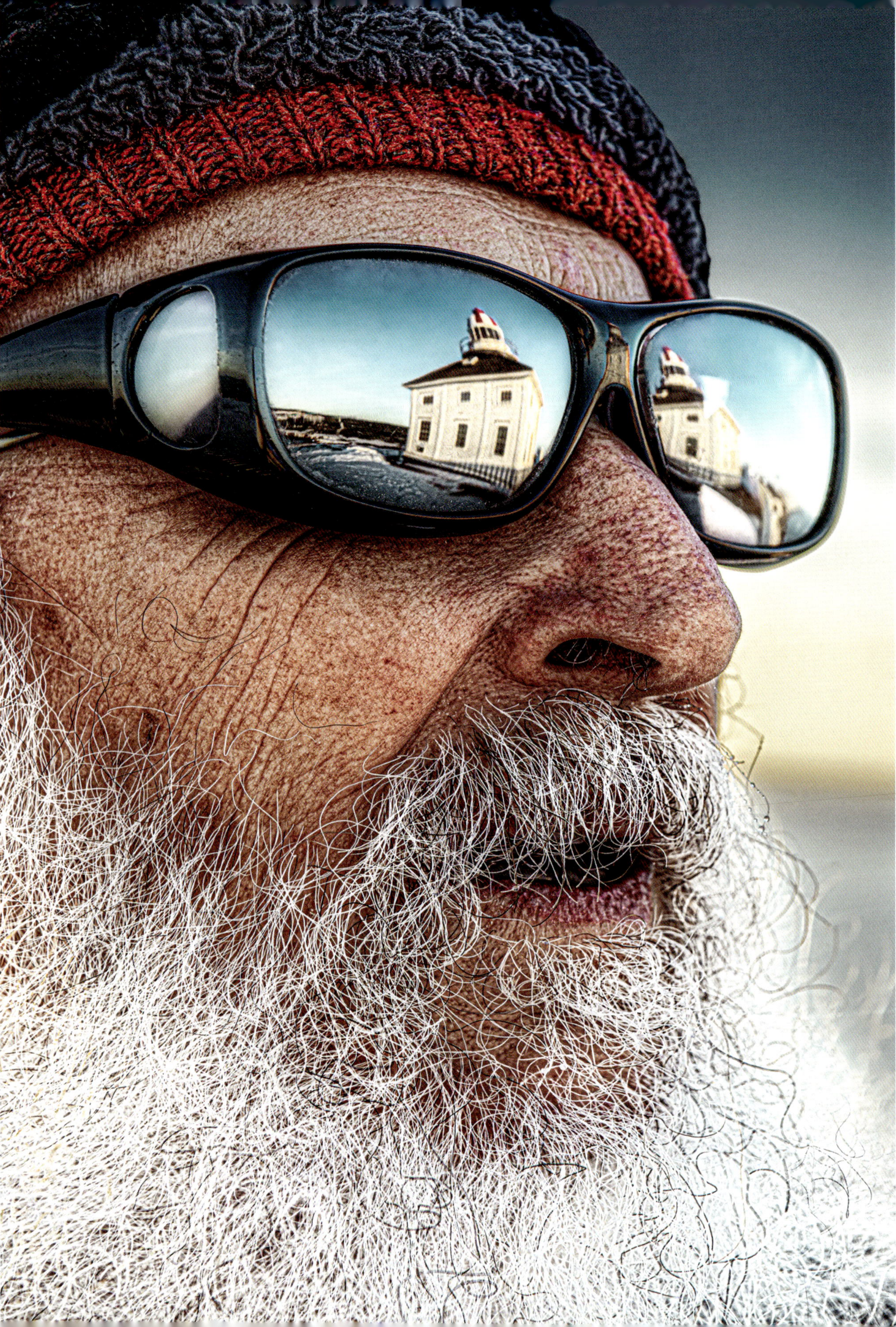

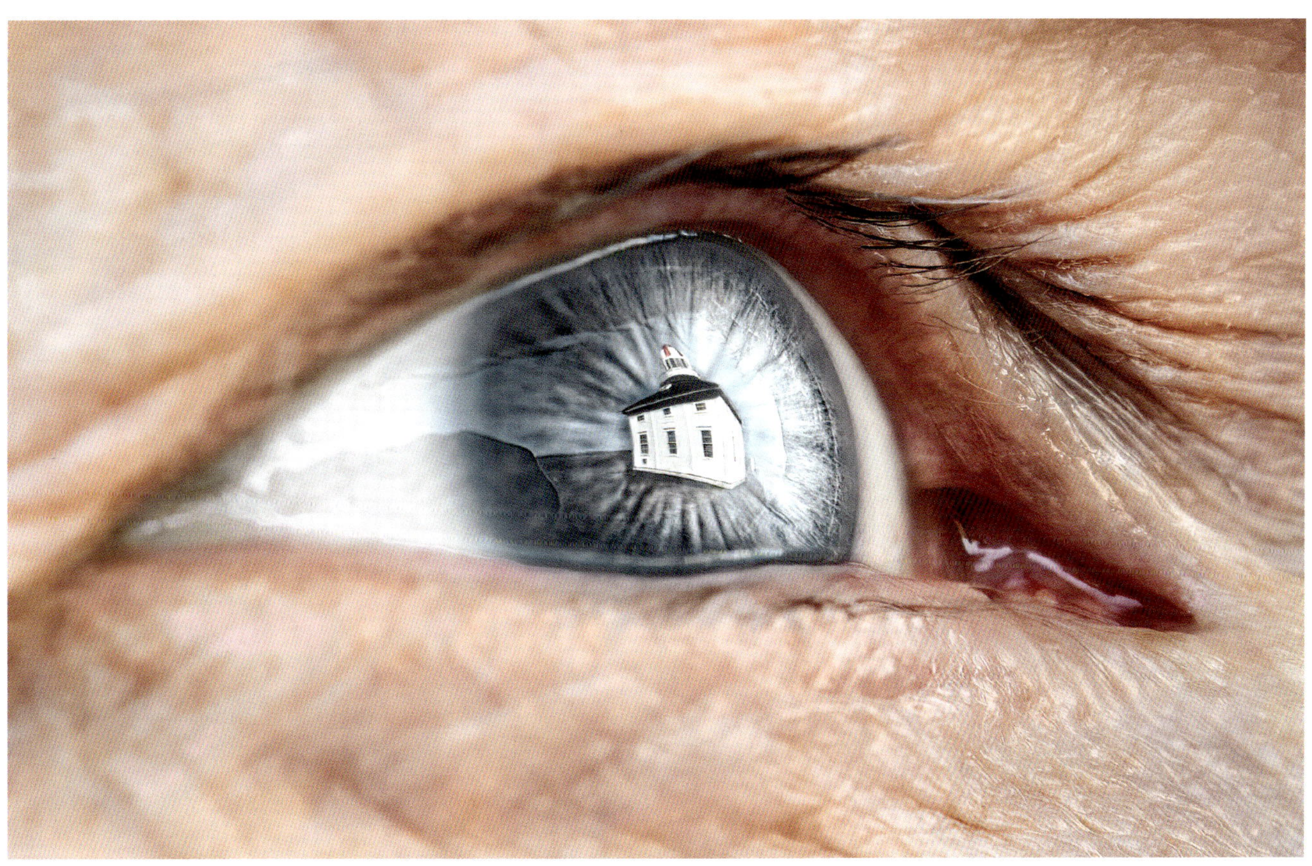

OPPOSITE

THE LIGHTHOUSE AND A TRUE NEWFOUNDLANDER
Robert and I went to Cape Spear early one morning. The lighthouse was bathed in early-morning sunlight and reflected in a true Newfoundlander's eyes.

YEAR: 2021

ABOVE

BABY-BLUE EYE I visited Cape Spear lighthouse, on Canada's easternmost point of land, with Robert. The lighthouse was reflected right in the middle of his baby-blue eye. Eyes are so magical that the iris looks like a miniature of the galaxy. This is not a composite photo, but a single-shot image.

YEAR: 2021

RIGHT

NAKED HISTORY Are we naked in front of history, or is history naked in front of us? The newspaper is the *Youth's Companion* from February 12, 1914. It is a real edition in my collection.

YEAR: 2022

OPPOSITE

SORROW Sorrow is soft. Sorrow is tender. Sorrow is like a veil. It gently shrouds your changing face and your eyes, which once had a soft look and shadows deep.

YEAR: 2023

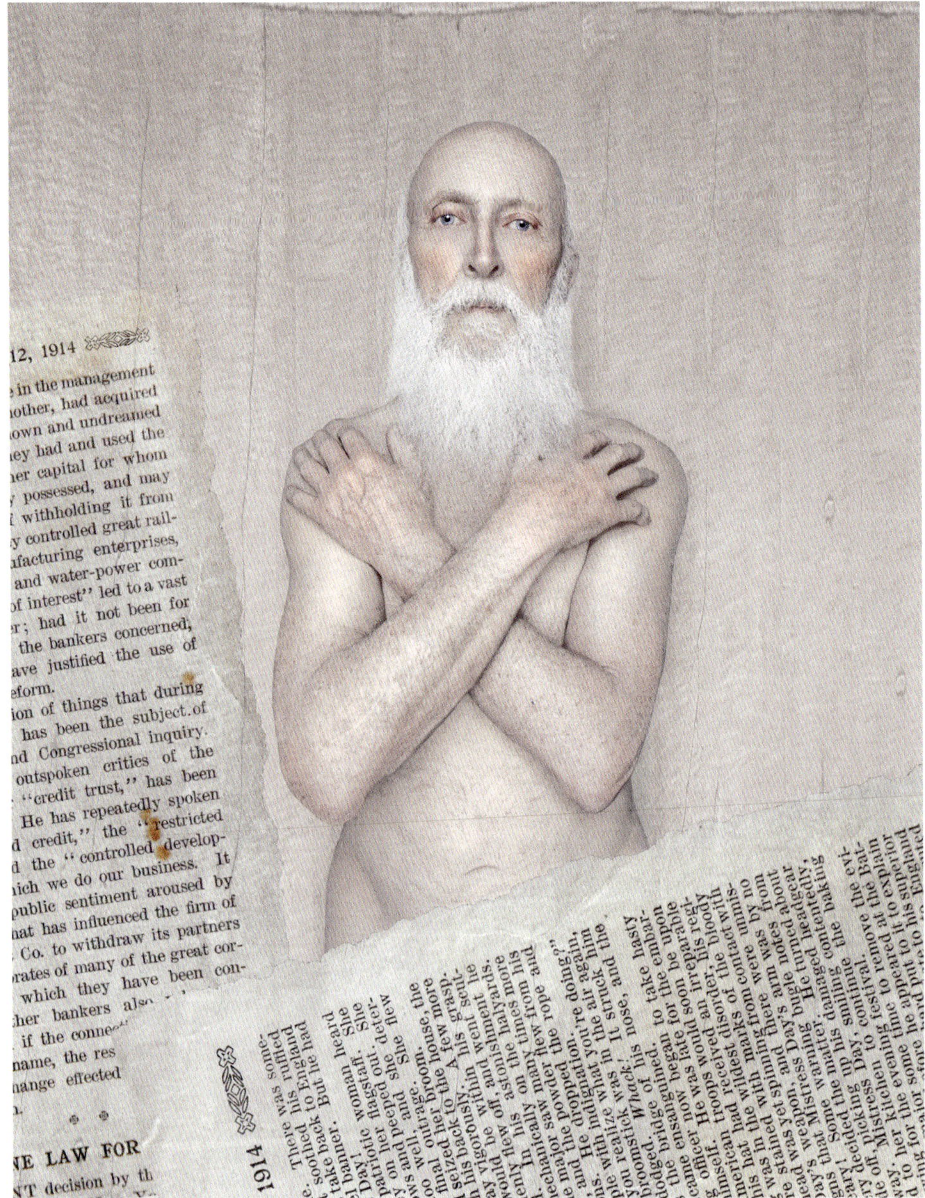

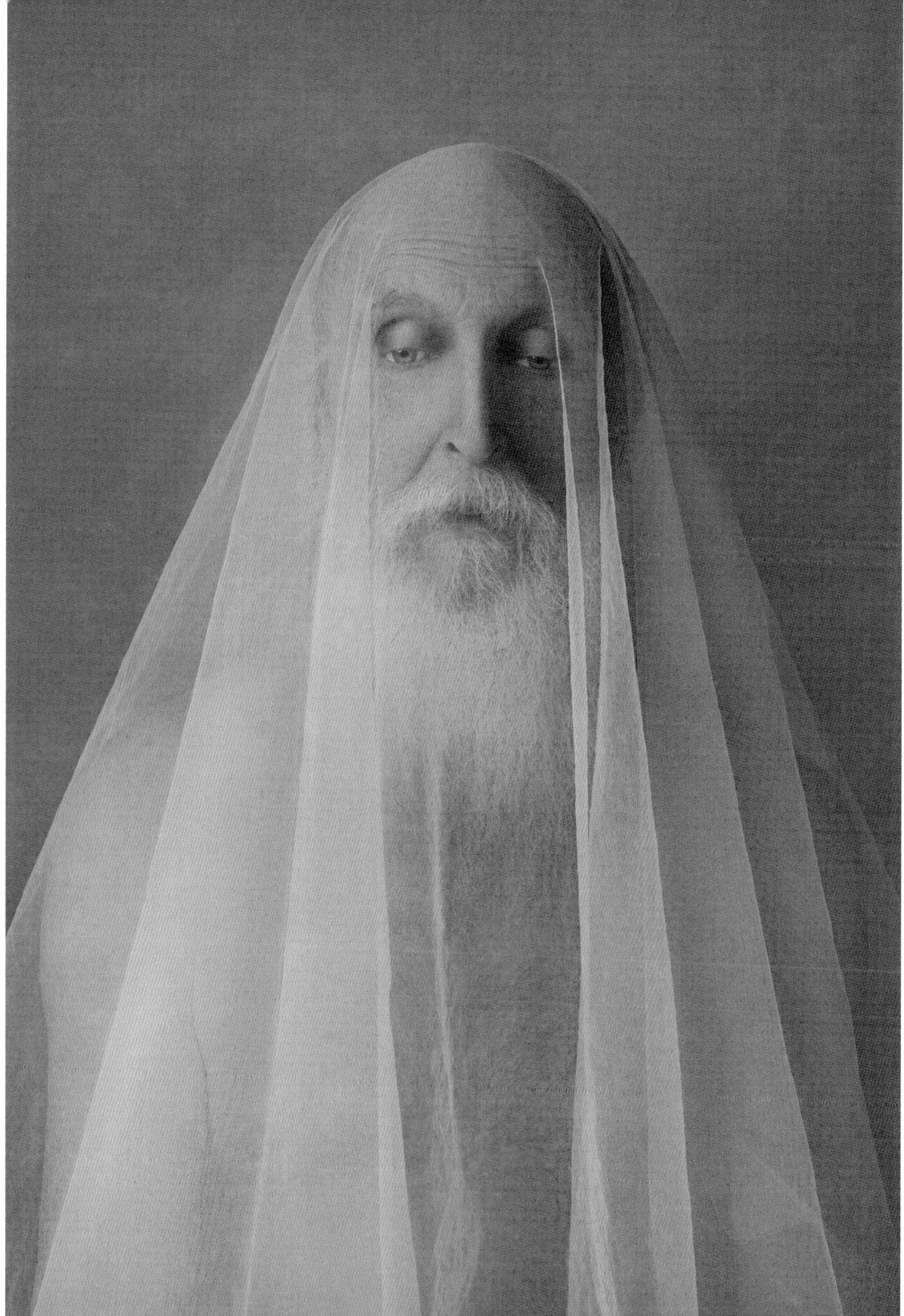

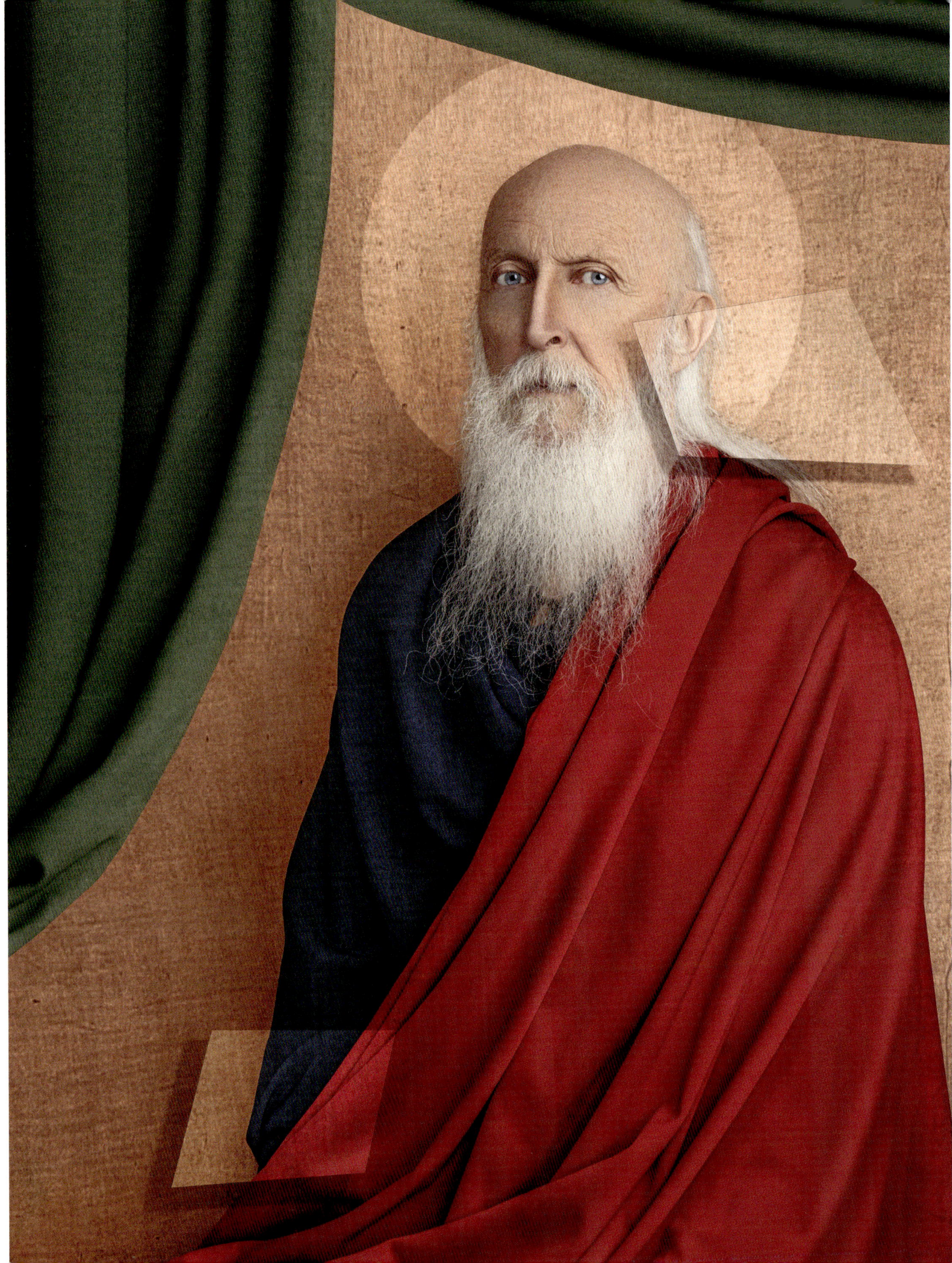

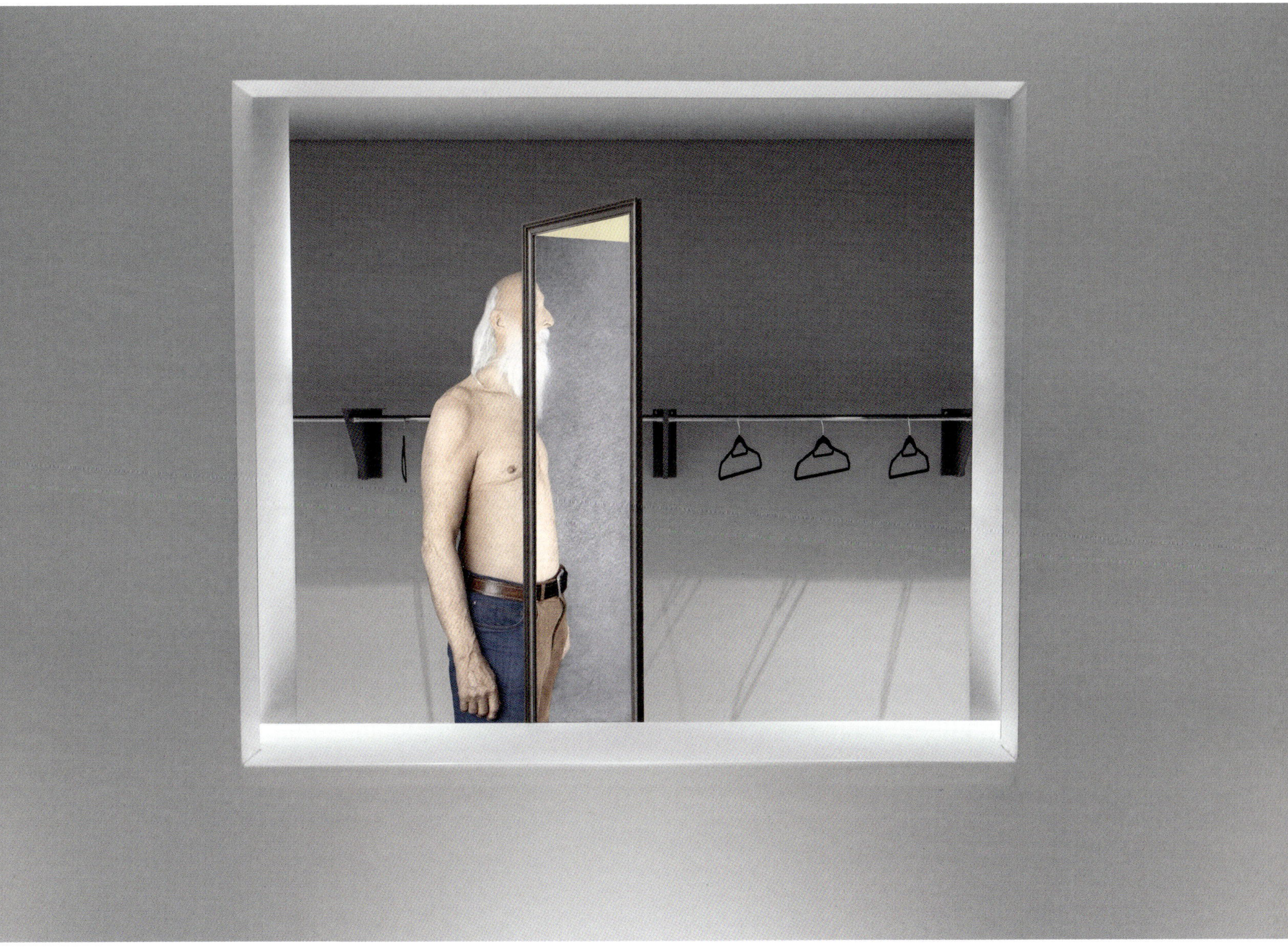

OPPOSITE

SEGMENTS OF A SAINT

Not everyone can be a saint, but we have elements of saintliness within us. This image is inspired by gold-ground Renaissance paintings.

YEAR: 2023

ABOVE

AN EMPTY COAT CHECK

A coat check with no coats: only Robert and a mirror.

YEAR: 2023

MR. SWEET

Robert has liked eating sweets since he was little. One story was that one day, little Robert walked to Bowring Park from Cashin Avenue with his friends. They kept eating Hershey Bells on their way to the park. You could track them from Cashin all the way to Bowring Park by the chocolate wrappers they left behind. They ate so many Hershey Bells that they began to feel sick as soon as they arrived in the park, and they had to walk back home: no park visit on that day.

YEAR: 2023

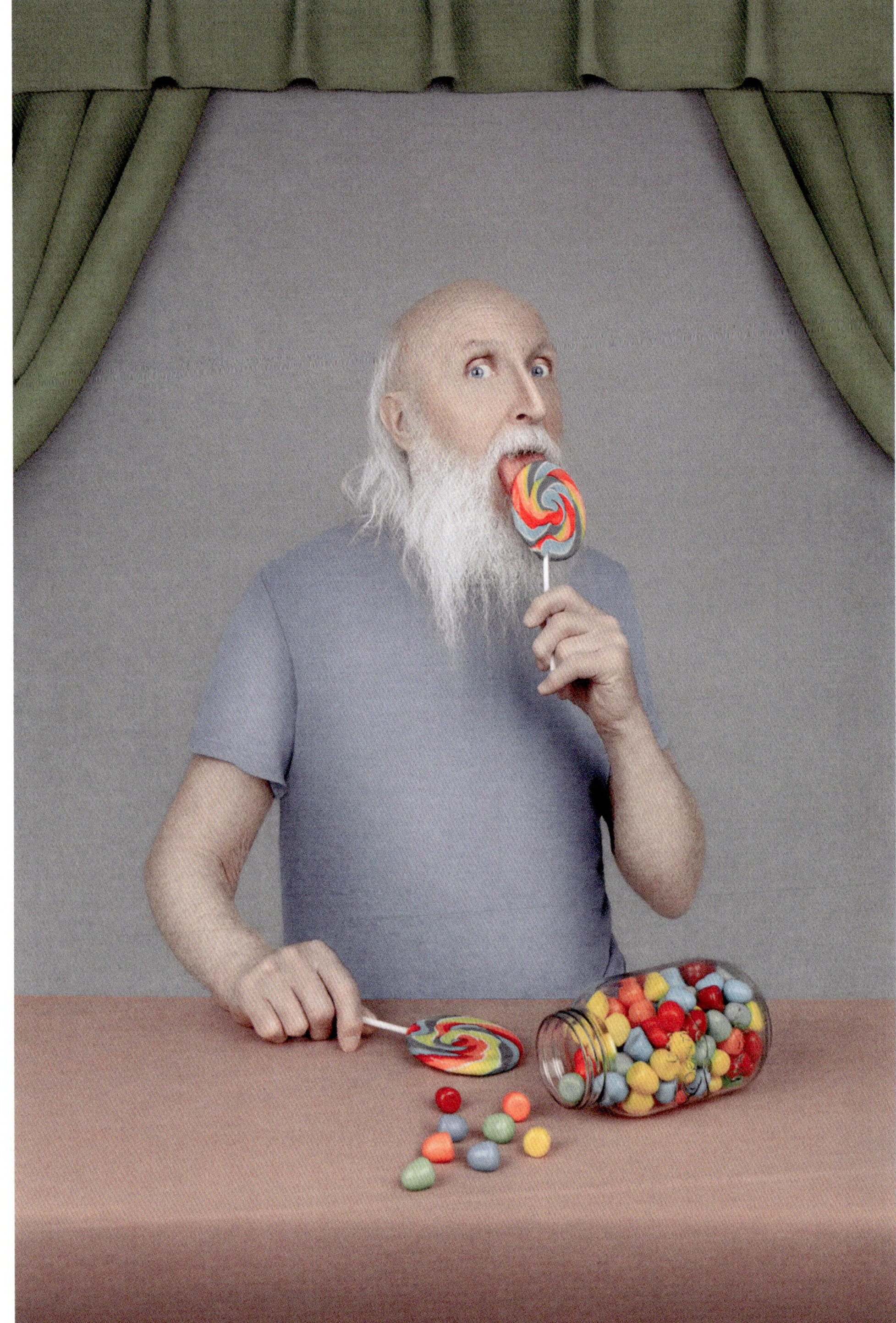

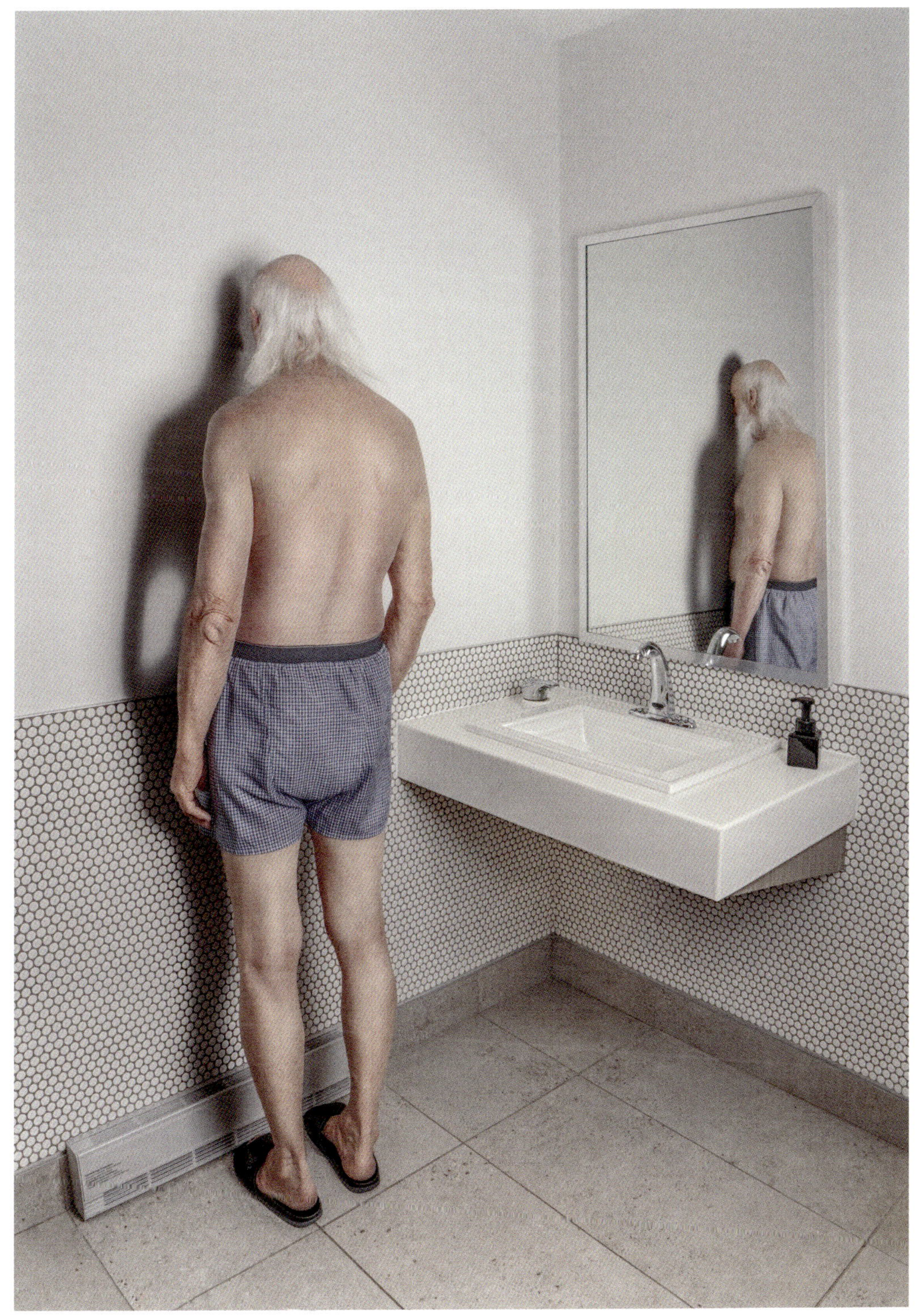

FACING YOURSELF

Sometimes it is difficult to face yourself, and that is why a lot of us choose not to.

An interesting detail: Robert's face and shadow in the mirror are different from the ones in front of the mirror.

YEAR: 2023

RIGHT

THE MILKMAID IN FERRYLAND

This photo of Lori Pittman is inspired by and pays tribute to Johannes Vermeer's painting *The Milkmaid* (1658), which is a masterpiece of the Dutch Golden Age. Lady Sara Kirke owned and operated a dairy at the Colony of Avalon in the 1630 and the 1640s. Archaeologists have recovered many ceramic milk pans and butter pots in the Colony of Avalon, now known as Ferryland.

YEAR: 2022

OPPOSITE

THE MAID AND HER BELLARMINE JUG

I took this portrait when my friend Lori Pittman was working in her seventeenth-century-style kitchen in the Colony of Avalon as a heritage interpreter. This portrait is inspired by Pieter Bruegel the Elder's painting *The Peasant Wedding* (1567).

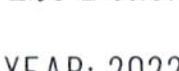

YEAR: 2022

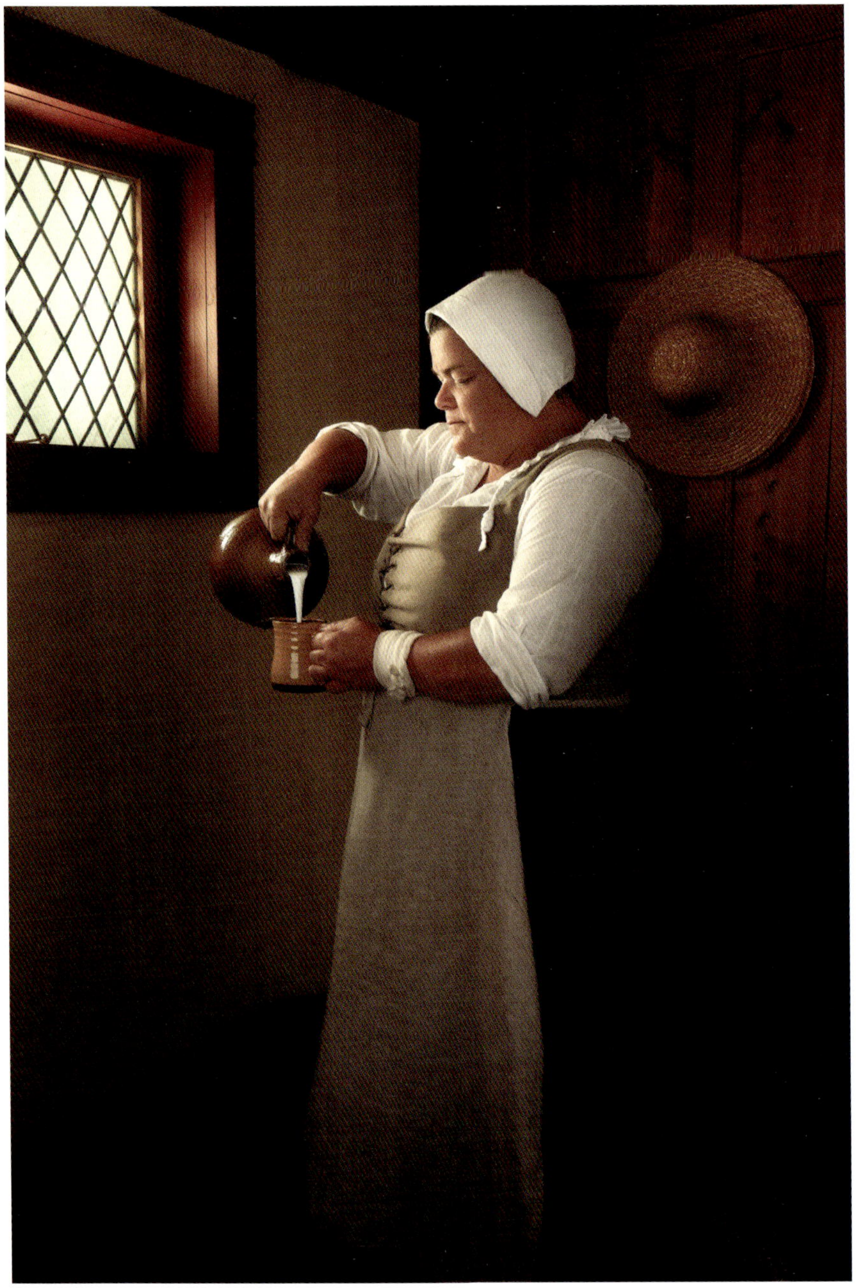

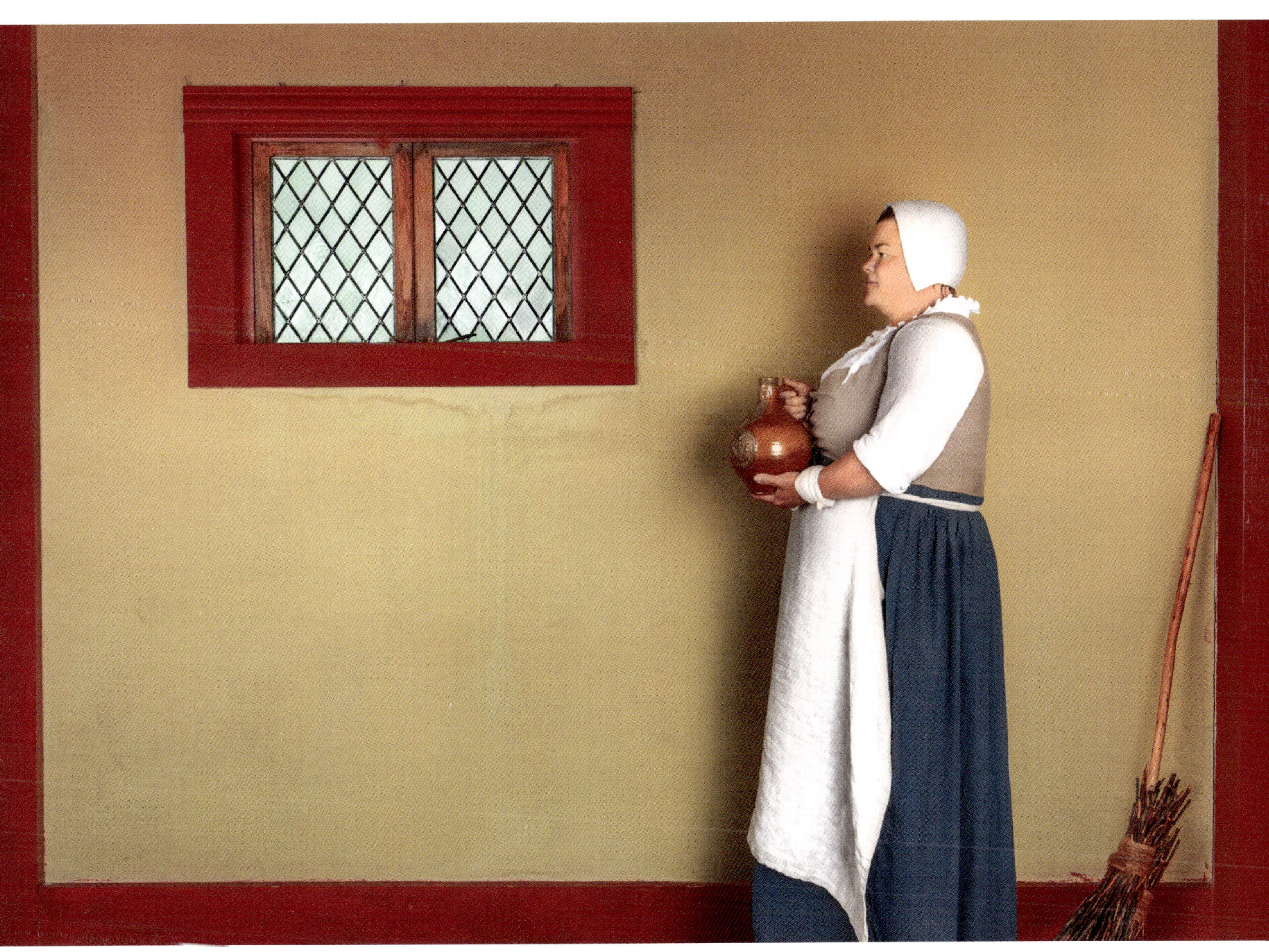

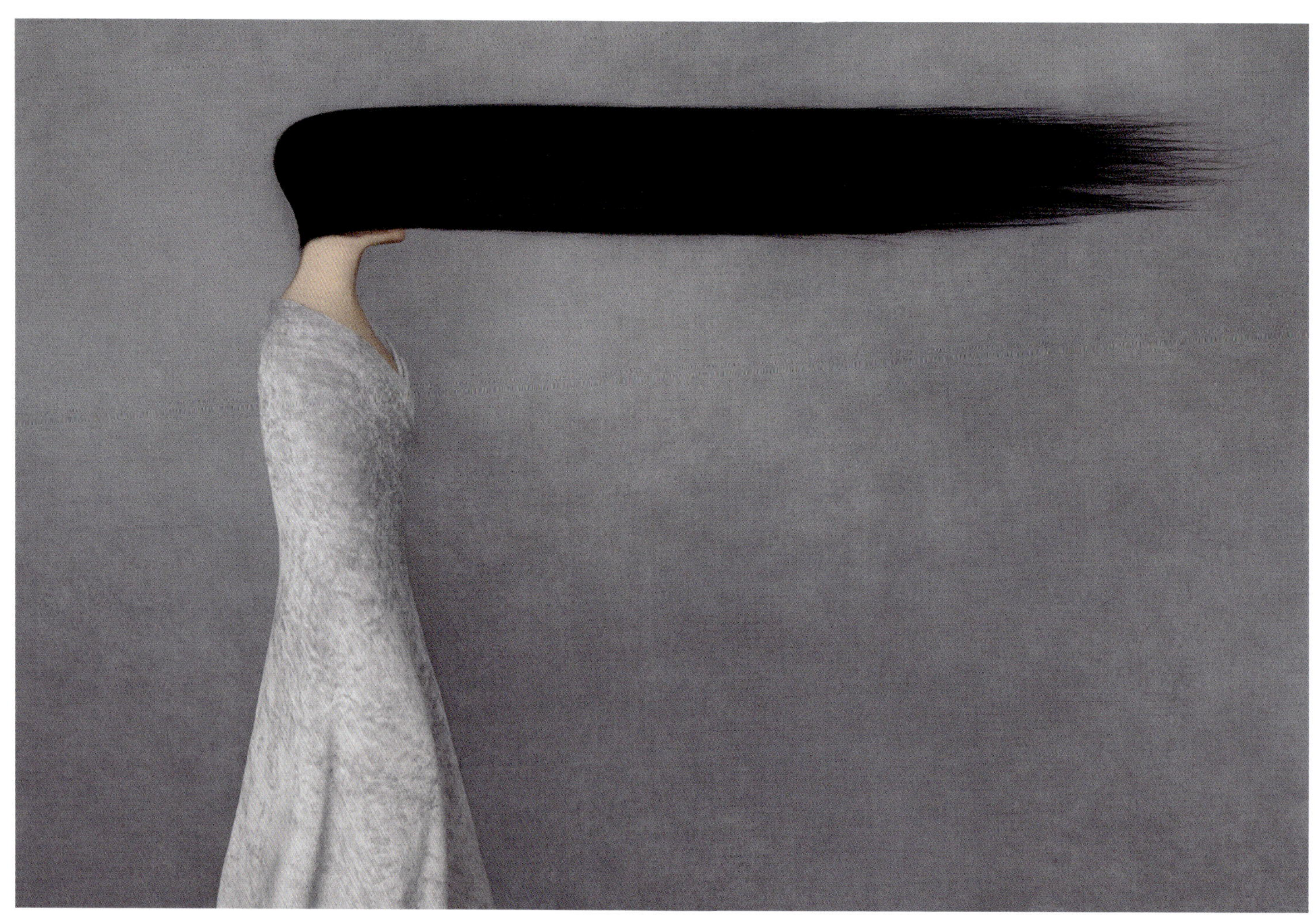

ABOVE

VESSEL FOR TIME This is my conceptual self-portrait. I trimmed my body to the shape of a vessel or a bottle. Our bodies are vessels for time. All the time that we spend fills our bodies. We are the result and embodiment of the time we have lived and experienced. In this portrait, my hair, which hasn't been cut for more than ten years, is the result and the embodiment of the past decade.

YEAR: 2023

OPPOSITE

THE HOODED MAN This artwork is inspired by the portrait of Girolamo Savonarola by Fra Bartolomeo (c. 1498).

YEAR: 2023

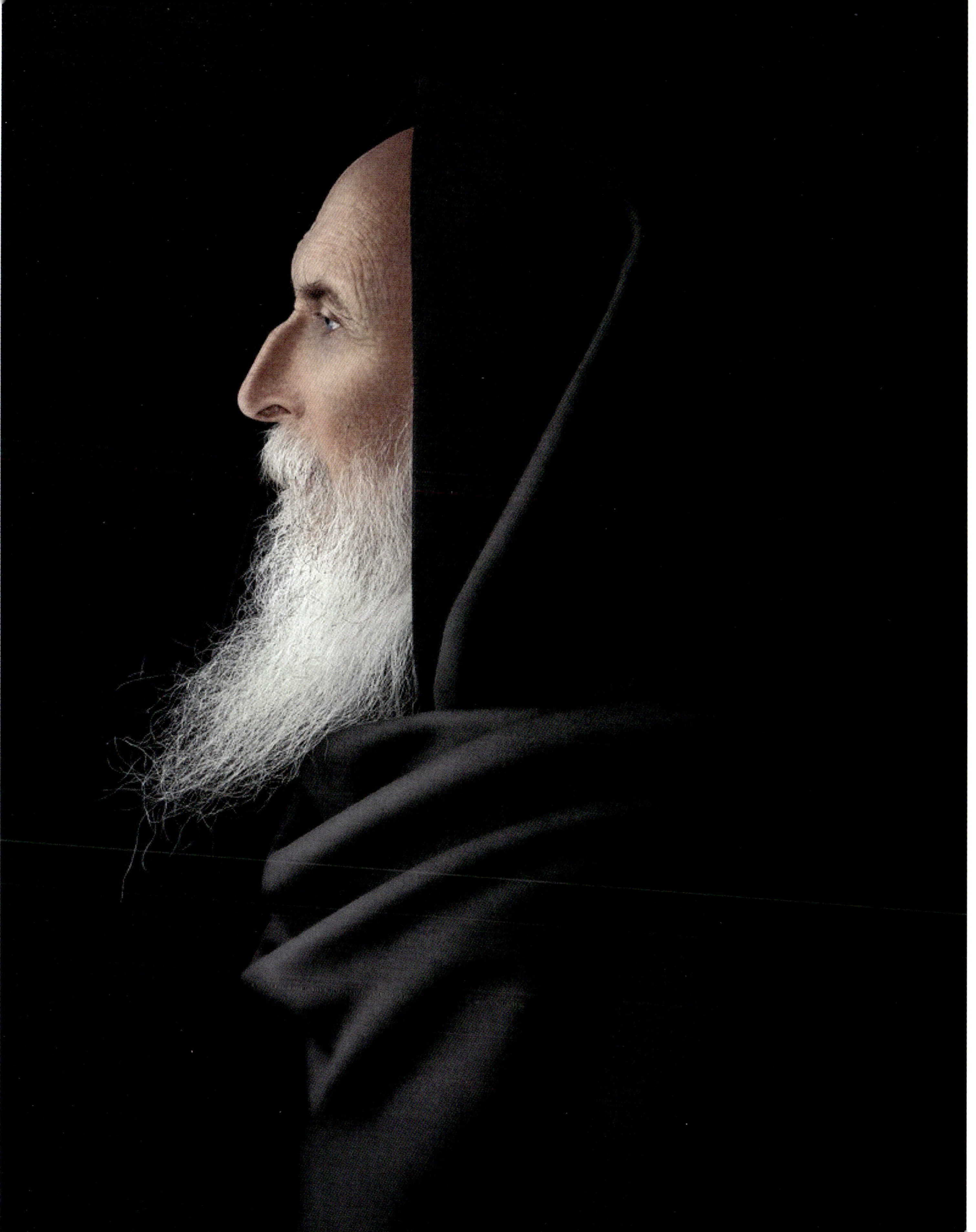

SERIES: AT HOME

When I came to Newfoundland in 2018 as an international student, Robert Tilley was the first friend I made, and through the years, he has become my best friend. I visit his home regularly. I took this series of photos from late 2020 to 2021, presenting daily life at his home, which he built more than forty years ago in a small fishing village in Newfoundland called Brigus South. In these photos, he plays, rests, cooks, and reads. I try to present everything in its real daily-life context. Through my photos, you can see the lifestyle of an elderly Newfoundlander, with its routines and its unique elements. This series also includes two photos taken in the Tilley House, Robert's family house, built in 1858 in Elliston by his great-great-grandfather. This house used to be his home when he was a child.

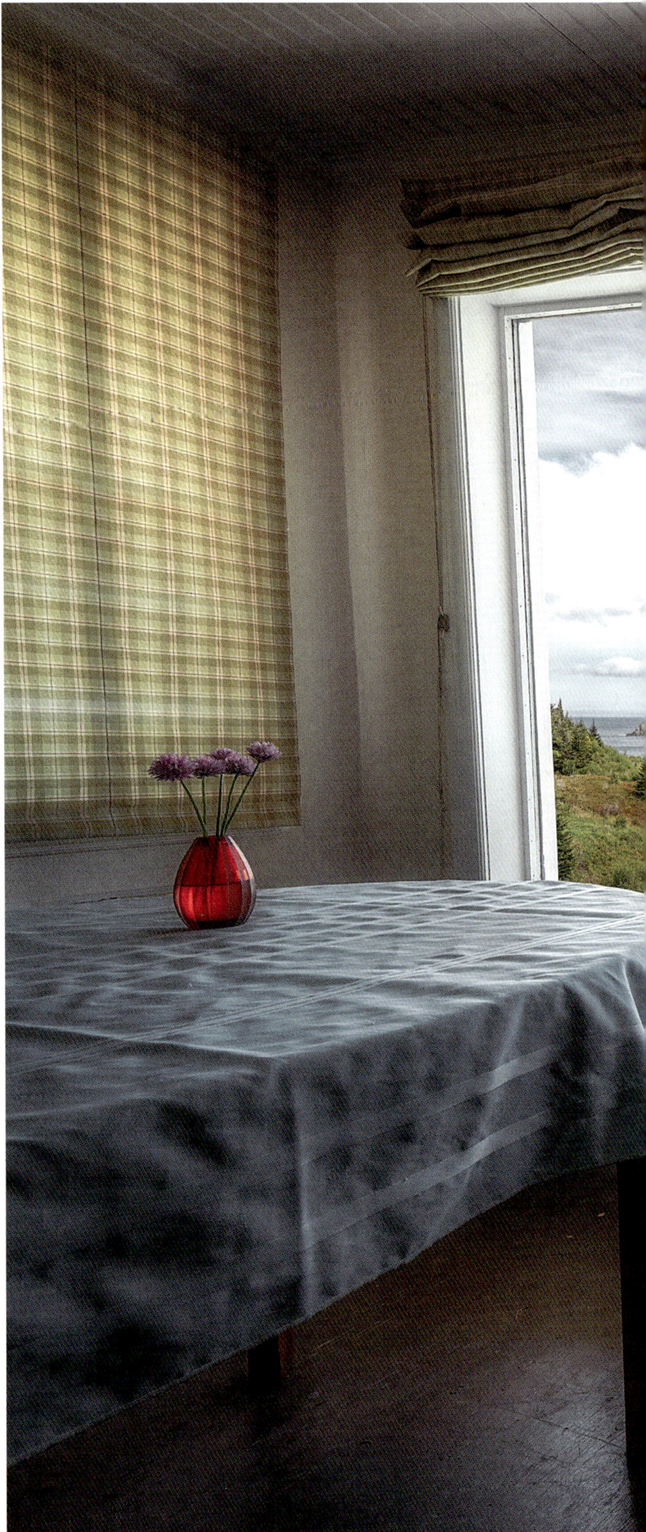

THE VIEW Robert is enjoying the view from the window of his home. He is taking a break from chores in the woods, so he is still in his workwear. The dining table on the left belonged to his parents. The white house next to him, which you can see from the window, belonged to his grandmother. The cliff in the window is Brigus Head, the landmark of Brigus South, where Robert's home is situated. This is Robert's home, where nature, people, past, and present are all nicely woven together.

YEAR: 2021

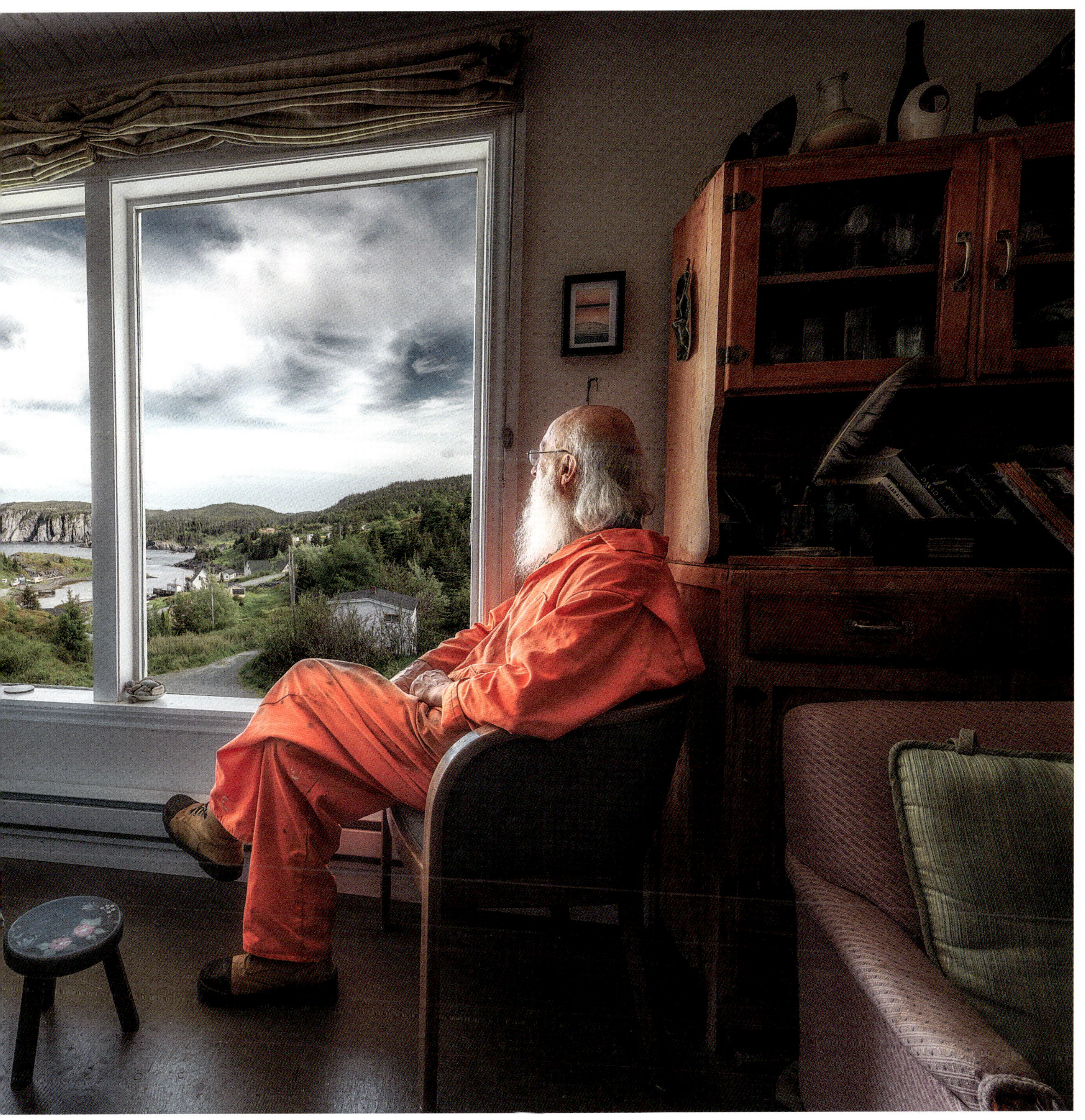

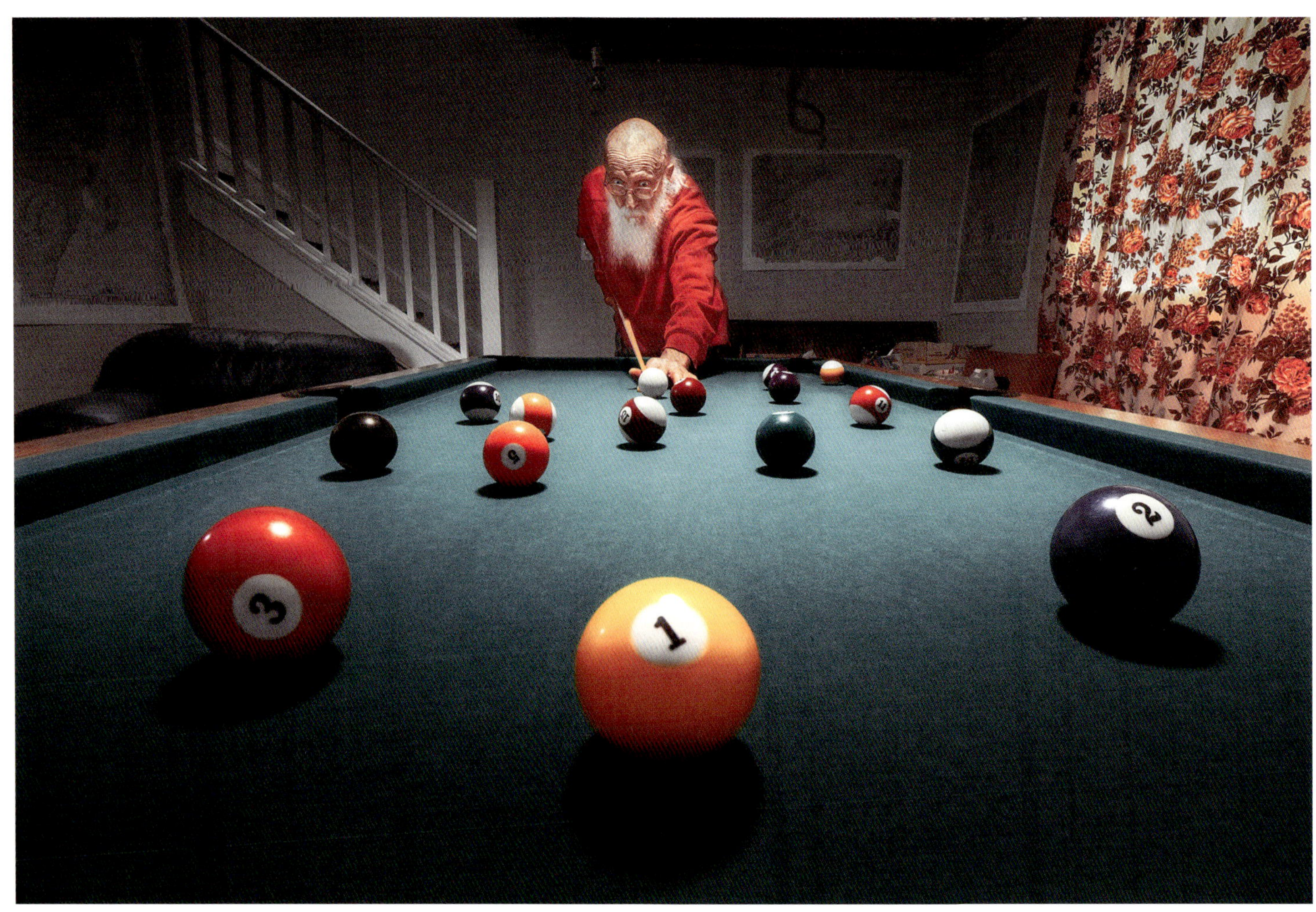

PLAY TIME Robert has a pool table in his house. Though he doesn't play often now, he's still a good shot when he picks up the cue. The antique maps on the wall were printed in the mid-nineteenth century, and they belonged to Robert's grandparents. This is Robert's home, where old-time memories mingle with modern fun.

YEAR: 2021

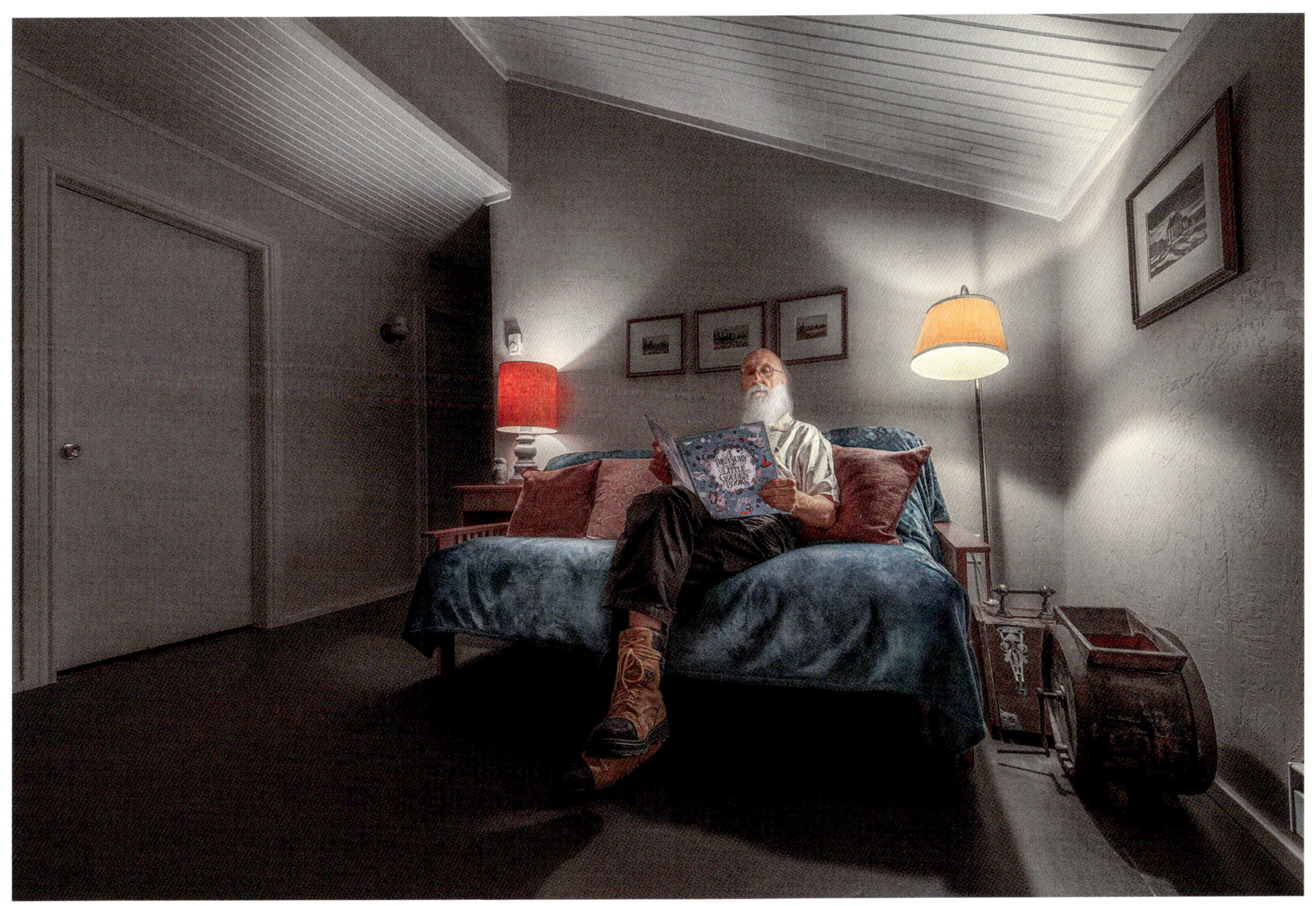

READING TIME Robert is reading a forty-year-old Golden Book, which his children used to read when they were little. The two rooms to his right used to be his children's bedrooms. Now they have grown up and left home and have their own families. The two antique objects to his left (one is a storage box and the other is a cream churn) belonged to his grandparents and date from the early nineteenth century. In Robert's home, memories of different generations are woven together.

YEAR: 2021

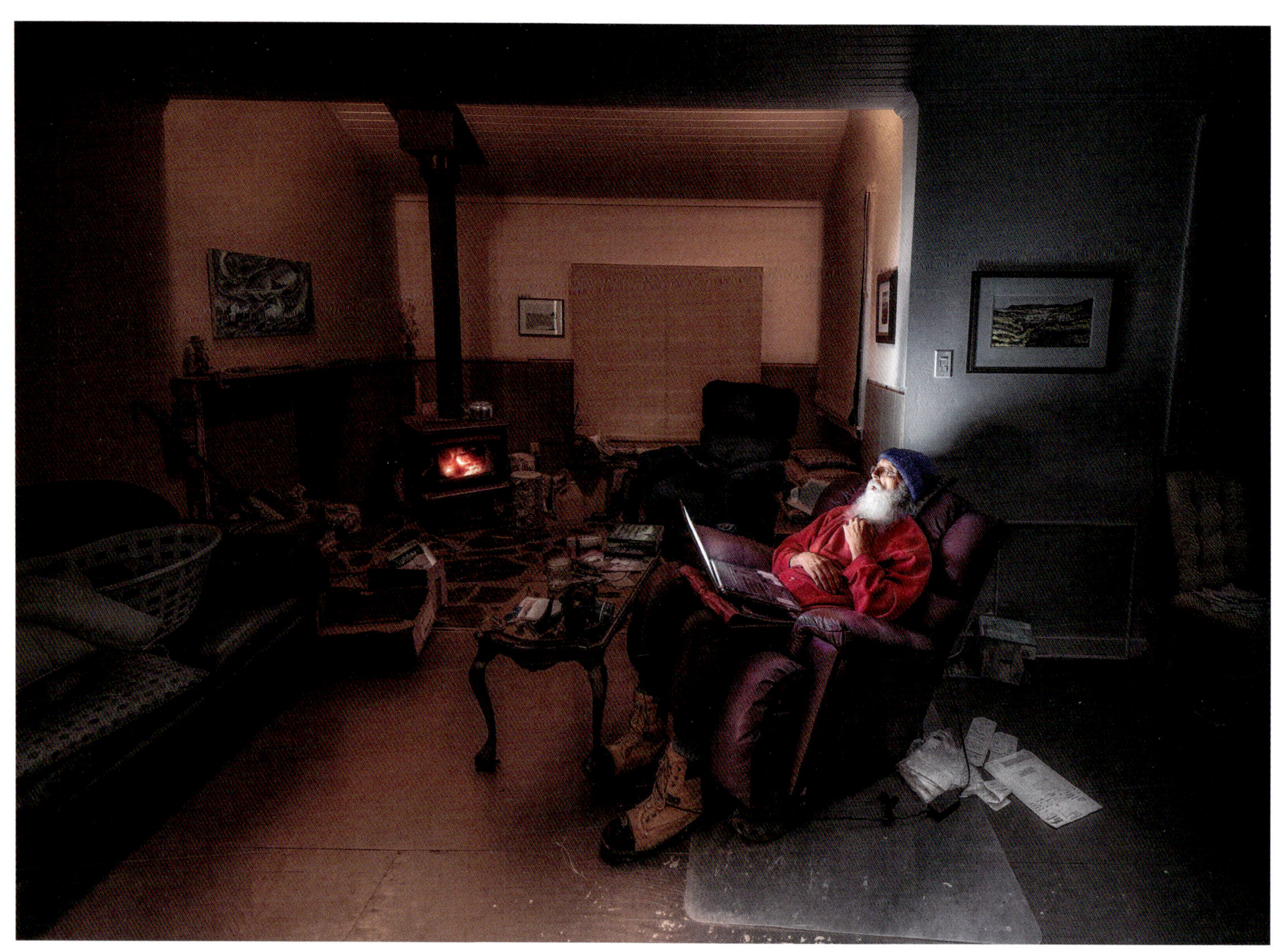

A CHRISTMAS STORY Robert is dozing off on his own chair at home. Nothing here was set up for a photograph, but everything fell by chance into the frame: Christmas is around the corner and Santa is exhausted from preparing gifts. He fell asleep in his chair when he was double-checking the lists on his laptop to make sure no one was forgotten. Some printed gift lists are scattered on the floor behind his chair, and the boxes for the gifts are beside the couch.

YEAR: 2020

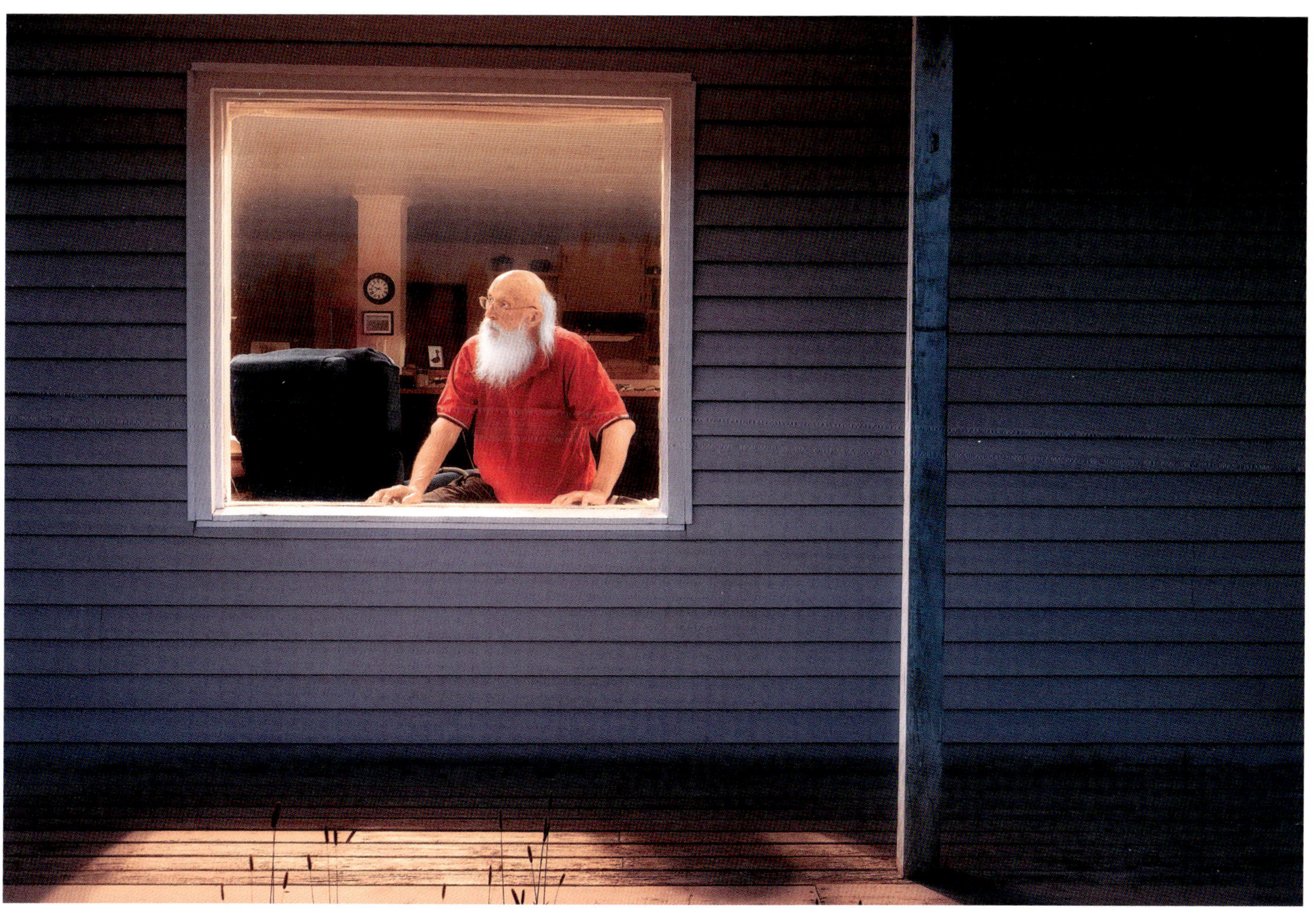

LOOKING OUT Robert is looking out from the window of his home, which he built forty-three years ago. If you look inside the window, you will find more than one Robert, representing his movements in the house.

YEAR: 2021

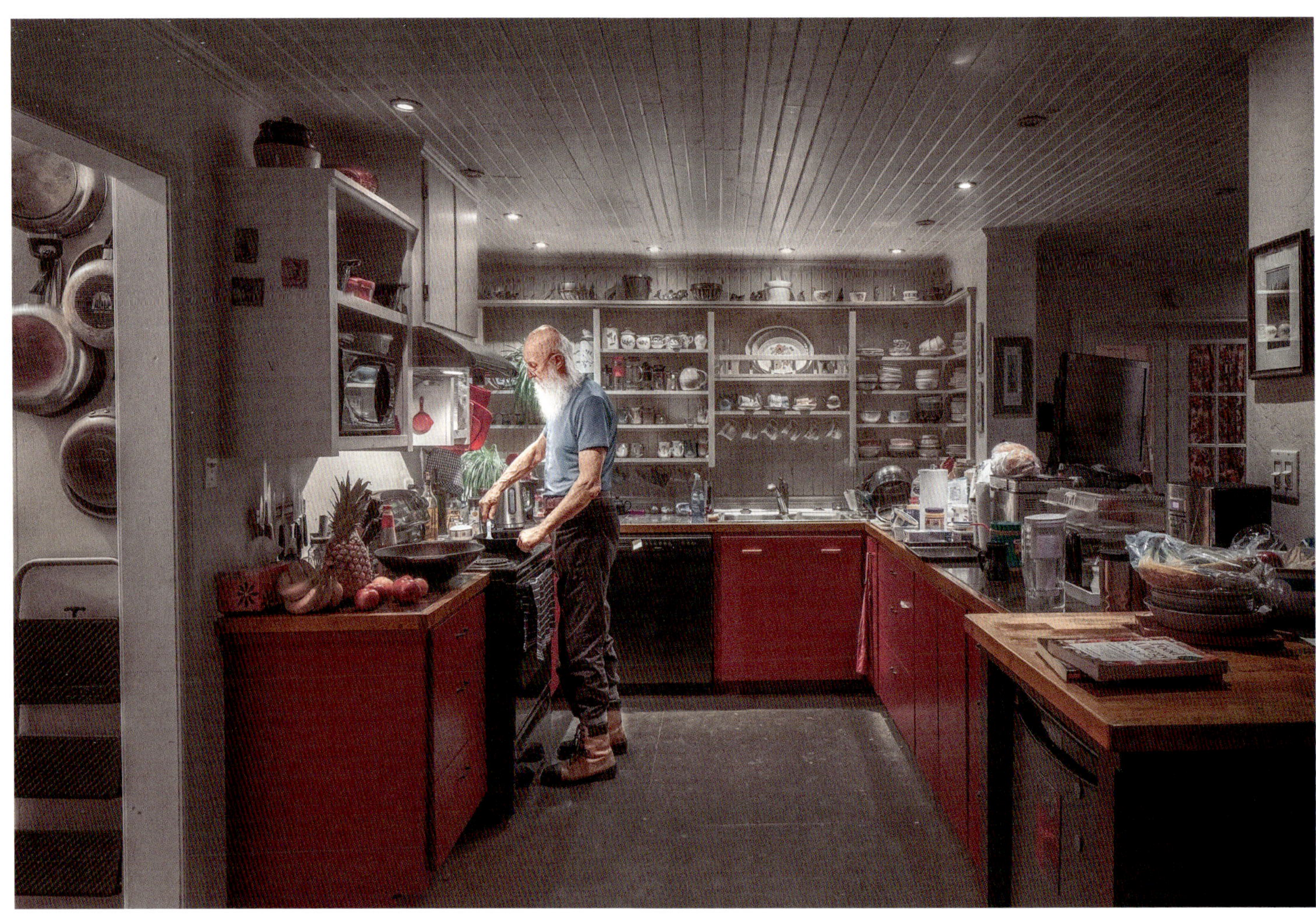

COOKING SUPPER Robert is cooking supper at home with a forty-year-old cast-iron pan he bought when he married. Some of the neatly arranged kitchen wares on the shelves belonged to his late parents and were their wedding gifts around eighty years ago. Robert built the sturdy red wooden counters with solid marble countertops more than forty years ago, when he built his home.

YEAR: 2021

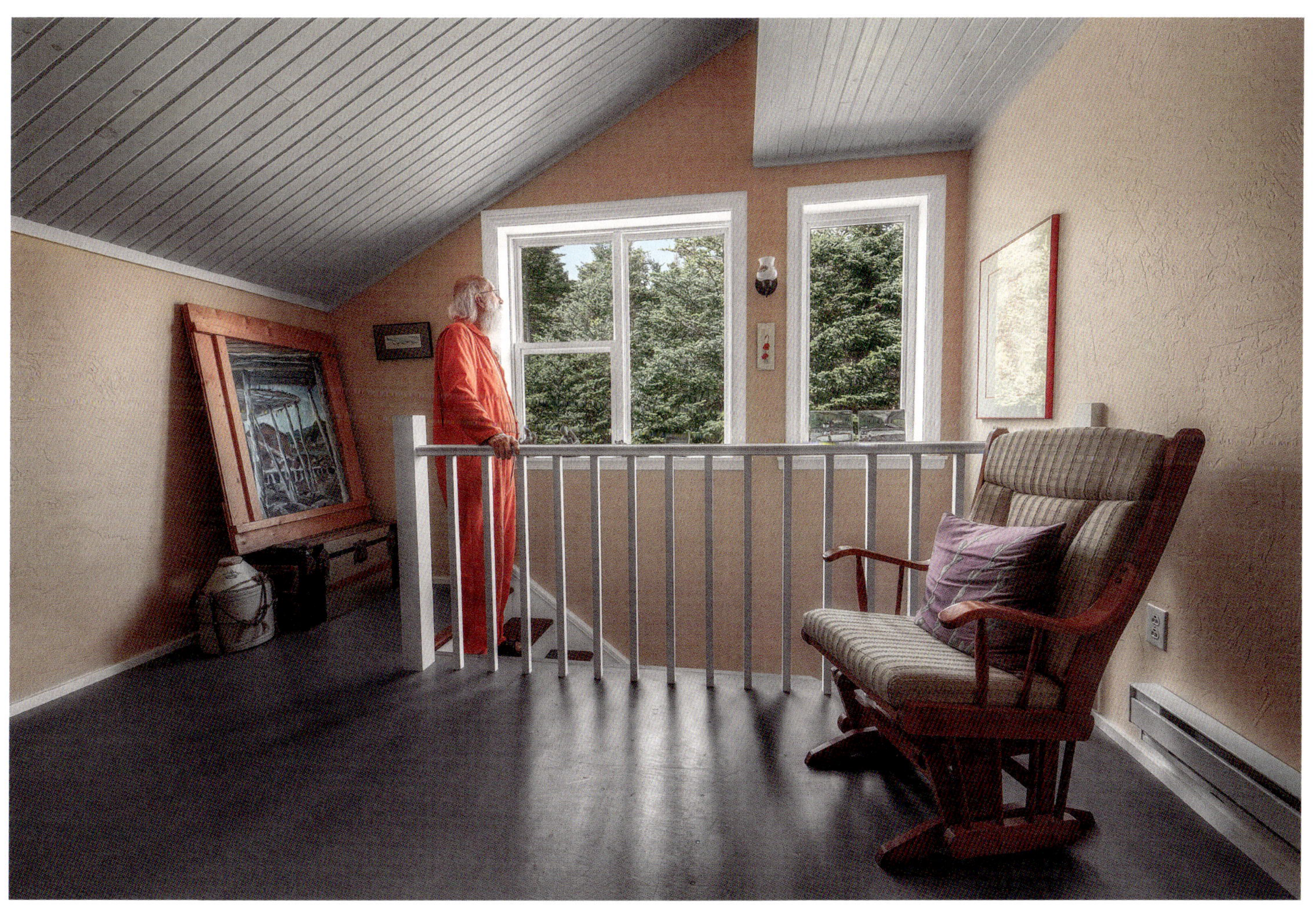

GET TO WORK This is a hot summer afternoon in Brigus South. After a short break on the rocking chair on the second floor of his house, Robert is ready to go downstairs and get to work in the woods around his house. Though he is over seventy now, he has been working inside and outside his house almost every day. "Work keeps me alive," Robert says.

YEAR: 2021

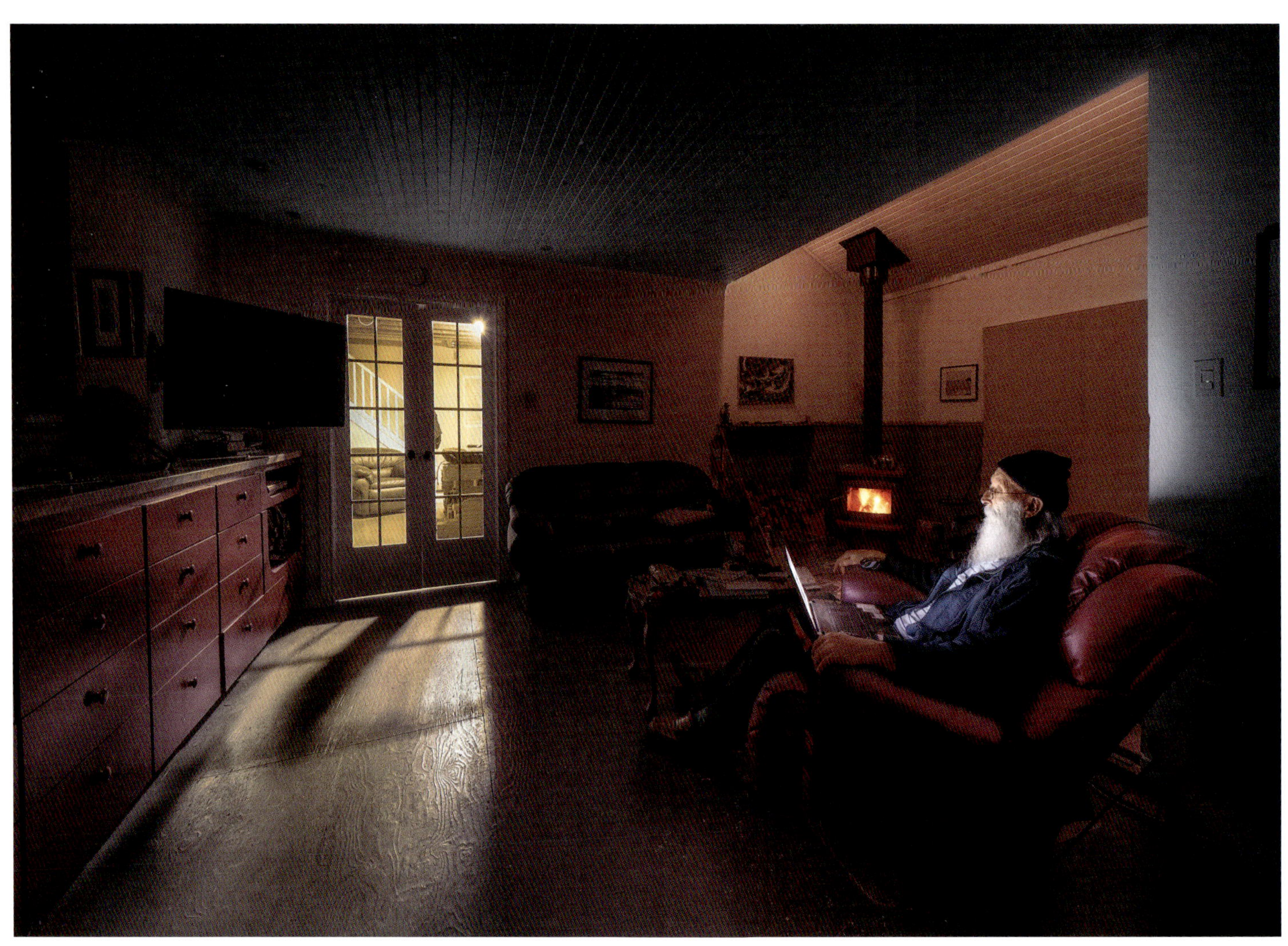

A RELAXING NIGHT This is a peaceful and relaxing night; Robert is sitting in his chair, as usual, posting his photos of scenery on Facebook. This is his main entertainment, besides watching TV. "I built my own home, and now I am relaxing in it," Robert says.

YEAR: 2021

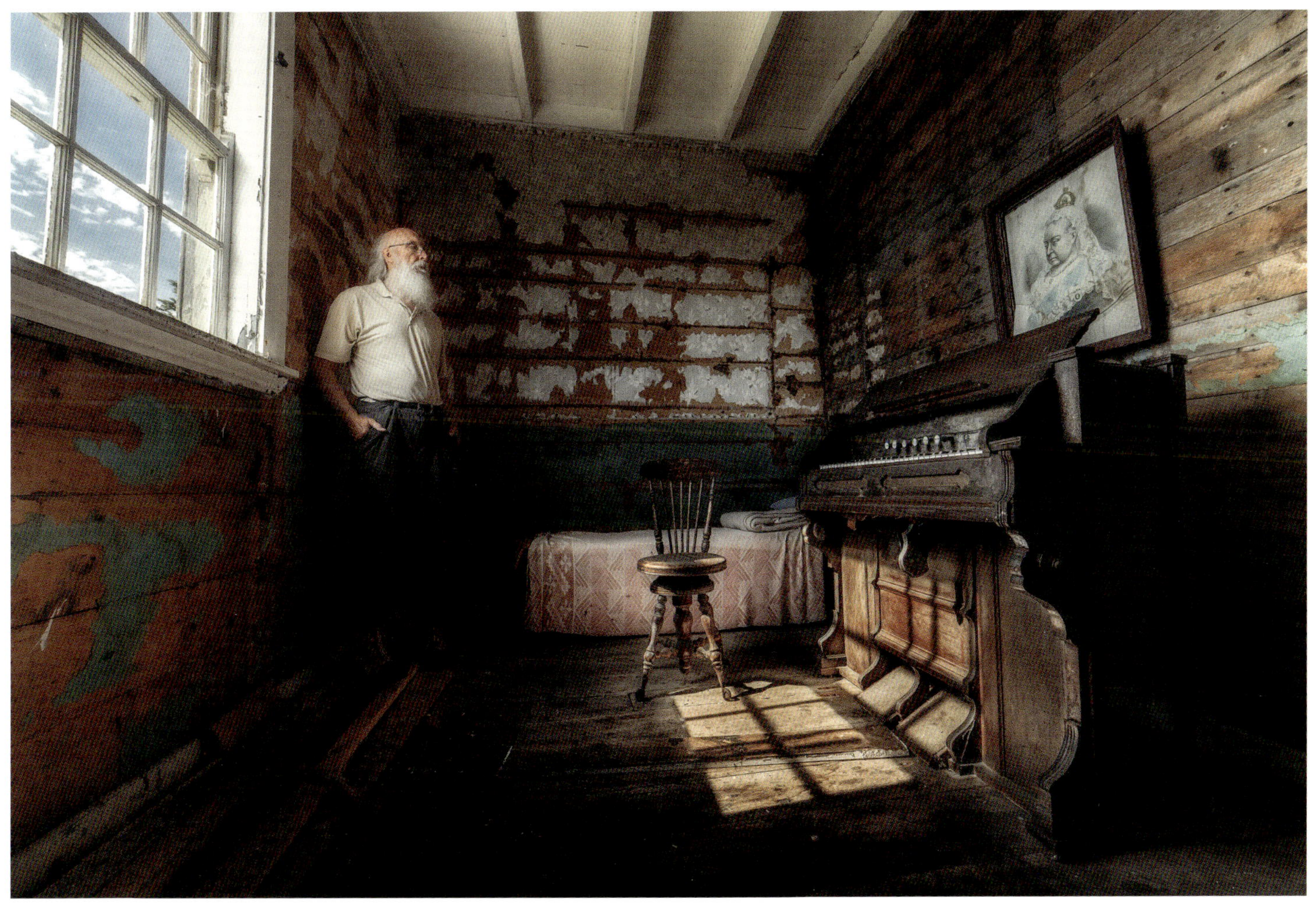

THE PARLOUR OF TILLEY HOUSE Robert is in the parlour of Tilley House, his old family home, which was built in 1858 by his great-great-grandfather. The picture on the wall is Queen Victoria, the great-great-grandmother of Queen Elizabeth. Time seems to freeze here. The afternoon sunshine is shining through the window, right on this Victorian organ. The organ has been silent for six decades, since the last resident of Tilley House moved out.

YEAR: 2021

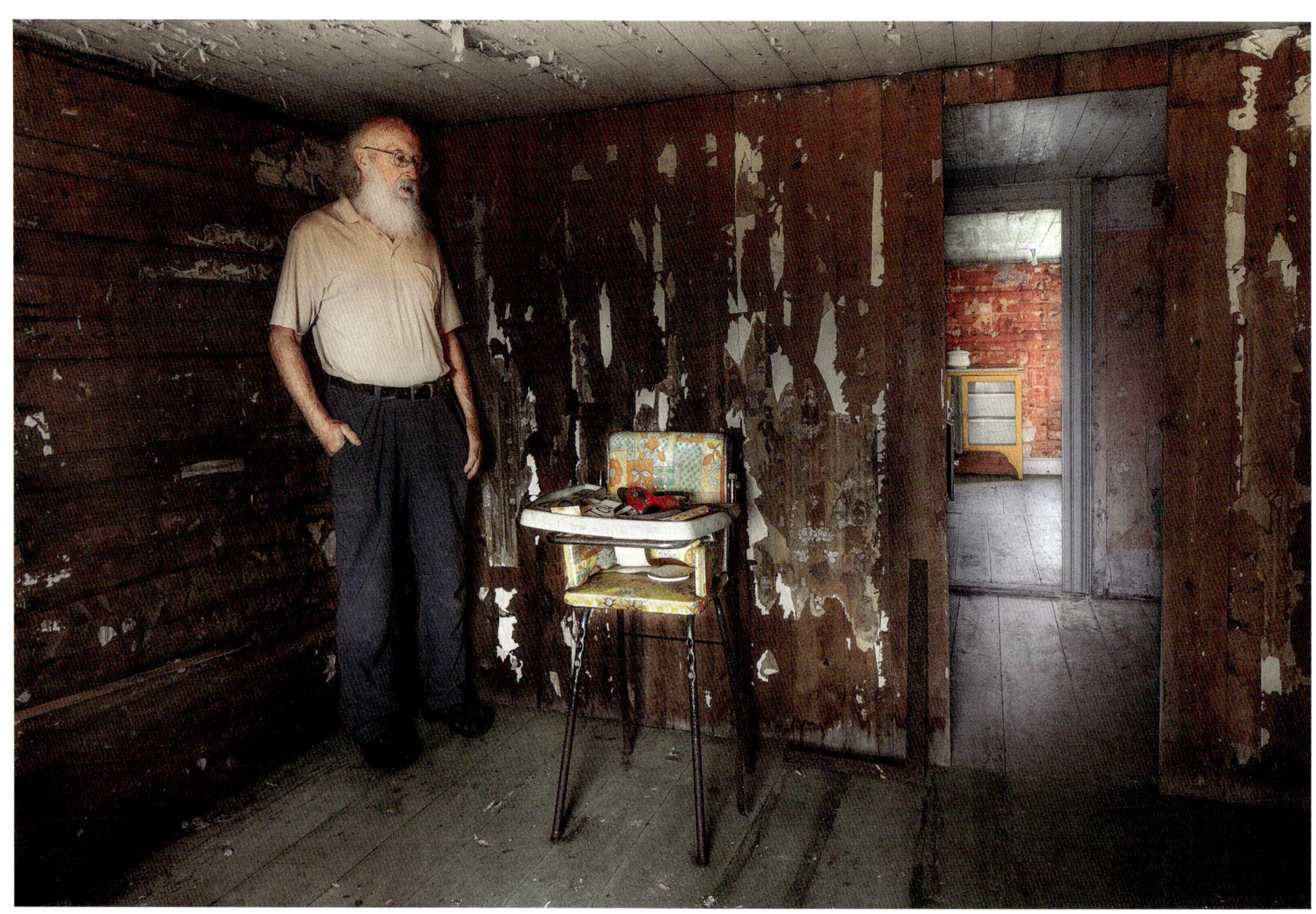

BABY CHAIR Do you still have your baby chair? Robert Tilley does. He is standing in Tilley House beside the baby chair he used more than seventy years ago. The belt on the chair belonged to his late grandfather, who was born in 1882. Robert's grandmother moved out in the 1960s, and since then this house has been vacant. You can see the other end of the house through the doors, one door after another. It feels as if these doors are leading us to another space, maybe back to Robert's childhood.

YEAR: 2021

SERIES: SKIN TO SKIN

In this photo series, I explore the bonds between people and places. I focus on Robert and his home as a specific case and present my works in a conceptual way. We all have skin, and objects have their skin too. The wallpaper is the skin of the wall. When the skin of the wall touches Robert's skin, the bond is revealed.

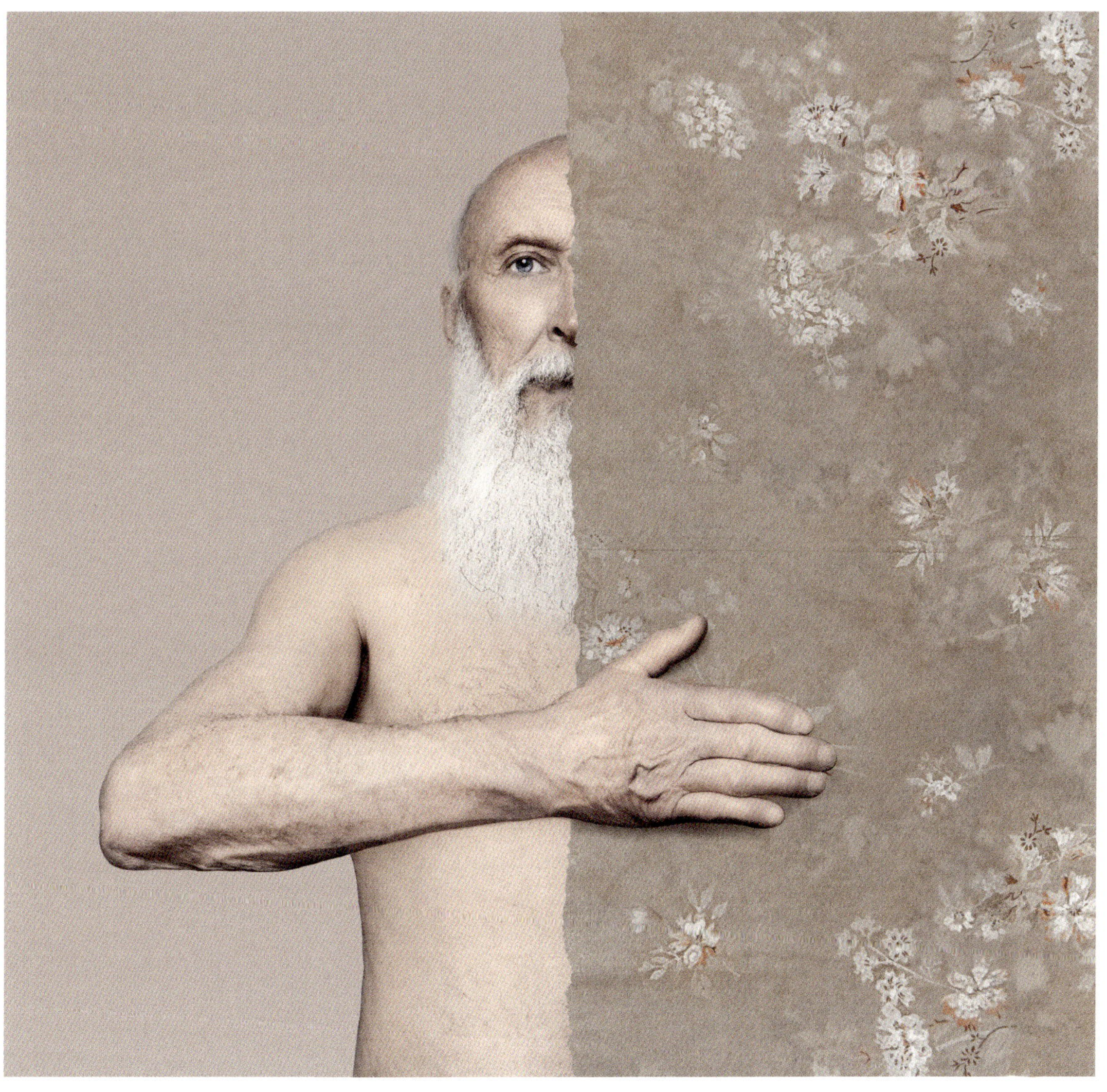

PREVIOUS

SKIN TO SKIN PART I

The wallpaper in this photo is from Robert's family home, Tilley House. The wallpaper is a century old.

YEAR: 2022

RIGHT

SKIN TO SKIN PART II

The wallpaper in this photo is from Robert's home in Brigus South; the wallpaper is more than forty years old.

YEAR: 2022

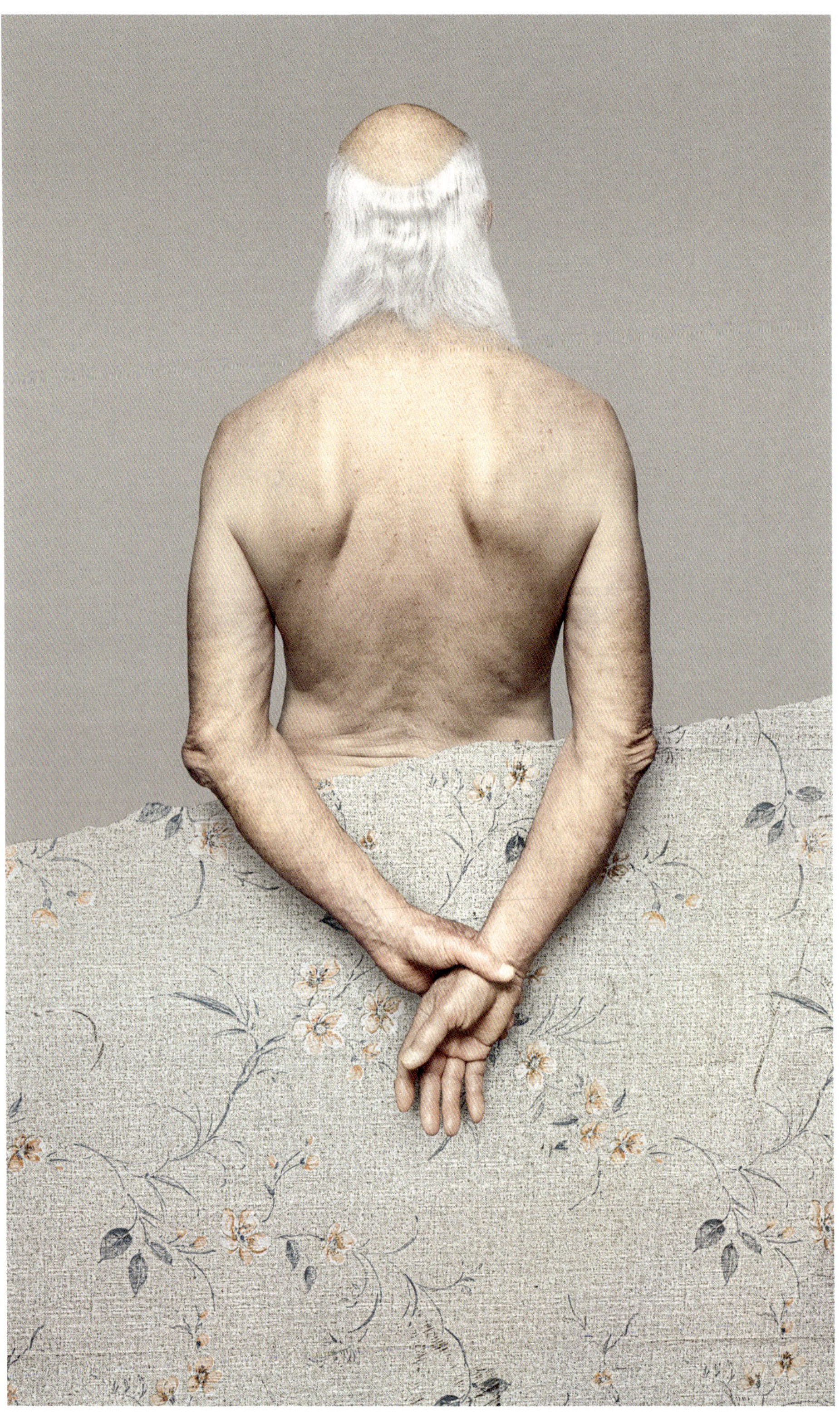

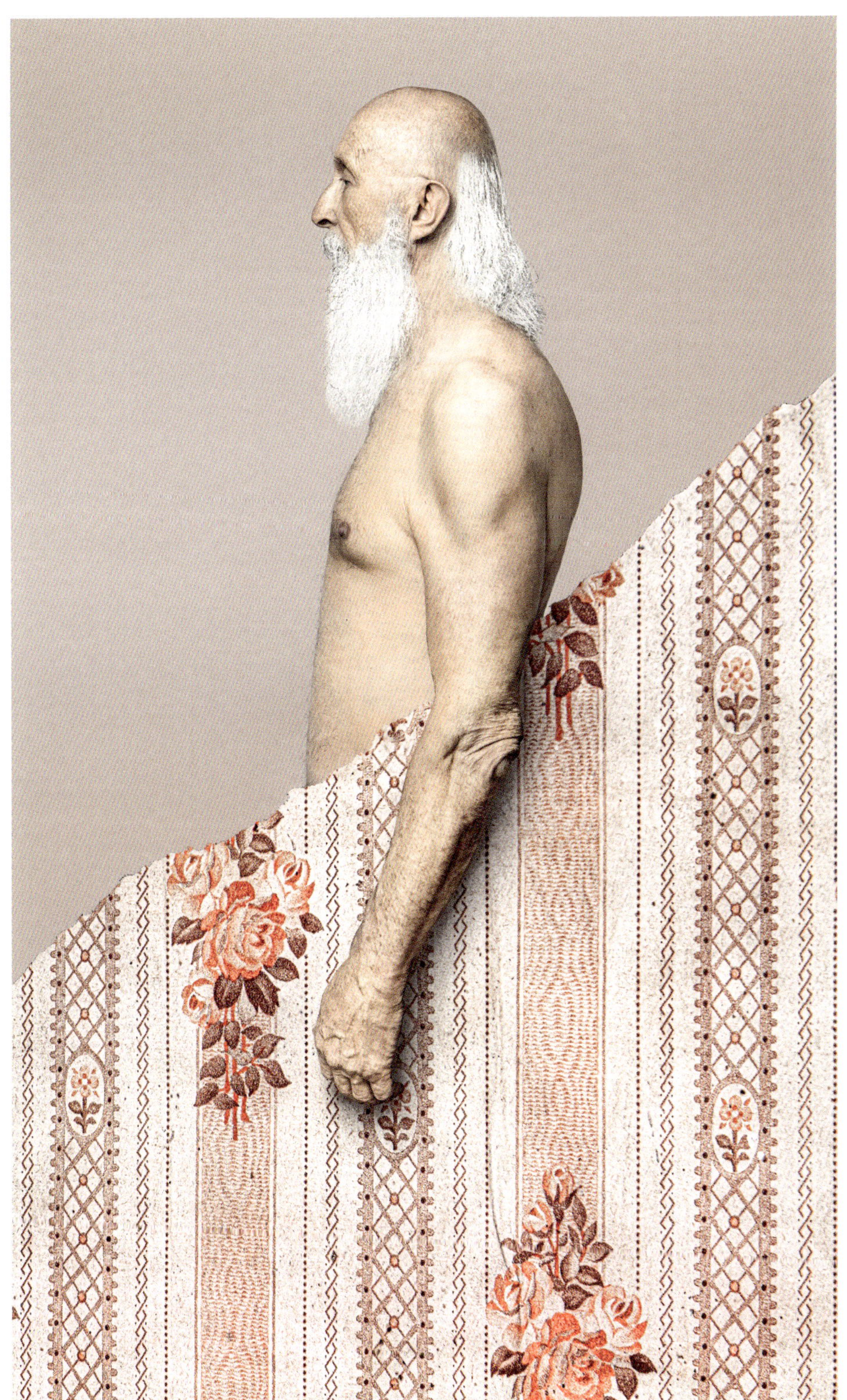

SKIN TO SKIN PART III

The century-old wallpaper in this photo is from Tilley House.

YEAR: 2022

SERIES: TEMPTATIONS

This series is inspired by *The Son of Man*, painted by Belgian surrealist painter René Magritte in 1964. The apple and the flying veil could both be interpreted as symbols.

RIGHT

TEMPTATIONS PART I

Desire is rising.

YEAR: 2022

OPPOSITE

TEMPTATIONS PART II

Temptations are swirling.

YEAR: 2022

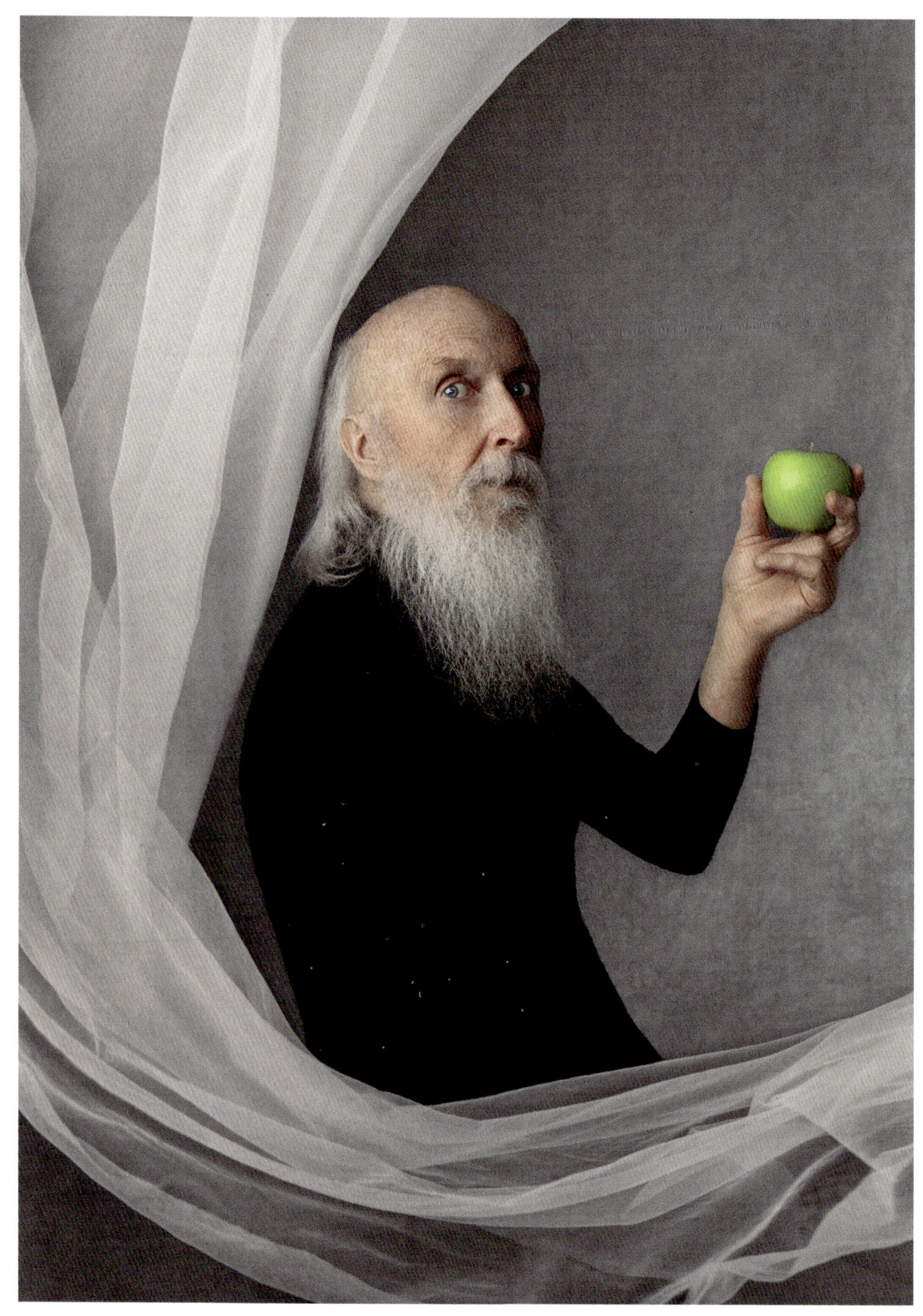

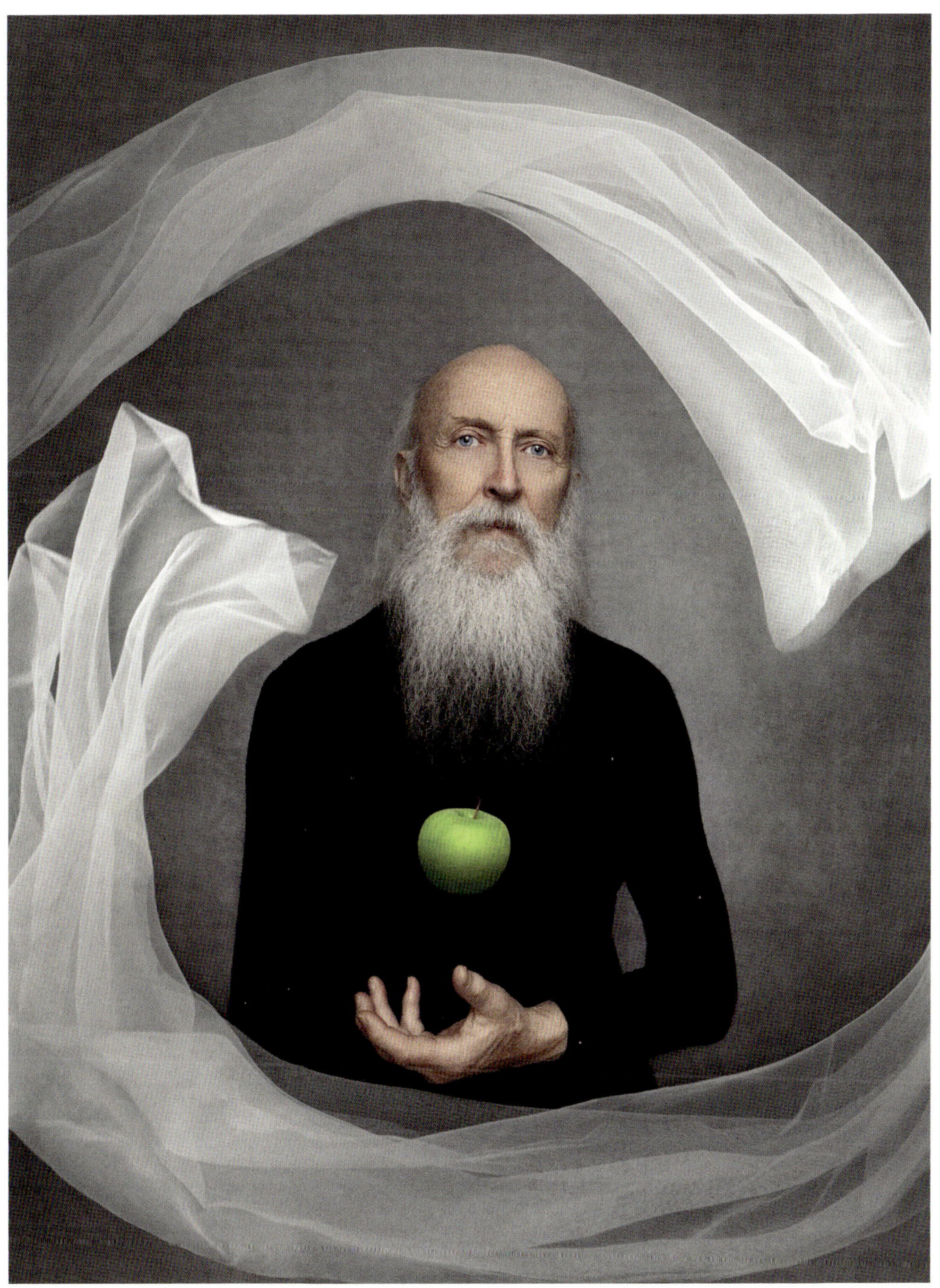

FOLLOWING LEFT

TEMPTATIONS PART III

Temptations are various. Which one do you pick? Robert is modelling for this portrait. Except for the fruit and Robert's skin, the other parts of the image, including his hair, are absolutely grey, just in different shades. Their saturation is 0, and the RGB = 1:1:1. That is to say, except for the fruit and Robert's skin, this is actually a black-and-white image. Interesting, isn't it? I would like you to feel the beauty of the grey.

YEAR: 2022

FOLLOWING RIGHT

TEMPTATIONS PART IV

Temptations are right there. Do you choose to see them or not?

YEAR: 2022

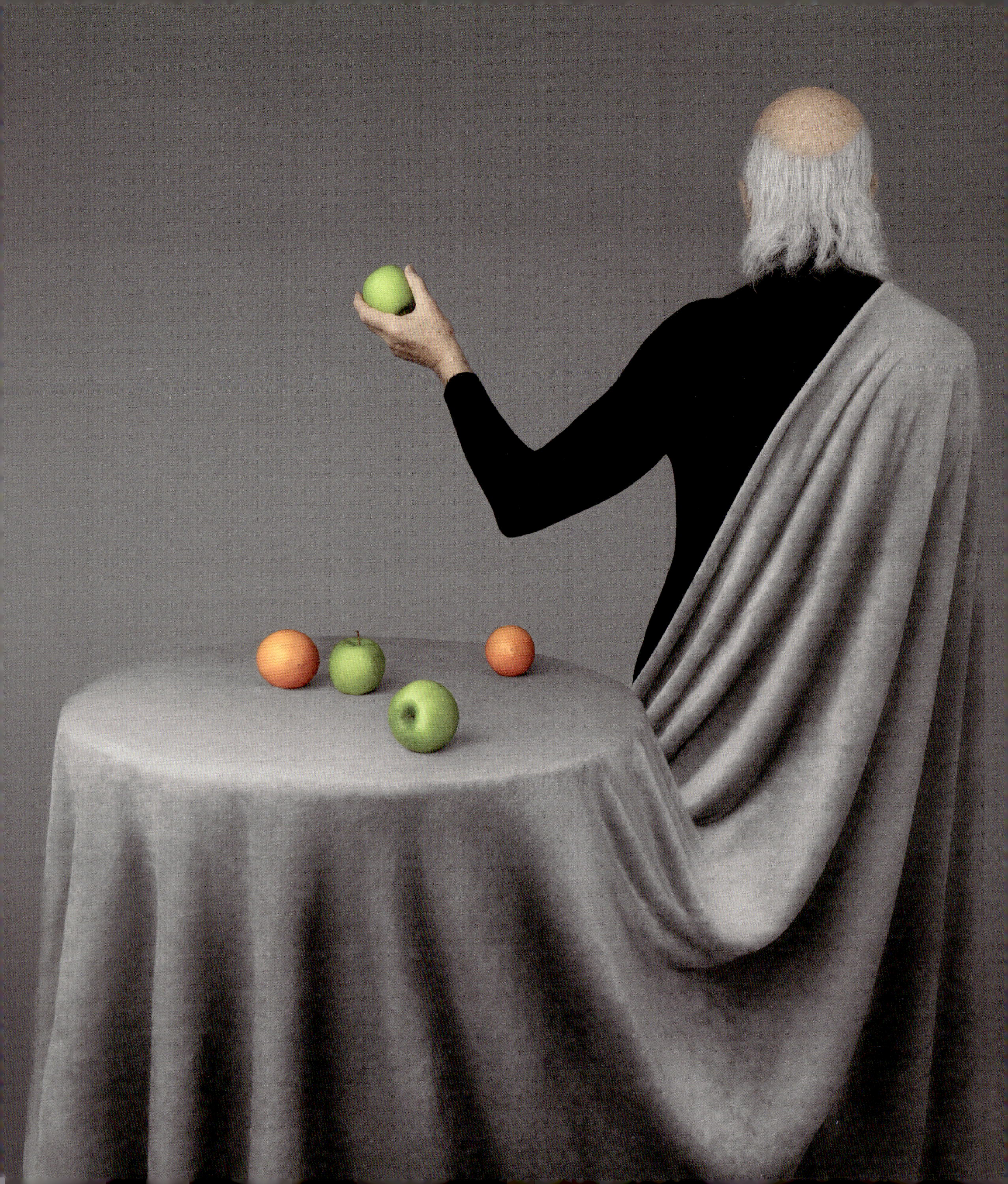

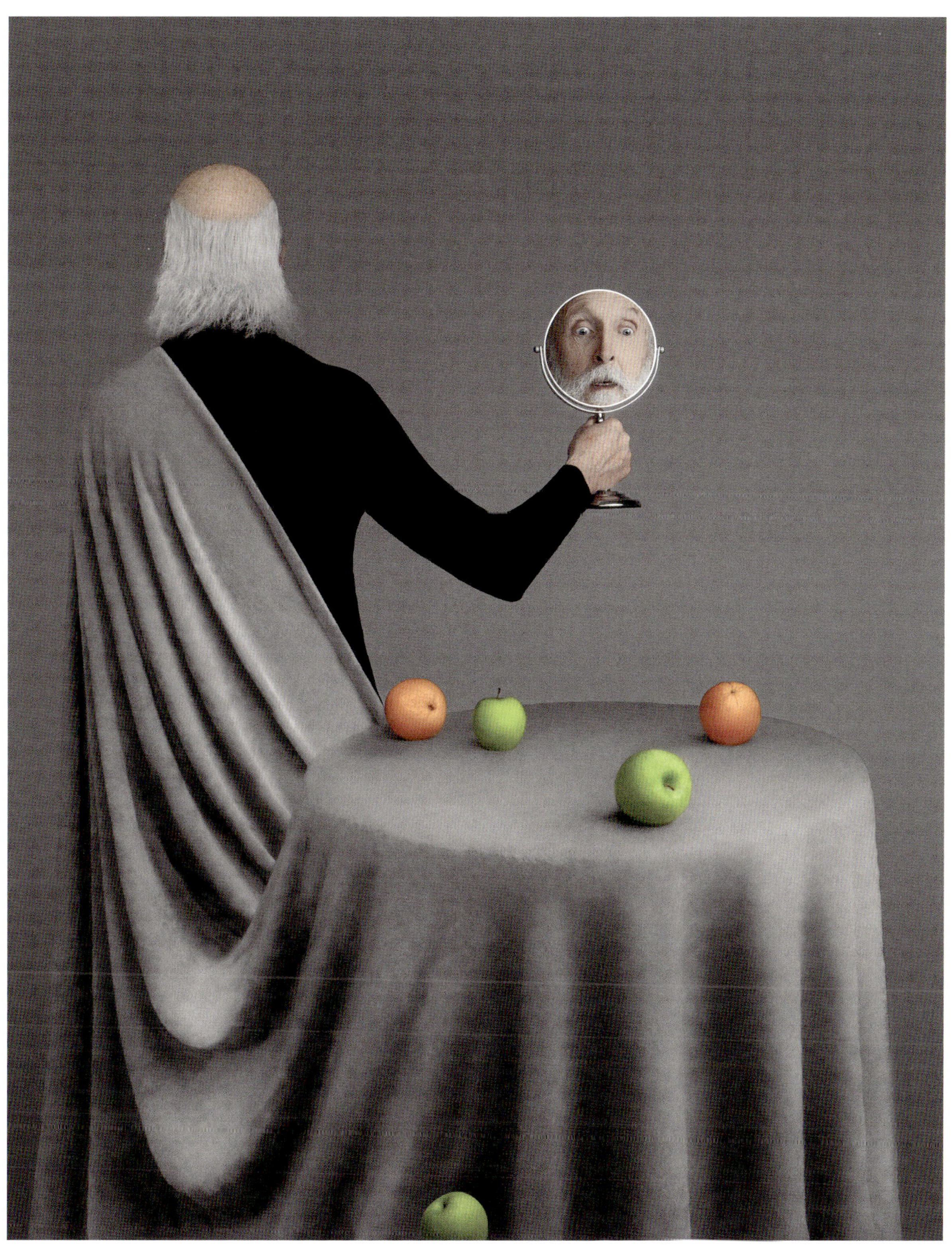

SERIES: A TRIPTYCH

This series includes three portraits of Robert under a flying veil. The behind-the-scenes story is that when I took this photo, I set the timer on my camera and waved the veil in the air. I tried nearly a hundred times before I got a satisfactory result. Thanks to Robert for his patience.

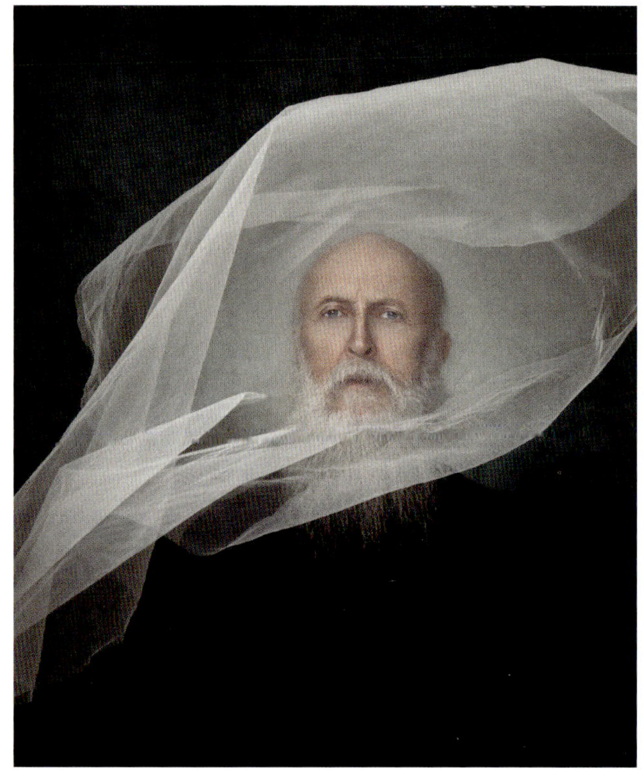

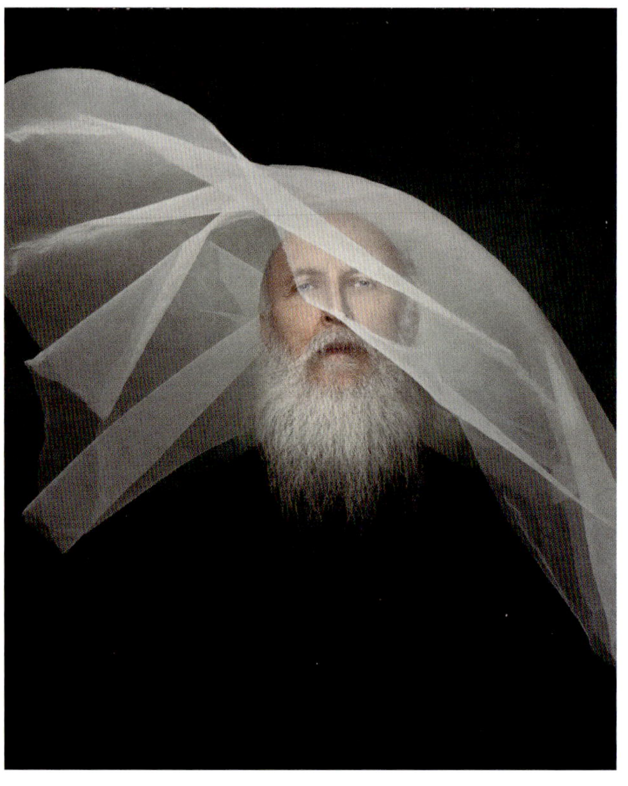

TOP
A TRIPTYCH PART I: VEILED
YEAR: 2022

OPPOSITE
A TRIPTYCH PART II: HUSHED
YEAR: 2022

BOTTOM
A TRIPTYCH PART III: UNVEILED
YEAR: 2022

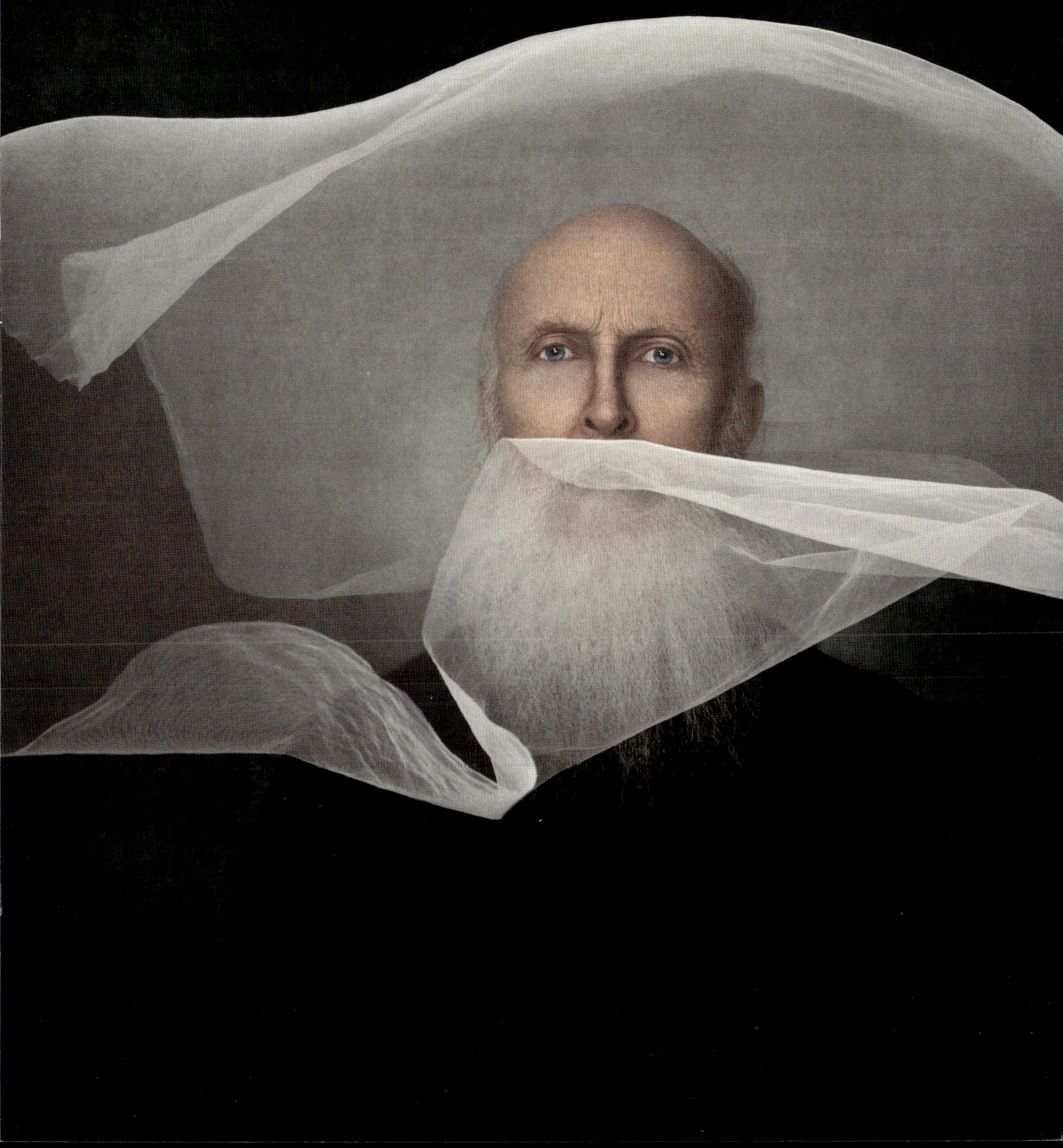

MULTIPLE ROBERTS IN RAINDROPS I took this photo in the fall of 2017, when I first came to Newfoundland as a tourist and met Robert. Robert was driving me around the city in his car. We stopped for a break and it suddenly began to rain. Robert was standing outside the car and his face was reflected in the raindrops on the windshield. One Robert became multiple reversed Roberts. I captured this moment from the passenger seat. This is one of my first photos of Robert. I took it with a very basic camera, the only one I had at that time. I didn't know much about photography then, and really didn't think I would become a photographer. Life is magic.

YEAR: 2017

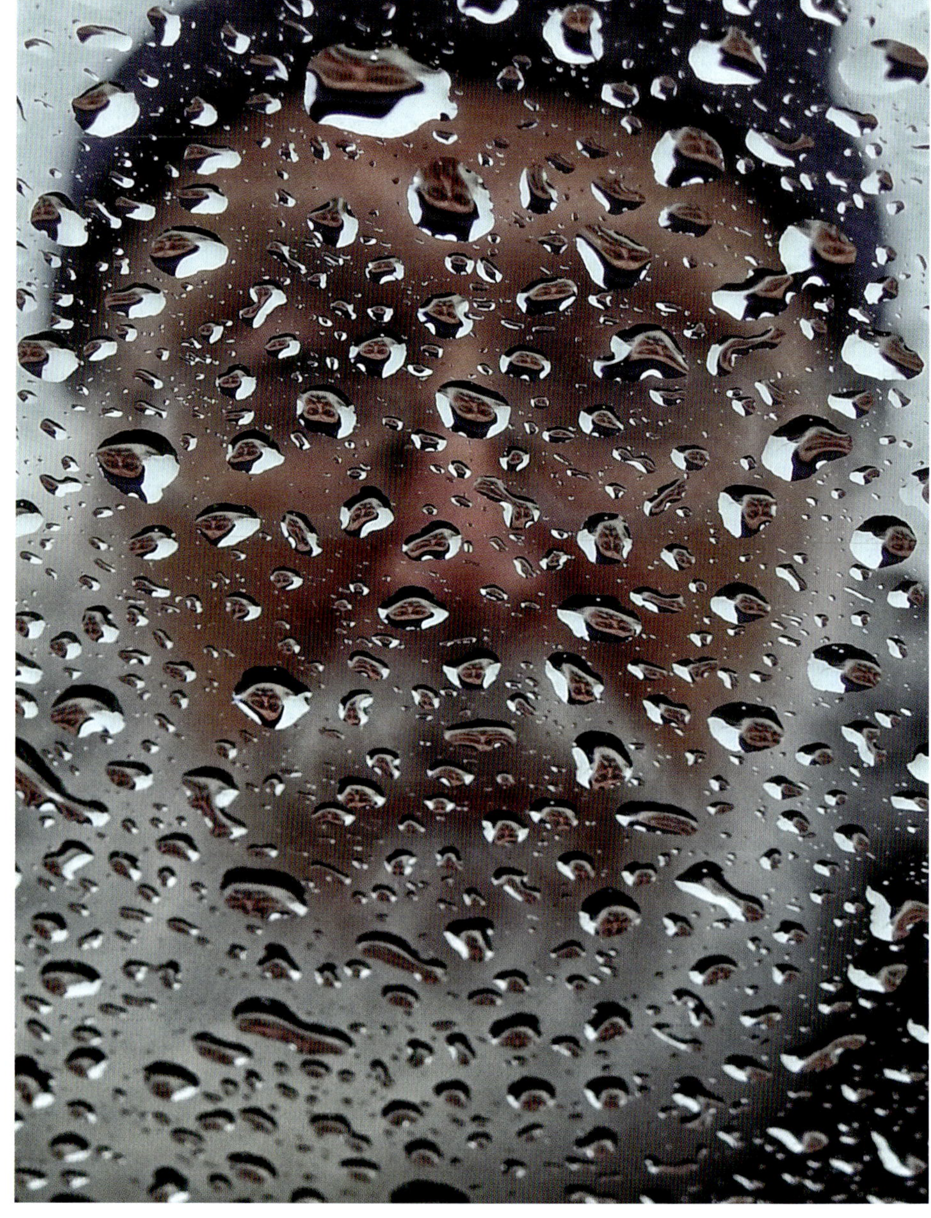